FAIR EMPLOYMENT STRATEGIES IN HUMAN RESOURCE MANAGEMENT

FAIR EMPLOYMENT STRATEGIES IN HUMAN RESOURCE MANAGEMENT

Edited by
Richard S. Barrett

Q

Quorum Books
Westport, Connecticut • London

Library of Congress Cataloging-in-Publication Data

Fair employment strategies in human resource management / edited by
   Richard S. Barrett.
         p.   cm.
   Includes bibliographical references and index.
   ISBN 0–89930–986–0 (alk. paper)
   1. Discrimination in employment—United States. 2. Discrimination
in employment—Law and legislation—United States. 3. Employment
tests—United States I. Barrett, Richard S.
   HD4903.5.U6F35   1996
   658.3—dc20   95–50464

British Library Cataloguing in Publication Data is available.

Library of Congress Catalog Card Number: 95-50464
ISBN: 0–89930–986–0

First published in 1996

Quorum Books, 88 Post Road West, Westport, CT 06881
An imprint of Greenwood Publishing Group, Inc.

Printed in the United States of America

The paper used in this book complies with the
Permanent Paper Standard issued by the National
Information Standards Organization (Z39.48–1984).

10 9 8 7 6 5 4 3 2 1

Copyright Acknowledgments

The editor and publisher gratefully acknowledge permission to reprint the
following chapters:

Chapter 12 by Richard S. Barrett, adapted from Barrett, R. S. (1995). Employee
selection with the performance priority survey. *Personnel Psychology, 46,* 653–662.

Chapter 33 by Richard S. Barrett, adapted from Barrett, R. S. (1992). Content
validation form. *Personnel Management, 21,* 41–52.

To Shirley, my wife,
to our progeny, Andy, Tracy, and Laura,
and to their progeny

Contents

Preface   xi

I: Development of Standards

1   Fairness and Public Policy in Employment Testing: 3
    Influences from a Professional Association
    Wayne J. Camara
2   Ethical Issues and Dilemmas in Fair Employment Strategies   12
    Rodney L. Lowman

II: Content Validity

3   Job Analysis   23
    Richard S. Barrett
4   Content Validation   27
    Irwin L. Goldstein and Sheldon Zedeck
5   Content Validity, Face Validity, and Quantitative Face Validity   38
    William C. Burns
6   Content Validation Form   47
    Richard S. Barrett
7   Multiple-choice Tests   57
    Richard S. Barrett

III: Empirical Validity

8   Criterion-related Validity   67
    Richard S. Barrett

9   Interpreting the Correlation Coefficient   73
     Richard S. Barrett
10   How Much Does a Test Validation Study Cost?   88
     Lance W. Seberhagen
11   Validity Generalization   94
     Neal Schmitt

               IV: Selection Procedures
12   Simulations   107
     Richard S. Barrett
13   Person-environment Congruence   112
     Richard S. Barrett
14   Situational Judgment Tests   119
     Mary Ann Hanson and Robert A. Ramos
15   Assessment Centers   125
     Sarah E. Henry
16   A Legally Defensible Interview for Selecting the Best 134
     Gary P. Latham and Christina Sue-Chan
17   Personality Assessment   144
     Robert Hogan
18   Employment Drug Testing   153
     Stephen D. Salyards and Jacques Normand
19   A Modern Approach to Minimum Qualifications   164
     Lance W. Seberhagen
20   Background Data for Personnel Selection   171
     Garnett S. Stokes and Cheryl S. Toth

               V: Testing Women
21   Physical Ability Testing for Employment   183
     Joyce Hogan and Ann M. Quigley
22   Gender Issues in Employment Testing   192
     Mary L. Tenopyr

               VI: Impact on Protected Classes
23   Adverse Impact   201
     Richard S. Barrett
24   Alternative Selection Procedures   208
     Richard R. Reilly
25   Sliding Bands: An Alternative to Top-down Selection   222
     Sheldon Zedeck, Wayne F. Cascio, Irwin L. Goldstein,
     and James Outtz

VII: Legal and Regulatory Concerns

26 The Equal Employment Opportunity Commission and   237
    Other Government Agencies
    Donald J. Schwartz
27 Interpreting the Ban on Minority Group Score Adjustment in   246
    Preemployment Testing
    Paul R. Sackett

VIII: Compliance with Title VII and Related Laws

28 Related Federal Acts: Americans with Disabilities Act and   259
    Age Discrimination in Employment Act
    Richard S. Barrett
29 Zetetic for Testers   264
    Richard S. Barrett

IX: Litigation

30 Case Preparation for the Plaintiffs   271
    Kent Spriggs
31 The Industrial Psychologist as an Expert Witness in   280
    Testing Cases
    R. Lawrence Ashe, Jr.
32 The Expert Witness and the Attorney   285
    Richard S. Barrett
33 Cooperative Efforts among Potential Adversaries   293
    Lawrence R. O'Leary

Suggestions for Further Reading   301
Name Index   305
Subject Index   309
About the Contributors   313

Preface

Since the passage of the Civil Rights Act of 1964, selection psychologists and personnel specialists have designed new techniques for evaluating applicants and employees for selection, promotion, and downsizing. There are two basic objectives of this effort: to improve the quality of the work force and to reduce arbitrary barriers to employment of members of protected classes.

This book is a practical compendium of what practitioners have learned; it is not a scientific treatise or theoretical statement. It includes differing points of view from which readers can select what seems most appropriate for their needs. Accordingly, I have asked practitioners in the field to share what they have learned in any aspect of the selection process, including specific selection techniques, arguments for or against various practices, and any new information that would be useful to professionals and nonprofessionals concerned with selection. In approaching potential contributors, I told them that it is not necessary that the authors agree with each other or with me — the field is far from having a settled repertoire of procedures and concepts that are accepted universally as valid and fair.

The prime focus of the book is to bring together, for the benefit of practitioners, the collective experience of professionals who have worked to develop economically, socially, and legally viable procedures for selection, promotion, demotion, and downsizing. Special attention is paid to assuring the fairness of treatment to classes protected under several laws: racial and ethnic minorities, women, the disabled, and older workers.

The book describes and evaluates useful procedures and demystifies the concepts that have been developed, with respect to Title VII of the Civil Rights Act of 1964, as amended in 1972 and 1991; Uniform Guidelines on Employee Selection Procedures; Questions and Answers to Clarify and Provide a Common Interpretation of Uniform Guidelines on Employee Selection Procedures; Americans with Disabilities Act; and Age Discrimination in Employment Act.

This book is not intended as a substitute for many excellent articles and texts in the field or for legal counsel. Therefore, it sometimes includes abridged versions of longer papers covering the same points by the authors. Those of you who want more detail and a more thorough review of the literature with detailed references are invited to get in touch with the authors directly.

This book is based on the efforts engendered by Section 703 h of Title VII of the Civil Rights Act of 1964, known as the Tower Amendment, named after its sponsor, Senator John Tower, which reads: "[It shall not] be an unlawful employment practice for an employer to give and act upon the results of any professionally developed ability test, provided the test is not designed, intended, or used to discriminate because of race, color, religion, sex, or national origin."

The meaning of Title VII was clarified by the unanimous decision of the Supreme Court in *Griggs v. Duke Power Company* (1971), which reads, in part: "The Act proscribes not only overt discrimination but also practices that are fair in form but discriminatory in operation. The touchstone is business necessity. If an employment practice which operates to exclude Negroes cannot be shown to be related to job performance the practice is prohibited. . . . What Congress has forbidden is giving these devices and mechanisms [tests] controlling force unless they are demonstrably a reasonable measure of job performance."

Title VII and the *Griggs* decision were elaborated by the Uniform Guidelines on Employee Selection Procedures, supplemented by Questions and Answers to Clarify and Provide a Common Interpretation of Uniform Guidelines on Employee Selection Procedures. This book is a compilation of the results of efforts to improve selection and to comply with these mandates.

There are nine sections and a list of selected readings.

Section I, Development of Standards, presents a history of fair employment law and standards from the perspective of the American Psychological Association and a discussion of ethical issues from the point of view of the Society of Industrial and Organizational Psychology.

Section II, Content Validity, describes the job analysis necessary to produce and defend a selection procedure on the basis of content validity, followed by three perspectives on the issue. This section ends with a discussion of the special problems of multiple-choice tests.

Section III, Empirical Validity, addresses the issues and some of the statistics involved in establishing the criterion-related validity of a selection procedure. The cost of a validation study is examined. The correlation coefficient and the value of a given validity coefficient are illustrated by diagrams. Validity generalization, a controversial issue, is discussed with reference to the ability to generalize the results of validity studies through meta-analysis.

Section IV, Selection Procedures, describes procedures that have been developed to go beyond the traditional multiple-choice tests of aptitude and achievement, unplanned interviews, and questionable personality tests.

Section V, Testing Women, addresses both physical and psychological testing as they apply to women.

Section VI, Impact on Protected Classes, opens with a discussion of how adverse impact is determined followed by a description of ways to reduce it without destroying the validity of the selection procedure.

Section VII, Legal and Regulatory Concerns, discusses the procedures and rules of the Equal Employment Opportunity Commission and the issues of race norming raised by the Civil Rights Act of 1991.

Section VIII, Compliance with Title VII and Related Laws, contrasts the Americans with Disabilities Act and Age Discrimination in Employment Act with Title VII of the Civil Rights Act. "Zetetic for Testers" is a checklist in the form of questions based on the Uniform Guidelines and the Americans with Disabilities Act.

Section IX, Litigation, sets forth different views of the relation between the attorney and the expert witness. It advocates cooperative efforts between potential adversaries in developing selection procedures that satisfy all interested parties.

There is a list of suggestions for further reading for those who want a deeper presentation on specific topics.

REFERENCES

Age Discrimination in Employment Act of 1967 (Pub.L. 90-202) (ADEA), as amended, 29 U.S.C. 621 *et. seq.*

Americans with Disabilities Act of 1990 (Pub.L. 101-336) (ADA), as amended, 42 U.S.C. 12101 *et. seq.*

Civil Rights Act of 1991 (Pub.L. 102-166) (CRA).

Equal Employment Opportunity Act of 1972 (Pub.L. 92-261).

Questions and Answers to Clarify and Provide a Common Interpretation of Uniform Guidelines on Employee Selection Procedures, *Federal Register* 43, no. 166, 11996–12009 (1979).

Title VII of the Civil Rights Act of 1964 (Pub.L. 88-352), as amended, 42 U.S.C. 2000e *et. seq.*

Uniform guidelines on employee selection procedures, 29 C.F.R. 1607 (1978).

I

DEVELOPMENT OF STANDARDS

1

Fairness and Public Policy in Employment Testing: Influences from a Professional Association

Wayne J. Camara

PUBLIC POLICY IN EMPLOYMENT TESTING WITHIN THE AMERICAN PSYCHOLOGICAL ASSOCIATION

The American Psychological Association (APA) has more than 125,000 members and affiliates and is organized into four directorates, which largely parallel the interests of its members: practice, science, education, and public interest. Testing issues are the responsibility of the Science Directorate; however, testing and assessment issues are sufficiently important to professional practice, public interest, and education to require formal oversight mechanisms across four directorates and governance areas at APA. In developing policy positions on issues concerning fairness and employment testing, these constituencies often have substantially different perceptions and values.

Generally, applied and academic industrial psychologists align with the Science Directorate in developing positions that are based on appropriate research and reflect appropriate practice. Public interest constituents primarily reflect a desire to ensure that employment practices are fair and that psychology assumes a broader agenda in advocating for ethnic, gender, and other forms of equity across outcomes. APA's practitioner constituency generally does not attempt to represent industrial psychology and is, instead, driven by the needs and desires of licensed clinicians. As a constituency, practitioners within APA generally are less concerned about issues of employment testing and fairness discussed in this chapter. However, many clinical psychologists within

APA continue to advocate for restrictions that would limit many forms of industrial practice (e.g., executive development, use of personality tests) to licensed clinicians despite any lack of expertise and training in industrial/organizational (I/O) psychology.

In developing public policy positions, APA does not necessarily require formal mechanisms for approval from its constituencies. Rather, consensus is required across the association's directorates and governance groups, which often can be obtained through discussions among staff or members serving on key committees or boards representing the respective constituencies. In cases in which such consensus cannot be obtained in a timely manner, the association may not adopt a formal position.

Two of APA's 50 divisions are concerned primarily with the development of policy in areas of employment testing and fairness. The Society of Industrial and Organizational Psychology (SIOP) (Division 14 and Division 5: Evaluation, Measurement, and Statistics) both have members with expertise in measurement and employment testing and remain active within APA governance. Members of these two divisions often are involve in the development of APA policies affecting employment testing. Individual members of APA can influence greatly the policy positions of the association directly through communication with staff and members serving on various governance groups within the association or indirectly through its divisions. As a membership organization, APA must be responsive to its members, and practitioners in I/O psychology can be most effective when they organize and insist on APA support in certain areas. Often, a single, clearly articulated communication from one member may be adequate to initiate staff action on a particular issue, and repeated and insistent urging from an APA division or a small but vocal group of members quickly will get the attention of APA's senior staff.

THE UNIFORM GUIDELINES ON EMPLOYEE SELECTION PROCEDURES

In 1966, the Equal Employment Opportunity Commission (EEOC) issued the predecessor Uniform Guidelines on Employee Selection Procedures (hereafter, Uniform Guidelines). A number of psychologists, nearly all of them APA members, participated in panels assembled by EEOC to assist in this initial work. The resulting guidelines adopted the existing standards. A second set of more detailed guidelines was issued by EEOC in 1978; however, this document has been criticized by industrial psychologists for its prescriptive approach, promotion of differential validity, and call for independent validity studies for each population subgroup.

When a common set of Uniform Guidelines on Employee Selection Procedures (Equal Employment Opportunity Commission [hereafter EEOC], 1978) was under development in 1977–78, as well as when the U.S. House of Representatives conducted hearings on a possible revision of the Uniform Guidelines in 1978, APA formally responded to opportunities for comment. Ad hoc committees representing both APA and SIOP reviewed various drafts of the 1978 document and provided input, much of which was not incorporated into the final document. In congressional testimony, APA Executive Officer Leonard Goodstein (1985) noted that psychologists maintained a unified commitment to equal employment opportunity but that "there is considerably less of a consensus . . . regarding the appropriate course to pursue in the near future with respect to the Guidelines." Psychologists were divided between those who supported retaining the Uniform Guidelines in their present form and those who supported a revision to reflect recent research and scientific progress. Psychologists who favored the former (including APA's testing committee) viewed the Uniform Guidelines as compatible with the *Standards for Educational and Psychological Testing* and feared that a revision could result in weakening the document. SIOP supported a revision, feeling that significant progress had been made in a number of specific areas and that the document no longer represented good contemporary practice in personnel selection. APA's 1985 testimony presented four major technical issues that divided the psychologists in relation to the Uniform Guidelines and proceeded to list both sides of the argument (quite unusual for congressional testimony but characteristic of APA's difficulties in reaching a timely consensus on issues of fairness in employment testing): validity generalization, differential prediction, validity requirements and documentation, and utility analysis. Generally, SIOP argued that the current Uniform Guidelines did not adequately permit and weigh validity generalization and utility analysis and were in error in requiring fairness studies, defining construct validity, and discussing acceptable types of validity evidence.

EMPLOYMENT TESTING AND
FAIRNESS IN THE COURTS

Prior to *Watson v. Fort Worth Bank and Trust* (1988), APA had never participated as an amicus in any court in an employment discrimination case involving a challenge to tests because the issues before the court often were seen as only peripherally relevant to psychology and prior cases involved direct challenges to standardized tests, the subject of strong controversy across the various constituencies within APA. In *Watson v. Fort Worth Bank and Trust*, the Science Directorate and its testing committee supported the association's submission of an amicus curiae brief (APA, 1987). The resulting brief made several points relevant to employment testing and was, arguably, somewhat persuasive in the court's decision, which cited the brief in extending the same disparate impact theory of discrimination (*Griggs v. Duke Power*, 1971) to subjective procedures:

Subjective procedures can be scientifically validated and are "amenable to the same psychometric scrutiny" as objective procedures. APA cited the applicability of the Test Standards (APA, 1985) to interviews and rating scales and argued that the court's choice of analysis under Title VII should not turn on whether the challenged employment practices are subjective or objective.

The subjective procedures used by the employer in this case were not shown to be scientifically valid, and the Test Standards and Principles provide adequate guidelines for how such devices could have been validated.

There is no professional or scientific justification to treat subjective and objective devices differently in imposing validation requirements. In fact, APA went further in arguing that not imposing essentially the same technical standards for both types of procedures would provide a covert means for discrimination. (APA, 1987)

Justice Blackmun, in concurring with the majority, cited APA's argument regarding holding subjective procedures to the same psychometric scrutiny as objective procedures. However, he also implied that less formal means may be appropriate in establishing job relatedness of subject procedures (depending on the type and size of the business in question and the particular job functions).

APA's brief was criticized for not addressing the difficulty in establishing technical reliability for subjective procedures and the extent that such procedures would have to be completely restructured and "objectified" to meet professional standards; confusing subjective practices with decision processes; not adequately evaluating the cost, burden, and time required to design, quantify, and validate subjective procedures; and going well beyond its stated purpose of "informing the court on psychometric issues" by stating that the public policy goals of Title VII would be thwarted if subjective processes are not held to rigorous scientific standards.

APA (1987) also became involved in *Price Waterhouse v. Hopkins*, a case involving sex discrimination in promotional decision making in which evidence was based primarily on sexual stereotyping in the workplace. This Supreme Court case examined the burden of proof in mixed-motive cases. The Women's Legal Defense Fund urged APA to submit a brief in this case, and much of the evidence accepted by the lower courts regarding sexual stereotyping was based on testimony by an APA psychologist with expertise in this area.

APA's brief in this case supported the argument that sex discrimination, based upon evidence of sexual stereotyping, was a partial basis for Hopkins' failure to be promoted to partner at Price Waterhouse. The brief notes that three factors promote stereotyping in employment settings: the rarity of the stereotyped individual within the setting, the ambiguity of criteria used in evaluation, and the paucity of other information available to inform a decision.

The Court agreed to review *Wards Cove Packing Co., Inc. v. Antonio* the day after it released its decision in *Watson*. This case provided the court with an opportunity to further sort out the many issues concerning the burden of proof that remained unanswered from its earlier decisions. APA declined to seriously consider involvement in the *Wards Cove* case because the legal issues primarily concerned the burden of proof in disparate impact cases — issues not considered of specific relevance to the expertise of psychologists. Ultimately, the Court held that the burden is placed on plaintiffs to prove that an employer has not met standards for business necessity when using employment practices having discriminatory effects.

THE CIVIL RIGHTS ACT OF 1991

Within weeks of the Court's decision in *Wards Cove Packing Co., Inc. v. Antonio*, legislation was introduced that would partially overturn that ruling. In 1990, APA stated that the definition of business necessity in proposed legislation did not conform to accepted scientific standards in testing, proposed that "manifest relationship" (from *Griggs v. Duke Power Co.*) replace "significant relationship," and recommended a definition of business necessity that would restore the standard established in *Griggs* and prevent quotas: "The term 'required for business necessity' means shown to be: (1) predictive of or significantly related to work behavior(s) comprising or relevant to the job or job family for which the procedure or combination of procedures is in use, or (2) representative of one or more important components of the job, or (3) otherwise manifestly and demonstrably job related" (Camara, 1990).

Throughout 1989–91, Science Directorate staff worked actively in advising legislative staff and other groups on the merits and appropriateness of proposed legislative language. Schneider (1991) testified on behalf of APA, noting problems with the terms "significant relationship," as it is commonly associated with a statistically significant relationship, which would exclude content validation approaches; "successful" job performance, which could be construed as dichotomizing the construct and establishing a minimal standard, rather than viewing performance as a continuous variable; and "job performance," which needed to be more broadly defined to include concepts such as employee absenteeism, turnover, trainability, and so on (p. 2).

SIOP was also active during both 1990 and 1991 in working with APA staff on these issues and asserting their own positions on respective versions of the legislation. Their comments generally were consistent with those of APA, but their concerns often were more detailed. However, after extensive efforts by organized psychology to influence the above issues, it is perhaps Section 106 of the Civil Rights Act of 1991, introduced fairly late in the debate, which presents the greatest concerns to most I/O practitioners. This section prohibits the adjustment of scores, use of different cutoffs, or other methods of altering the results of tests on the basis of race, color, religion, sex, or national origin. This section was embraced largely by Democrats and Republicans as a politically expedient solution to charges that the legislation was a "quota bill" and the political flap that involved within-group scoring on the General Aptitude Test Battery (GATB) (discussed below). One remaining concern presented in both the Civil Rights Act of 1991 and the Americans with Disabilities Act (ADA) concerned the statement that personnel selection techniques having a disparate impact must be "job related for the position in question." Industrial psychologists immediately notified APA of concerns that such wording could be construed to imply that both laws require criteria to be related to a specific "position" held by an incumbent, rather than one of a class of related jobs. APA attempted to clarify this issue with the White House, Departments of Justice and Labor, EEOC, and lawmakers in correspondence of March 11, 1992 (Camara, 1992), which stated:

Relative to the use of the phrase "position in question," (1) job relatedness showing involving jobs, job classes, or job families are scientifically acceptable and should satisfy the requirement indicated by the language "job-related for the position in question" in both the ADA and Civil Rights Act of 1991; (2) it is not necessary to re-establish job-relatedness for similar jobs or job classes or families; (3) evidence of expected progression to higher level or more complex jobs or job classes or job families is appropriate; and (4) any interpretation of the Civil Rights Act of 1991 (or the ADA) that does not permit job-relatedness showing of these types is inconsistent with generally accepted principles and practices of personnel psychology. (p. 31)

The association entered this position into public record in anticipation of litigation that might arise over this ambiguous issue.

WITHIN-GROUP SCORING

At a time when Civil Rights legislation was a subject of continued discussion, the use of within-group scoring emerged as the lightning rod for debates on fairness, quotas, and the federal government's role in such affairs. At issue was the use of separate norms for minorities and nonminorities for reporting scores and referring applicants who take the GATB. This practice, labeled "race-norming," resulted in rank ordering applicants based on their percentile score produced from within-group norms.

A committee of the National Research Council had defended this practice for the GATB, but amid the politics of the time (e.g., a *Washington Times* headline read "employers required to fake test scores to favor minorities"), the Bush administration suspended both the practice and the use of the GATB. The association's statement generally reflected the shock and outrage expressed by a number of industrial psychologists over the suspension of a valid testing program in favor of less valid and more subjective practices, irrespective of their opinions regarding within-group scoring. In writing to the Department of Labor, APA stated that job referrals must be made whether the GATB is used or not and that there are no known alternatives that are as valid and economically useful as the GATB; there is no apparent scientific or economic justification for the suspension of the GATB. APA noted that increases in the validity and utility of a referral system should not automatically be compromised by focusing primarily on reducing score differences among racial or ethnic groups.

SIOP's scientific affairs committee examined the use of subgroup norms and issued a technical paper that concluded that test score adjustments (that aid in making valid decisions) should be permitted, provided that such adjustments do not increase the adverse impact of the test. Test score adjustments that either fail to increase the validity of tests or decrease the validity of tests do not have a firm scientific justification, although they may be justifiable on the grounds of advancing specific public policies.

AMERICANS WITH DISABILITIES ACT

Legislation on ADA and the Civil Rights Act generally ensued during the same time, and only a handful of industrial psychologists expressed any interest or concern about ADA during this time. The goals and objectives of ADA were overwhelmingly supported by rehabilitation psychologists, with industrial psychologists raising considerable concerns over the definitions of "impairment," "qualified examiner," and "reasonable accommodations."

APA argued that requests for reasonable accommodations in pre-employment screening should be made prior to the assessment, but that employers should routinely inform all applicants of the intent of ADA and that reasonable accommodations be available if they are unable to complete the described preemployment tasks. APA also left the door open for challenges after assessment, including retesting or canceling test scores, noting the reluctance of persons with disabilities to self-disclose.

Several APA divisions submitted individual comments. Division 5 and SIOP took decidedly different approaches, raising a number of concerns regarding existing language and calling for increased clarity and specificity in addressing many issues involving testing persons with disabilities. For example, SIOP stated that prior self-disclosure was essential and should be required prior to participation in the pre-employment screening process. SIOP argued for language that would clarify reasonable accommodation and permit measures of personality traits and physical characteristics related to the essential functions of the job to be included in acceptable preemployment inquiries. Division 5 opposed the definition of mental disabilities and questioned the absence of criteria for use in this diagnosis and resulting accommodations. Division 5 (APA, 1991) issued perhaps the most comprehensive statement on testing under ADA that addressed concerns in four areas: equating different forms of tests, standardization of tests, flagging scores on modified tests, and psychological evaluations designed to predict job behavior, which are not medical examinations. APA's comments were heavily criticized by I/O practitioners.

In 1993–94, the APA Science and Practice Directorates worked collaboratively to clarify when a preemployment selection device is considered a medical examination. In May 1994, APA's Practice and Science Directorates developed a statement for EEOC that argued that a test should be classified according to the purpose for which it is being used and that physical ability and personality tests are appropriate for preemployment when they assess job-relevant abilities, skills, or traits.

CONCLUSION

APA policy is developed to broadly reflect the perspectives of psychologists and promote the relevance of psychology as a science, profession, and respective public interest concerns. The specific policy position taken by APA on a given issue reflects the views and perspectives of the constituency that promotes the issue and the internal directorate within APA that is most actively involved in the issue.

Issues concerning employment testing and fairness are generally of concern to both the Science and Public Interest Directorates within APA. In certain debates, public interest constituencies have directed or actively participate in these debates because they sense the issue is of sufficient relevance (e.g., ADA, the Bell Curve debate, *Larry P.*); in other issues, fairness has appeared somewhat more removed from the major issue (e.g., Goals 2000). In the end, APA policy is nearly determined as much by which parties decide to play in an issue as it is by the substantive content of an issue.

Individual members can have an impact on APA policy development by making their views known to the executive staff of APA, members serving on APA governance groups (e.g., its testing committee), and leaders of Divisions 5 and 14. When a constituency actively voices a concern about proposed legislation or a court case, the potential for APA involvement increases dramatically. APA policies have been and will continue to be the subject of controversy both from within industrial psychology and testing and outside that audience. This is as much a result of the nature of the process and organizational structure as it is of the demands of public policy that insist on a dichotomization of complex issues with a minimum of explanation.

REFERENCES

American Psychological Association, Division 5 (1991). Response to call for comments from the EEOC on implementation of the Americans with Disabilities Act. Washington, DC: Author.

American Psychological Association (1987). Amicus curiae brief in support of the petitioner. *Watson v. Fort Worth Bank and Trust*, p. 13.

American Psychological Association (1987). Amicus curiae brief in support of the respondent. *Price Waterhouse v. Hopkins.*

Camara, W. J. (1995). *APA involvement in employment testing and litigation: Historical overview.* Unpublished paper (available from the author).

Camara, W. J. (1992). You say job, I'll say position. *The Industrial and Organizational Psychologist, 30,* 29–32.

Camara, W. J. (1990). Correspondence to the U.S. House of Representatives Education and Labor Committee on the subject of the Civil Rights Act of 1990.

Civil Rights Act of 1991 (Pub.L. 102-166) (CRA).

Goodstein, L. (1985, October 2). Testimony before the U.S. House of Representatives Education and Labor Committee, Subcommittee on Employment Opportunities on the subject of the Uniform Guidelines on Employee Selection Procedures.

Larry P. v. Riles, 495 F. Supp. 926 (N.D. Cal. 1979) appeal docketed. No. 80-4027 (9th Cir., Jan. 17, 1980).

Schneider, B. (1991, March 5). Testimony before the U.S. House of Representatives Education and Labor Committee on the subject of the Civil Rights Act of 1991.

Standards for educational and psychological testing. (1985) Washington, DC: American Psychological Association.

Uniform guidelines on employee selection procedures, 29 C.F.R. 1607 (1978).

Wards Cove Packing Co., Inc. v. Antonio, 109 S.Ct. 3115 (1989).

2

Ethical Issues and Dilemmas in Fair Employment Strategies

Rodney L. Lowman

One of the defining characteristics of a profession is that, in addition to its members having at least minimal mastery of a defined and delimited body of knowledge (the boundaries of which often are fiercely guarded from encroachment by other professions), its members agree to abide by a particular ethical code of conduct. In return for membership in the profession, which bestows financial and other privileges, including high prestige, the member agrees to engage in certain behaviors and to refrain from engaging in others. He or she also accepts and agrees to espouse a particular set of values when engaged in that profession.

Concerning the extremes of behavior, consensus of appropriate behavioral guidelines is not difficult to obtain. Presumably few would contend that it is ethical (i.e., behaviorally appropriate) for a therapist or physician to have sex with a client, for a scholar to falsify research data, or for an expert serving as a professional witness intentionally to distort or misrepresent factual information. Professions might vary in the extent to which behavioral prescriptions are enforced or complaints of ethical malfeasance rigorously investigated, but about the inappropriateness of extreme behavior, there is little disagreement.

Controversial or emerging areas of practice and those in which competing values vie for influence invite ethical controversies and dilemmas (see, e.g., Eyde & Kowal, 1987; Eyde & Quaintance, 1988; London & Bray, 1980). In attempting to assure fair employment strategies, for example, the issues are complex and the ethical course of behavior not always obvious. Consensual agreement on appropriate standards of practice may, therefore, not easily be reached (see, e.g., Society of Industrial/Organizational Psychologists, 1985). The issue is complicated further by the fact that many different professionals, whose specific ethical principles or practices are not always consistent with one another, can be involved in fair employment cases.

In this chapter, written from the perspective of a psychologist involved, among other areas, in helping to identify ethical behavior in the practice of psychology in organizational contexts (Lowman, 1985), I consider ethical principles, dilemmas, and cases related to fair employment strategies. I attempt to demonstrate that it is the professional's obligation in any emerging area such as this one to make clear all assumptions and, at the least, to be explicit on the assumptions he or she has made.

SOURCES OF ETHICAL COMPLEXITY

The primary source of ethical guidance for psychologists is the ethics code of the American Psychological Association (APA) (1992). Other professions (e.g., law, medicine) are guided by their own mandated codes of behavior. The psychologists' ethical code identifies a number of aspirational and enforceable standards intended to guide the professional practice of psychology both in presently well-defined areas of practice and in emerging ones.

The ethical principles of psychologists are, perhaps, the best developed guidelines to professional behavior yet developed for any social science discipline. They articulate both desired and prohibited behavior, setting both an aspirational and an enforceable standard. Although the ethical standards of the APA technically apply only to the 100,000-plus members of that association, in practice, most states have adopted by law the APA ethics code in their licensure statutes. Psychology, as a profession of scientific origins, strives to define acceptable behavior in terms emphasizing objectivity, truthfulness, and candor, approaches that are expected to prevail in the forensic as well as the research context (see, e.g., ethical principles 7 and, particularly, 7.04, APA, 1992, p. 14). Although very explicit ethical guidelines are articulated in many areas of professional psychological practice, especially those concerning psychotherapy, it is not a distortion to state that there has been rather little guidance provided specifically on ethical issues in fair employment practice. At best, the professional is left to abstract the issues of fair employment practice from principles established in other contexts and for other types of problems. Nonetheless, the need is more for applying existing principles than for creating new ones, because no ethics code possibly can cover all applications, especially as practice becomes more complex and diversified.

In this chapter, I discuss some applications to fair employment testing of existing psychological ethical guidelines and attempt to identify ethical dilemmas and difficulties ranging from the obvious to the more subtle. The aim is to assist the practitioner in understanding how the ethical guidelines of at least one profession, psychology, would apply to fair employment strategies.

I will present sample cases to illustrate how the psychologist's ethical code might apply to issues arising in fair employment contexts. All cases in this chapter are composites or otherwise disguised in order to disguise the identity of the participants. They are provided for purposes of training and stimulating thought, not case resolution.

CASE 1. CONSIDERING ADVERSE IMPACT

Facts

A psychologist worked with an organizational client in a heavy manufacturing industry to design a new hiring selection procedure. The procedure included a test of mechanical reasoning that, according to the research literature and the psychologist's own experience, had adverse impact on females (the females taking the test were selected at a proportionately less high level than the males). A review of the literature for this ability showed a sex difference to occur in almost all samples. Still, the test had good validity coefficients (correlations between the test and criterion measures) with a variety of samples and jobs similar to the one being selected for.

The psychologist in this case set up a selection program using the mechanical reasoning test as the primary selection device. He did not consider alternative tests because he had used it to his clients' satisfaction in many other settings, he felt that this one had the highest validity coefficients, and he believed that what the test measured was most tied theoretically to primary duties of the jobs being selected for. It was not the psychologist's practice to do outcome studies in the specific applications, because the organizational client did not wish to pay for such efforts and the psychologist accurately surmised that the sample sizes would be too small to assure reliable findings. He felt that validity generalization could be used as the basis for defending the measure against any litigation. However, the psychologist also did not examine the empirical impact of his selection procedures on gender or race in the final hiring decisions. When, over time, adverse impact predictably obtained, the Equal Employment Opportunity Commission (EEOC) eventually brought charges against the company when their ratios of males to females actually became less favorable to women. In learning of the action taken against the company, the psychologist urged an aggressive legal counterattack on the grounds that the test had validity for the task at hand.

Interpretation

The psychologist in this case appears to have erred in failing to consider, or to advise his organizational client to consider, the need to take adverse impact into account when instituting a selection device or program. As APA's ethical principle 1.14 states: "Psychologists take reasonable steps to avoid harming their . . . clients . . . and to minimize harm where it is foreseeable and unavoidable" (APA, 1992, p. 1601). In this case, the psychologist had an ethical obligation to have been knowledgeable about the potential effects of adverse impact on a company and should have worked with the organization's managers to help them make an informed decision about how to balance the twin needs of validity and affirmative action. Failing even to consider the actual obtained results with the recommended test was especially problematic. Without necessarily abandoning the selection device, the psychologist might have recommended that the company use more than one kind of test (including other measures such as those of general cognitive ability, which are less likely to have adverse impact) or might have helped the company to consider affirmative action policies in which the most qualified of the female candidates might have been selected. In addition, the psychologist could have encouraged the company to institute vigorous recruiting policies to increase the pool of qualified female applicants so that persons able to perform the job well could be hired.

CASE 2. NOT-SO-EXPERT WITNESS TESTIMONY

Facts

A psychologist consulted with an organizational client that subsequently became involved in litigation concerning a particular employment issue. During the ensuing trial, a psychologist from one side was pitted against one from the other. One testified that the work of the other was shoddy and unprofessional, citing several minor flaws with the research analyses. However, the testimony was presented in such a manner to suggest that these issues, all trivial, had much greater import on the overall result than was actually the case. The result was a misleading impression, seemingly carefully nurtured, that the work done by the defendant's psychologist was entirely unprofessional.

Interpretation

Theoretically, a court proceeding is a search for truth. In fact, in the U.S. system of adversarial justice, the role of a trial often is anything but a disinterested search for truth. Experts are pitted against experts, and the result often is confusing to jurors and judges alike. Professionals serving as expert witnesses nonetheless retain an obligation to testify in an accurate and nonmisleading manner. The APA ethics principles stipulate: "In forensic testimony and reports, psychologists testify truthfully, honestly, and candidly and, consistent with applicable legal procedures, describe fairly the bases for their testimony and conclusions" (APA, 1992, p. 1610).

CASE 3. CONFIDENTIALITY OF TESTING MATERIALS

Facts

For a variety of reasons, including past employment procedures, a psychologist's client company came to the attention of the EEOC. The EEOC, as part of its initial review procedures, demanded, under threat of subpoena, copies of the original, name-identified records for a selection project and also copies of the tests employed. Releasing the tests would have violated the test publishers' terms of copyright and potentially would have resulted in sensitive psychological information (test scores) being released without the permission of the applicants. The psychologist insisted that the records not be released without identifying information being protected and that tests not be released to unqualified personnel.

At first, the EEOC staff made efforts to comply with these restrictions. However, when it became apparent that the procedures worked out to protect the identity of the applicants were cumbersome, they changed back to their original stance and demanded copies of name-identified records. In addition, they insisted that the tests themselves be given to the EEOC, although there was no qualified expert at the EEOC's regional office to interpret the tests.

The psychologist contacted the test publishers, whose attorneys reluctantly agreed to the release. Although the tests were ultimately provided as requested to the EEOC, steps were taken to increase the EEOC staff's awareness of confidentiality restrictions and copyright protections of the testing material. In this case, the psychologist did what could be done to protect confidentiality of tests and consumers of tests. By a release being obtained from the test publishers, grounds for copyright infringement were avoided. Nonetheless, the behavior of the EEOC representatives proved them to be unknowledgeable about confidentiality demands of professionals and unwilling to change their agency's policies to accommodate them. The review of complex psychological tests by unqualified persons is no less egregious a problem when conducted by a government agency than by an unqualified professional.

Implications

Too often psychologists are forced to compromise ethical standards by the nonnegotiable demands of the EEOC for receiving data in a particular way. The insistence, for example, that individual EEOC examiners, who rarely are trained testing professionals, have the right to examine tests on an item-by-item basis (EEOC, 1994) or that organizational clients provide copies of tests themselves without assuring proper protection of copyright restrictions and protecting the test from inappropriate disclosure creates needless complications for psychologists and other professionals attempting to behave professionally. Yet, the EEOC itself is an employer of psychologists and other technical experts, and these individuals do not abdicate their ethical obligations when they assume such positions. Agencies in general and psychologists employed by such agencies in particular own an ethical obligation to assure that their procedures for conducting investigations and litigation do not violate professional standards. In certain jurisdictions, introduction of specific tests and test items into a court proceeding is prohibited by law. Psychologists employed by organizations like the EEOC need to take steps aggressively to protect the integrity of the tests with which their agency's employees come into contact. For example, the APA ethical standards (principle 2.02b) state, in part: "Psychologists refrain from misuse of assessment techniques, interventions, results, and interpretations and take reasonable steps to prevent others from misusing the information these techniques provide. This includes refraining from releasing raw test results or raw data to persons . . . who are not qualified to use such information" (APA, 1992, p. 1603).

CASE 4. CURIOUS, IF NOT SPURIOUS, DATA

A psychologist, presuming to represent the best interests of her company client, presented in a contested employment selection trial correlation coefficients between selection tests and outcome measures that strained all credibility. Whereas the usual magnitude of correlation between a criterion measure and a valid selection procedure is positive but moderate (say, correlations in the +.30s), this psychologist testified under oath that the correlations between predictor and outcome were very high (generally in the +.90s). Such findings were not in keeping with those typically found in the literature. When challenged on this result, the psychologist steadfastly maintained that her data were accurate but refused to allow objective outside researchers to review her data or collected evidence. Another psychologist attempted to replicate these findings in another sample and found a positive, but much more modest, correlation pattern.

After the trial, an ethics charge was brought against the psychologist by an expert witness for the other side. The charge was sustained when the psychologist admitted to an impartial review panel that she had "through oversight" inflated the magnitude of the correlations to further her client's case when it became clear that the evidence on which the enthusiastic conclusions had been drawn was scientifically unacceptable.

OTHER ILLUSTRATIVE EXAMPLES

The cases so far presented illustrate the diversity of types of ethical concern and behavioral problems from the obvious to the complex. In the next section, I will illustrate other dilemmas that professionals may encounter.

Bias, Let Me Count the Ways

An expert may be engaged and asked to perform technical analyses but with restrictions placed on what the psychologist can analyze or consider. Professional psychologists should seriously question and generally decline such arrangements, because partial analyses may obscure important limitations of the data.

Similarly, the work of psychologists may be obscured by a partial reporting of obtained results. Reporting only positive or significant results when there are also negative ones is problematic. Generally, psychologists should report all relevant findings, both supportive and not supportive of the case.

Misleading results also may obtain by inflation of correlation coefficients by correcting for restriction in range when there is none or using an inappropriately low estimate of reliability of the criterion measure. Both tactics can be misleading in suggesting a larger relationship between predictors and criterion than is appropriate.

Finally, and, hopefully, rarely, outright falsification of data occasionally happens. Such behavior obviously is unethical.

Shy Ghosts

Sometimes these cases involve an unidentified expert, sometimes called a "ghost expert," whose identity is unknown to the psychologist asked to perform the analyses. Such experts may direct or comment on the work of hired psychological consultants. Concerning the use of undisclosed expert witnesses, client organizations might do better to identify to the expert the identity of all involved experts, because certain experts may be known for particular biases or prejudices. Moreover, allowing certain experts to criticize the work of others without opportunity for recourse or rebuttal is potentially problematic.

Abusive Discovery

Either side to litigation may create inappropriate delays in a fair employment litigation process. Although such tactics may be common legal maneuvers, they strain psychologists' ethics. Reported practices in this area include "losing" data that are on hand, presenting data in an incomprehensible format when clearer data are on hand, or asking the other side for overly detailed information that is difficult and expensive to assemble but that has no known value.

Overall, there are many opportunities for abuse by and of psychologists in fair employment cases. Psychologists who take their ethical obligations seriously decline to engage in false, misleading, or inappropriate practices and do not condone the behavior of those who do. They decline opportunities, even when financially rewarding, that involve compromises to their ethical standards. As Plato put it, "It is better to suffer wrong than to do wrong."

REFERENCES

American Psychological Association. (1992). Ethical principles of psychologists and code of conduct. *American Psychologist, 47,* 1597–1611.

Equal Employment Opportunity Commission. (1994). Enforcement guidance: Pre-employment disability-related inquiries and medical examinations under the Americans with Disabilities Act. Washington, DC: Author.

Eyde, L. D., & Kowal, D. M. (1987). Computerised test interpretation services: Ethical and professional concerns regarding U.S. producers and users. *Applied Psychology: An International Review, 36,* 401–417.

Eyde, L. D., & Quaintance, M. K. (1988). Ethical issues and cases in the practice of personnel psychology. *Professional Psychology: Research and Practice, 19,* 148–154.

London, M., & Bray, D. W. (1980). Ethical issues in testing and evaluation for personnel decisions. *American Psychologist, 35,* 890–901.

Lowman, R. L. (Ed.). (1985). *Casebook on ethics and standards for the practice of psychology in organizations.* Bowling Green, OH: Society of Industrial/ Organizational Psychology. (Withdrawn from publication; revision to be published in 1996).

Society of Industrial/Organizational Psychology. (1985). *Principles for the validation and use of personnel selection procedures* (2d ed.). Bowling Green, OH: Author.

II

CONTENT VALIDITY

3

Job Analysis

Richard S. Barrett

Job descriptions are fundamental to the development and validation of selection procedures, especially those that are justified on the basis of content validity. The requirements of a job description seem simple. It should describe the important work behaviors or work products in enough detail so that a reader can understand what is done on the job and the complexity and importance of the major job duties. Next the Knowledge, Skill, and Ability (KSAs) and, sometimes, other attributes required to perform the job duties should be described in behavioral terms.

A flaw in the writing and interpretation of the Uniform Guidelines on Employee Selection Procedures (1978, hereafter Uniform Guidelines) has led to a proliferation of task analyses, in which dozens of specific activities are defined and then rated for importance and other characteristics. Task analysis sometimes is carried to unrealistic extremes that contribute little to the validity of the selection procedure while diverting attention and funds from the basic objective, that is, developing fair, job-related selection procedures.

JOB DESCRIPTION

There is no prescribed way to analyze a job. Interviews may be conducted with incumbents, supervisors, or other knowledgeable employees. Observations at the workplace may be augmented by training of the job analyst about the job. All that is required is that an effective method be used and described.

The degree of completeness is determined by common sense, because the amount of detail is not specified. The important behaviors should be described; the trivial and obvious may be ignored. The term "behavior" is not limited to physical activities or the production of physical products; it includes less visible activities such as those involved in analyzing problems and making decisions. There should be enough narrative detail so that a person who knows the world of work but does not know the job would understand what is done.

A major flaw in some job descriptions is a lack of meaningful detail. For example, a reference to interviewing in the complex job of social service casework says only this: "Interviews clients in home or office. . . . Interviews applicants for service to children and persons referring cases of children needing care or supervision." This is scarcely enough to guide the development of a content-valid test.

Some organizations, by policy, do not have job descriptions or deliberately keep them vague in an effort to deflect critics or unions who may use more complete and accurate information to further their own objectives. Whether this is a wise strategy for the employer is not for me to say, but it does interfere with developing and defending selection procedures.

Importance is usually measured by subject matter experts, who divide 100 percentage points among a list of 10 to 15 major job duties. Ideally, the list should be exclusive and exhaustive. Such lists are hard to write, but most raters can handle a little ambiguity. It is advisable to have the ratings performed by several subject matter experts, because there are likely to be a few who divide up the percentages idiosyncratically. Graphic rating scales generally are too subject to response set to be useful.

Section 14 B(3), Job Analysis or Review of Job Information, of the Uniform Guidelines (1978) suggests the use of "frequency of performance" as a possible basis for judging importance. Generally, there is a close connection between time spent and importance, but not always. Sales representatives may spend several hours a day driving between customers, but the purpose of the job is to convince the customer to place an order. The extreme discontinuity between time spent and importance occurs in firefighting. The major purpose of a fire department is putting out fires, but employees spend only 3–5 percent of their time in this activity.

When the job analysis also identifies the KSAs, they must be defined and the relationship between each knowledge, skill, or ability and each work behavior, as well as the method used to determine this relationship, should be provided.

Knowledge, skill, and ability are defined behaviorally in Sec. 16:

Knowledge — A body of information applied directly to the performance of a
    function

Skill — A present, observable competence to perform a learned psychomotor act

Ability — A present competence to perform a behavior or a behavior that results in an observable work product.

Despite the efforts in the Uniform Guidelines (1978) to require operational definitions, some test developers revert to vague generalities. One test development agency produced a list of 875 job elements for state troopers, including good memory, ability to project authority, lack of prejudice, pride, compassion, no narcolepsy, ability to conform, and ability to light flares.

Over the years, however, the use of KSAs has changed. Some test developers do not list them at all, relying only on the description of the job duties. Others are more specific and behavioral and, therefore, more useful.

TASK ANALYSIS

Perhaps because Section 15C(3), Job Analysis, of the Uniform Guidelines (1978) mentions "the associated tasks" or simply because test builders want to protect their flanks, the Uniform Guidelines have been interpreted to mean that task analysis is required. Task analysis starts with compiling a list of dozens of discrete job elements, eliminating the least important, and then rating the survivors on several scales. Question and Answer Number 77 clarifies the issue:

Q. Is a task analysis necessary to support a selection procedure based on content validity?

A. A description of all tasks is not required by the Guidelines. However, the job analysis should describe all important work behaviors and their relative importance and their level of difficulty. . . . The job analysis should focus on the observable work behaviors and, to the extent appropriate, observable work products, and the tasks associated with important observable work behaviors and/or work products. The job analysis should identify the critical or important work behaviors that are used in the job, and should support the content of the selection procedure.

Despite this disclaimer, countless hours and thousands of dollars have been wasted in developing and evaluating hundreds of tasks, sometimes for the simplest jobs.

CONCLUSION

The job description is the foundation on which content-valid tests are built and provides useful information for content validation efforts. If it is needed later to convince a court that the selection procedure really is job related, it should communicate enough information to inform the court on what is done and the importance and complexity of the major job duties.

There are several shortcuts. Many jobs already have been described. Much time and effort can be saved by cooperative efforts in which an employer takes advantage of the work already done by another.

Dividing up 100 percentage points among major job duties is quicker and more accurate than task ratings, which sometimes use ten-point scales, more than most people can handle.

Narrative descriptions of duties can communicate complexity better than graphic ratings.

The Uniform Guidelines (1978) define KSAs in terms of the ability to perform job functions. There is little value in ratings for police officers on memory, basic math ability, integrity, observation, and perceptiveness (among a total of 22 traits). It may be possible to show that the measures of these traits are related to success on the job through an empirical study, but their value cannot be assumed.

Even with the best job description, it usually is necessary to collect additional information to develop and, later, justify a specific selection procedure. The job description provides the framework but not the details that are required.

REFERENCES

Questions and answers to clarify and provide a common interpretation of the uniform guidelines on employee selection procedures, 41 F.R. 11996 (March 7, 1979).

Uniform guidelines on employee selection procedures, 29 C.F.R. 1607 (1978).

4

Content Validation

Irwin L. Goldstein and Sheldon Zedeck

VALIDATION AND SELECTION SYSTEMS

The usefulness of any selection system, be it a written multiple-choice test, an interview, or a job simulation, begins with the question of validity. This is made particularly clear in the description of validity concerning test usage provided in the *Standards for Educational and Psychological Testing* (1985): "Validity is the most important consideration in test evaluation. The concept refers to the appropriateness, meaningfulness, and usefulness of the specific inferences from test scores. Test validation is the process of accumulating evidence to support such inferences" (p. 9). Although the evidence may be collected in a variety of ways, an essential point is that "validity" refers to the degree to which the evidence supports making inferences about probable job behavior based upon test scores. The *Principles for the Validation and Use of Personnel Selection Procedures* (Society for Industrial and Organization Psychology, Inc. [SIOP], 1987, hereafter SIOP Principles), make it clear that there are a variety of strategies that can be used to collect evidence concerning inferences about scores, one of which is a content-oriented strategy. An excellent review of the various validity strategies is presented by Schmitt and Landy (1993).

CONTENT-ORIENTED STRATEGIES

As stated in the Uniform Guidelines on Employee Selection Procedures (1978, hereafter Uniform Guidelines), "To demonstrate the content validity of a selection procedure, a user should show that the behavior(s) demonstrated in the selection procedure are a representative sample of the behavior(s) of the job in question or that the selection process procedure provides a representative sample of the work product or the job" (Sec. 14C(4)). A similar view is stated in the SIOP Principles (1987), where it is noted that content validity is an appropriate strategy when the "job domain is defined through job analysis by identifying important tasks, behaviors, or knowledge and the test . . . is a representative sample of tasks, behaviors, or knowledge drawn from that domain" (p. 19).

Thus, if it can be shown that the test measures the critical aspects of the job performance domain, inferences about job performance based on the test are justified. One way of conceptualizing this relationship is that if the test and the on-the-job performance domain are identical or interchangeable, inferences about the relationship of performance on the test and performance on the job could be made with considerable confidence. In most instances, it is not possible for the test and performance domain to be exactly identical. However, it is possible to design tests that simulate the job tasks such that the knowledges, skills, and abilities (KSAs) required to perform well on the test are the same KSAs that are required to perform well on the job. In other words, when there is congruence between the KSAs required to perform on the job and the KSAs required to perform on the testing instrument, then it would be possible to make inferences about how the test scores relate to job behavior. Such assumptions are clearly based on the degree of fit between the specific KSAs that are critical for job performance and the specific KSAs that are being assessed with the testing instrument.

However, to the degree that there are KSAs required for performance on the test that are not required for job performance, the test is contaminated, and inferences concerning the scores are more problematical. Contamination can occur when the wrong KSAs are tested because a detailed job analysis that accurately specifies the required KSAs has not been properly performed (the role of job analysis is described further below). An example of this problem experienced by the authors was a math test that required a candidate for the position of fire conservation ranger to perform certain advanced mathematical computations. It turned out that, per the job analysis, the test was supposed to examine the ability of the ranger to count the number of animal species in a physical area, but counting objects and performing advanced mathematical computations are not the same skill. Thus, it may be that the wrong persons were being selected for the job because the wrong KSAs were being tested; certainly, the behaviors required to perform well on the test were not the same behaviors required to perform well on the job. It may be that there is a general math ability that includes counting as well as mathematical computation performance; in other words, persons who perform well on one of these tasks will also perform well on the other because it is part of a general ability construct. However, as presented later in this chapter, content validation by itself is not an appropriate methodology for establishing constructs. What is needed for the test to select rangers is a test that focuses on the ability to count.

At other times, contamination occurs because the testing method itself introduces required KSAs that may not be critical for job performance. For example, a job analysis for the position of a lieutenant in a fire department might indicate that, when arriving at a fire scene, the lieutenant gives short orders indicating where the firefighters should place themselves and what equipment they should take into a fire. If, in the testing situation, the examinee is required to respond to the presentation of a fire scene by writing an essay concerning what he or she would do, there is the question of whether that is content valid, that is, if writing an essay requires KSAs that the job analysis indicates might not be relevant for the position of a supervisory firefighter. If the candidate is required to write the essay in perfect English and the exam is scored for spelling and the quality of the written essay, there are even more serious issues about content validity. If we added the fact that, in the fire department under study, the lieutenant does not perform any writing of essays or reports, then there is the further question of whether the examination format requires KSAs that are not required by the job. One strategy that was used to resolve this problem was to give examinees a tape recorder and instruct them to respond to the fire scene situations by speaking the directions and orders they would have given. This point is discussed in the SIOP Principles (1987), in which it is noted that, in order to minimize contamination, "Irrelevant components should be minimized" (p. 23). In any case, it should be apparent from these examples that, in establishing content valid tests, the job analysis needs to be very detailed and carefully performed. We will discuss that point further below.

Another aspect of content validity is that, if there are key aspects of the job that the test is expected to assess but it does not, the selection system can be, to some degree, deficient. For example, a job analysis might show that there are a number of important components to the job, ranging from the ability to communicate effectively with other individuals to the ability to read. Often, when testing large numbers of individuals (as sometimes happens in entry level tests, especially in the public sector), it is difficult to test the ability to communicate effectively, because this might require an individual assessment exercise. On the other hand, it is quite possible to test the ability to read with large numbers of individuals by employing paper and pencil methodology. Clearly, the question of deficiency is a matter of degree. If large, important components of the job are not tested, then questions arise about the degree to which the selection system is deficient. The question of how much of the job a selection system needs to measure in order to be considered acceptable is not easily determined, but clearly, the test developer must present a plan that shows that critical KSAs identified in the job analysis are being tested. This situation evolves into a more serious legal issue when the test developer only tests a small portion of the KSAs required for the job and the test produces serious adverse impact against protected class members, such as minorities or women. In these situations, it becomes the responsibility of the test developer to design innovative approaches that permit the testing of other important KSAs required for the job.

CRITICAL ISSUES IN ESTABLISHING CONTENT VALIDITY

The Role of Job Analysis

It is clear that one major difference in content- and criterion-oriented strategies is that, in content approaches, statistical correlational evidence is not collected to show that the scores on the test actually predict job performance (see Chapter 8, this volume, for further discussion). Rather, as discussed above, the evidence for content validity concerns the degree of congruence or overlap in KSAs between the critical job components and the test components. This places considerable stress on the completeness and accuracy of the job analysis, because it serves as the entire foundation for the content validity approach. Goldstein, Zedeck, and Schneider (1993) describe the type of detailed job analysis necessary for establishing a foundation for content validity. The critical components of the job analysis procedures that they describe include the following.

The final outcome of the job analysis needs to be a set of specific KSAs and a set of specific task groups or tasks to which the KSAs are linked. These groups of linked KSA-tasks provide the foundation for the design of content-valid tests. The specificity of the tasks and KSAs is required so that there is no misunderstanding about what is being tested and why the test requires the same behaviors as the job. The SIOP Principles (1987) recognize this issue by noting that "When ability is defined in this very specific way, content-oriented strategies may be sufficient. When referring to more general abilities such as reasoning or spatial ability, a construct-oriented strategy is likely to be necessary" (p. 19). The Uniform Guidelines (1978) similarly recognize this issue by stating that content-oriented strategies are not appropriate for demonstrating the validity of a selection procedure when they "purport to measure traits or constructs such as intelligence, aptitude, personality, commonsense, judgment, leadership and spatial ability" (Sec. 14C(1)). The issue related to specificity becomes clearer when one considers a general ability, such as the "ability to write." This issue is, of course, the same issue discussed in the above example concerning the forest conservation ranger and the construct of a general math ability. In this case, the ability is not described in a specific enough way to determine whether the behavior being tested is the behavior required to perform the job. For example, the "ability to write" could really mean any of the following: ability to compose clear and concise sentences and paragraphs in preparing a written report, ability to transcribe alphanumeric data accurately, ability to take notes describing an event that can be interpreted later, or ability to record information from records onto a standardized form.

Clearly, one would design different steps to measure performance for these different situations. However, if the job analysis produced a statement such as "ability to record information from records onto a standardized form" as opposed to "ability to write" or "ability to transcribe," the test developer can more easily construct an exercise that simulates the tasks and the requisite KSAs, with the end result being a content-valid test. Having specific information concerning the ability required and also having specific information concerning the tasks performed make it possible to design simulated exercises that call forth the critical KSAs necessary to produce the behaviors required on the job.

The collection of job analysis information requires a systematic approach that ensures that the information collected is truly representative of the job in question. This requires the design of a methodology to ensure that information is collected that captures the job (including both tasks and KSAs). It is helpful to think of job analysis as a series of accurate, multiple photographs. This is not a trivial exercise, because sometimes it is even difficult to determine what the actual target job is. For example, the use of standard job titles or a generic name for a job often is misleading, because it can mask a variety of jobs. The title of "administrative aide" in hospital management groups often includes a variety of jobs, including executive secretary, laboratory assistant, or personnel analyst. Similarly, the same job might vary considerably, depending on a number of factors, including where or when it is performed. Thus, an important step is defining the job in question and determining what information needs to be collected.

It is also necessary to determine what methods will be used to collect the job information so that the "photographs" truly capture the job. There are a number of methods that can be used in this process, such as job observations, interviews with individuals and panels, and surveys. Each of these techniques has different advantages and disadvantages. For example, interviews are subject to the interviewers' skills and biases, while mail surveys, under some conditions, might have low return rates. Good planning is needed to ensure the best use of a number of techniques to maximize the quality of the job analysis information. Harvey (1991) and Goldstein (1993) describe many of the different types of systems available for collecting such information.

It also is important to determine how to select representative members (both job incumbents and supervisors) from the organization to participate in the job analysis process. For example, if the job varies in the way it is performed from location to location or from shift to shift, it is important that individuals are selected who are able to represent that variation. Also, it is necessary to select persons who know how the job is to be performed; therefore, selecting persons with limited job experience or focusing on persons who are not good performers makes no sense. Another consideration is when to use incumbents and when to use supervisors in the job analysis process. We have found that incumbents are good at describing the tasks that they perform, while supervisors are better at describing the KSAs needed to perform the tasks. For these reasons, the individuals chosen usually are called "subject matter experts" (SMEs). Given how critical these individuals are to the process, it is important to have a plan that documents how these choices were made. Leaving the choice to a clerk or organizational representative without clear guidelines may lead to difficulties. For example, in such instances, you might end up with nonrepresentative SMEs — persons who are not strong performers are chosen because their employers do not want to have their best people off the job participating in the job analysis.

Also, it is important to represent the views of different groups of individuals, such as members of minority groups or women. In some instances, it is possible that these individuals perform the job in different ways or have different tasks to perform. For example, in one law enforcement agency, women were assigned to tasks in airports because their supervisors viewed those assignments as less dangerous. Regardless of your views concerning such assignments, failure to include women would have resulted in leaving out those tasks from the job analysis. In other cases, there is the view that some groups overrepresent the difficulty of certain tasks in order to make it more difficult for others to be selected for the job. Even if you believe there is general agreement on how the job is performed among all members of the work group, it will be very difficult to explain to group members and the courts why no members of these classes participated in the job analysis and why there are no data available on these issues.

In addition to the processes involved in collecting information concerning the tasks and KSAs required to perform the tasks, there is also a need for quantitative data on certain critical functions. Thus, in describing tasks, it is important to know which tasks are truly important to the job as well as which tasks are performed most frequently. Similarly, for KSAs, it is important to know which are important for job performance. Typically, this type of information is collected in survey format, in which it is possible to obtain independent judgments from a sample of people. One has a lot more confidence that a KSA is important when a group of 50 SMEs independently rated it as important and when there is little disagreement between them. In any case, it is necessary for the test developer to be able to show eventually that the test actually relates to important functions of the job, and the only way to do this is to have the information available.

Knowledges, Skill, and Ability in Terms of What Is Needed the First Day on the Job

When using content validity strategies, it is important to determine what an employee is expected to be able to perform or to know before placement on the job. Thus, the Uniform Guidelines (1978) note that "Content validity is not an appropriate strategy when the selection procedure involved knowledges, skills or abilities which an employee will be expected to learn on the job" (Sec. 14C(1)). Thus, another piece of information collected in the job analysis is whether employees are expected to have the KSAs in their repertoire before placement on the job or before being trained. Often, knowledge components, such as the knowledge of policies or rules or regulations, fall into the category of items that need to be learned once the employee is on the job. This means that, for entry-level positions, even knowledge that eventually will be critical for job performance will not be testable. If you discover that, in your job analysis for an entry-level job, there is considerable knowledge specified as important and needed the first day, a careful check should be done to ensure that mistakes have not been made.

As far as knowledge is concerned, even when it is needed on the first day, it is important to determine whether the knowledge is memory-type knowledge that incumbents are expected to have memorized and at their fingertips or whether it is the kind of knowledge that a person typically looks up when he or she needs it. There have been instances where an entire test has consisted of short-answer questions based upon candidates being asked to memorize an entire policy manual. In a number of these instances, it was determined that either the knowledge is not required the first day or the job incumbent virtually never memorizes the information but looks it up when it is needed. When that latter type of situation exists, the content validity of the examination becomes suspect. An option in such an instance would be to develop a test that asks questions about the knowledge but provides manuals and other job-related documents that the examinee can use while answering questions; this is similar to an open-book examination.

Detailing a Test Plan

When the job analysis is complete, a template is available consisting of information linking KSAs that are critical and needed the first day to tasks or task groups that are important and performed on the job. At this point, the test developer designs test components that reflect these KSA-task linkages. A test plan describes why the particular testing procedure is being chosen and how it corresponds to the data from the job analysis. Information needs to be provided to show that the test examines the critical KSAs that are needed the first day and that the simulations are based upon important tasks. Information also is provided to show that the tasks being designed are also those that the job analysis indicates give candidates the opportunity to show their performance on the critical KSAs.

The actual design of the test and answer keys is outside the scope of this chapter. However, it is a critical aspect of the process. Thus, for example, it is important to know that the wanted answers are really correct. It is not unusual for organizations to have conflicting policies that need to be sorted out, nor is it unusual for policies to change between the beginning of the job analysis and the actual test implementation. Also, there is the question of whether the level of difficulty is correct. The job analysis may specify that an individual needs a certain type of reading ability, but unless the level is carefully specified by checking materials in use in the organization, the test inadvertently may have the level set too high, thereby eliminating persons who could perform the job well. All of these types of concerns need to be checked. The process involves working carefully with representative SMEs from the organization. A list of many of these types of concerns is presented in Chapter 6. Also, the chapters in this book contain information on many different kinds of tests and procedures. The usefulness of any particular test depends on whether the particular procedure is useful for presenting the particular critical tasks and KSAs identified through the job analysis.

Establishing Content Validation,
or the Retranslation Process

Once the test has been developed, two critical sets of information exist: the job analysis and the test itself. It is clear that, if the process works properly, the test should stem from the job analysis and, therefore, should be content valid. However, the way to actually establish that fact is through a process known as "retranslation." For this process, a new group of representative SMEs who were not involved in the original development of the test are chosen. These individuals are asked to review each component of the test and the answers and then to indicate independently which KSAs generated by the job analysis are required to perform well on each test component. It, thus, is possible to collect data that establish which KSAs are being tested (and which are not being tested). These data also require a measure of whether the SMEs agree about these judgments. In addition, it is also possible to determine whether KSAs that were not intended to be tested are included. If those KSAs are not identified in the job analysis as important or are identified as KSAs that are not required the first day, then further test development changes are needed. For example, if test administration necessitates that the examinee write his or her response but the job does not require writing ability, a potential solution would be that the writing per se not be evaluated or scored. Examinees would be told this so that they would not be spending time constructing "perfect sentences" but, instead, could use shorthand, outlines, and so on to indicate their response.

A second retranslation is to have SMEs link the tasks identified in the job analysis to the tasks required in the test components. In this way, we learn about the representativeness of the test components to the job.

In summary, these processes help provide data concerning the content validity or content relevance of the test. They also provide critical information for the weighting of the test components. There are many different ways of setting up weighting systems, but the general principles are that the test components that test for the more important KSAs and the KSAs that are related to more tasks deserve more weight. Weighting schemes as well as cut scores are described in other chapters in this book.

DOCUMENTATION

We hope that it is clear that content validation strategies involve a process ranging from the choice of methods to the choice of SMEs to data collection techniques and so on. The Uniform Guidelines (1978) and the SIOP Principles (1987) make it absolutely clear that it is the responsibility of the test developers to maintain careful records and documentation. You need to be able to describe what happened, who did what, who participated, and so on. Failure to maintain such documentation makes it extremely difficult to provide support or evidence for the content validity process.

WHEN CONTENT VALIDATION STRATEGIES ARE MOST APPROPRIATE

It is clear that validation is a process and content validation is one strategy for obtaining information concerning validity. Obviously, the more evidence that is collected, the more comfortable the investigator should feel about making inferences concerning validity. Thus, when content validation evidence is provided along with criterion-related evidence, the case for validation is that much stronger. Similarly, it is true that when a content validity study is well-conducted, the evidence for support is much stronger than when a poor study is conducted. The same is also true for a well-conducted criterion-related validity study.

However, it is still possible to ask whether there are situations in which content validation strategies are likely to be your only option. Our experience is that there are a number of situations in which content validity may be the only strategy for developing information to support inferences about validity. One such situation occurs when the sample size is not large enough for a criterion-related validity study, such as when only small samples of persons are eligible for a particular promotion. In other instances, reliable criterion information cannot be obtained for a variety of reasons, such as the adversarial conditions that often occur as a result of fair employment practices lawsuits or union actions that forbid the collection of job performance information. In any case, whenever a content validity study is performed (or a criterion-related study, for that matter), a poorly conceived and executed effort does not contribute to the evidence toward establishing validity. Too often, content strategies have been used as a cheap and easy way to avoid the effort necessary for validation efforts. It now is abundantly clear that effective strategies for developing content-related evidence have evolved and that a poorly conducted effort does not serve the organization well.

REFERENCES

Goldstein, I. L. (1993). *Training in organizations.* Belmont, CA: Brooks-Cole.

Goldstein, I. L., Zedeck, S., & Schneider, B. (1993). An exploration job analysis-content validity process. In N. Schmitt & W. C. Borman (Eds.), *Personnel selection in organizations* (pp. 3–34). San Francisco, CA: Jossey-Bass.

Harvey, R. J. (1991). Job analysis. In M. D. Dunnette & L. M. Hough (Eds.), *Handbook of industrial and organizational psychology* (pp. 71–164). Palo Alto, CA: Consulting Psychologists Press.

Schmitt, N., & Landy, F. J. (1993). The concept of validity. In N. Schmitt & W. C. Borman (Eds.), *Personnel selection in organizations* (pp. 275–309). San Francisco, CA: Jossey-Bass.

Society for Industrial and Organizational Psychology, Inc. (1987). *Principles for the validation and use of personnel selection procedures* (3rd ed.). College Park, MD: Author.

Standards for educational and psychological testing. (1985). Washington, DC: American Psychological Association.

Uniform guidelines on employee selection procedures, 29 C.F.R. 1607 (1978).

5

Content Validity, Face Validity, and Quantitative Face Validity

William C. Burns

This chapter discusses some of the issues involved in the definition and use of content validity from two very different perspectives. In the first section, a professional perspective is used. The term "professional" is used in this chapter to refer to the standards that have developed over the past 50 years in the fields of industrial and organizational psychology, psychometrics, and educational tests and measurements. In particular, an attempt is made to identify and distinguish "quantitative face validity" as a less-than-acceptable substitute for content validity. Another form of pseudovalidity, identified here as "semantic validity," is also defined and discussed. The second section examines content validity as it is defined by the Uniform Guidelines on Employee Selection Procedures (1978, hereafter Uniform Guidelines). In attempting to translate content validity into regulations, the federal agencies approach the subject in a way that, at first, seems rather strange. The third section, which focuses on using content validity, attempts to explore how an employer can meet both professional standards and the requirements of the Uniform Guidelines.

THE PROFESSIONAL PERSPECTIVE

The Legal Climate

Equal employment laws, regulations, and guidelines have pressured employers using tests to develop evidence of their validity. Underlying these pressures in many cases is a substantial financial exposure. Public employers are probably under the most difficult set of constraints. Many have civil service regulations that require that a large number of "examinations" be developed and given each year involving both entry-level jobs and promotions. The amount and the complexity of the research that would be required to accumulate the evidence needed to demonstrate that the inferences from these test scores are valid are well beyond the resources and the budgets of the agencies involved. (The professional definition of validity is quoted at the beginning of Chapter 4.)

Probably the only feasible strategy open to these agencies if they wished to satisfy both professional and legal standards is to form consortia so that the costs of the research could be shared. Unfortunately, rather than adopt a research-based strategy, many agencies have decided to try to claim that their tests are content valid by stretching the definition of content validity well beyond professionally acceptable limits. The most primitive approach is referred to here as "semantic validity."

Semantic Validity

The process is simple. The exam writer does a job analysis and then labels the knowledges, skills, and abilities (KSAs) that he or she theorizes are needed to perform the job duties. The next step is to write test items and use the same set of labels that were used in the job analysis. The result is a single set of labels that are assigned to both domains. This result can be described to nonprofessionals as a demonstration that the content of the test is the same as the content of the job, and, therefore, the test is content valid. Some of these exam writers have used the term "rational validity" to enhance their claim to legitimacy. Although, when the process is described in this way and its absurdity seems evident, it can be surprisingly difficult to convince some laymen (e.g., judges) that it is not an acceptable showing of job relatedness. Even more difficult to challenge are the pseudovalidation strategies that are complex extensions of face validity.

Face Validity

Professionals consistently have distinguished between actual validity and face validity. Anastasi (1988) begins a section on face validity as follows: "Content validity should not be confused with face validity. The latter is not validity in the technical sense; it refers, not to what the test actually measures, but to what it appears superficially to measure. Face validity pertains to whether the test looks valid to the examinees who take it, the administrative personnel who decide on its use, and other technically untrained observers." Describing the "administrative personnel" or the "technically untrained observers" as subject matter experts

(SMEs) and asking them to offer an opinion on whether the test "looks valid" does not alter the methodology. A nonprofessional is being asked to determine whether the test is valid or not. Labeling the nonprofessional an SME does not transform face validity into an acceptable validation strategy.

Collecting the opinions of the nonprofessional SMEs on forms and asking them to assign numbers to their opinions produces "data" but does not remove the process from the face validity category. The data are simply a quantification of opinion. They allow the calculation of means, standard deviations, interrater correlations, and many other possible statistics. Once the trappings of empirical research are applied to the SMEs' opinions, it is easy to lose sight of the fact that they are, after all, the opinions of laymen about the degree to which the test looks valid to them.

The label "quantitative face validity" was chosen as a name for this procedure to emphasize the fact that, despite the "scientific" appearance of the report, it is still only face validity.

I have examined many of these reports. Although it is only an anecdotal finding, I have concluded that SMEs almost always will report that the test (or its individual items) looks valid to them. Thus, a quantitative face validity procedure almost invariably will provide apparent support for a validity claim. This is true regardless of whether the test is actually valid.

Defining Content Validity

Definitions of content validity by the Society for Industrial and Organizational Psychology and by the federal Uniform Guidelines are quoted at the beginning of Chapter 4. Notice that, in both cases, the key to the definition is the idea of a representative sample. Just as measures of relationships (such as the correlation coefficient) are at the core of evidence supporting criterion-related validity, the nature and quality of the sampling process are central in providing evidence of content validity. The most important implication of the centrality of the sampling process is the truism that whatever is sampled is a member of the domain from which the sample is drawn. Thus, the relationship between the sample and the domain is "same as." Because the test and the job domain sampled are the same, there is no need to collect empirical data to determine their relationship. The other aspect of the implied sameness between the test and the job domain is that, if they are not the same, then content validity cannot be demonstrated. The relationship between the two domains then must be determined using empirical research. This requirement is a frequent occurrence when a content-oriented test development strategy is used.

Content-oriented Test Development

As long as the critical difference between test development and test validation is recognized, content-oriented test development offers a rich set of possibilities for innovation. Simulations, theoretical measures that attempt to replicate the elements thought to underlie superior performance, and many other creative measurement approaches that can be derived from thoughtfully observing job content and job performance become possibilities. However, as with any other test development strategy, an empirical validation process then must determine that the inferences about job performance are valid.

What Is a Link?

In many of the situations in which it cannot be shown that the test items are sampled from a job domain and the test developer wishes to avoid the expense of empirical research, a procedure is devised to "link" the test domain and the job domain. Professionals know what sampling is and they know what a correlation coefficient is, but what is a link? A survey of dictionary definitions leads to the conclusion that it is some sort of connection. What are the methodological or psychometric characteristics of a link? How does one determine when an attempt to establish a link has failed? To say that a link as a scientific construct is well short of minimal professional standards is stating the obvious. The use of the word "link" or a synonym that claims to connect the job and test domains is an almost infallible indicator of semantic or face validity.

A Sophisticated Example of Apparent Content Validity

Chapter 4 is an excellent example of how some of these issues can come together. Most important, it is a creative, sophisticated approach by two eminent industrial/organizational psychologists with well-deserved reputations for excellence (see also Goldstein, Zedeck, and Schneider, 1993). It is a good model for content-oriented test development. The fire scene simulation is an example of the way that content-oriented test development can produce measures that, theoretically, should have higher validities than the standard ability and aptitude tests. The authors also point out some of the ways that content-oriented test development can go astray.

I would argue, however, that there is still one gap that needs to be closed. The support for the inferences required by the definition of validity rests entirely on judgments by professionals or the opinions of SMEs.

I have had direct experience with tests that were developed using the content-oriented approach but that produced opposite results. The Berger Programming Test, which begins by defining a small, highly abstract programming language, produced empirical validities well above programmer aptitude tests and standard ability tests. Exactly opposite results occurred in the development of a selection battery for power plant control room operators; a computer simulation that looked valid to both seasoned industrial/organizational psychologists and the SMEs who were consulted failed to show a relationship to job performance. More traditional ability tests showed substantial validities; therefore, neither the research design nor the performance measures were at fault. The problem was that, apparently, the simulation did not accurately simulate.

It is probably only a matter of time before enough examples of failed judgments and opinions have occurred to discredit what I believe to be a promising procedure. A way must be found to move the process from the quantitative face validity category to a methodology that could correct for overly enthusiastic professionals and the apparent positive bias of SMEs. Perhaps the best way to do this might involve a combination of synthetic validation and construct validation (Schmitt & Landy, 1993). Meta-analytic techniques eventually also might become useful. The specifics of how this might work are probably better developed by an evolutionary process based on real research than by an attempt to define them in the abstract. The general approach would be to focus on constructs covering parts of jobs and not trying to use the whole job as the unit.

THE FEDERAL AGENCY PERSPECTIVE

Content Validity as Defined by the Uniform Guidelines on Employee Selection Procedures

The Uniform Guidelines (1978) were written and adopted as regulations by the four federal agencies with Civil Rights enforcement responsibilities. Because these agencies disagreed sharply among themselves on some issues (content validity being one of them), the final wording was negotiated and, thus, is more convoluted than is desirable. There are actually two varieties of content validity discussed in the Uniform Guidelines. I shall refer to them as "classic" and "extended" content validity. The standards that are applied to them are, in some instances, substantially different.

Classic Content Validity

The theme that unifies all of the content validity documentation requirements is that the user is expected to provide the detail and specificity needed to relate clearly the content of the test to the content of the job so that the "inferential leap" is very small. The classic approach is appropriate only if a test can be constructed by taking a representative sample of job behavior(s) or of a work product. An example of a work product would be a properly welded angle joint as one item in a sample drawn from a welder's job, which is then used in a test for selecting welders. A work behavior is something that the worker does. The standards for demonstrating classic content validity require that all aspects of the test closely resemble the job. Classic content validity is essentially the same as the basic professional view.

Extending Content Validity to
Knowledges, Skills, and Abilities

The adopting agencies reacted to the comments that were received in response to the publication of a draft by attempting to specify how KSAs can be justified using content validity. The task of writing regulations that extend content validity to include KSAs is extremely difficult. The goal is to allow the situations in which content validation is appropriate and to require criterion-related validation in the situations in which it is not.

The Uniform Guidelines (1978) state that a user must show "that the selection procedure measures and is a representative sample of that knowledge, skill, or ability" (Sec. 14C(4)). Two conditions were added to cover the problem of a test's being valid with respect to a knowledge domain but the knowledge's not being needed for successful performance. The first is that the KSA can be "operationally defined" using the restrictive stan-dards in 14C(4). The second is a showing that the KSA is "used in and is a necessary prerequisite to performance of critical or important work behavior(s)" (Sec. 14C(4)). Another method used "to put a fence around KSAs" (Sec. 16(M), 16(T), 16C(A)) (as it was referred to at the time) was to define the three terms in a much more restricted way than their standard dictionary or professional definitions.

Many of the abuses of content validity are attributable to the use of broad dictionary definitions of KSAs, which, if accepted by the adopting agencies, would allow claims of content validity in almost any situation. In many of these situations in which content validity is inappropriately used, a criterion-related study would show that the test is, in fact, not job related.

Section 14C(1) of the Uniform Guidelines (1978) states that "A selection procedure based upon inferences about mental processes cannot be supported solely or primarily on the basis of content validity. Thus, a content strategy is not appropriate for demonstrating the validity of selection procedures which purport to measure traits or constructs, such as intelligence, aptitude, personality, commonsense, judgment, leadership, and spatial ability."

An extended version of this section is available at http:// www.burns.com on the Internet.

USING CONTENT VALIDITY:
THE EMPLOYER'S PERSPECTIVE

Content validity is paradoxical because, if it is appropriate, it should be used before any other validation design. However, in the great majority of situations, it is not appropriate. If the test is a sample and, thus, has a "same as" relation to a job domain, administering the test is equivalent to being able to obtain a performance evaluation before the decision is made to hire or promote. The validity coefficient equals the reliability coefficient. So, the recommendation to employers is, if you can use content validity, you should use it. The issues then focus on using it in accordance with professional standards and the Uniform Guidelines (1978). My assumption is that most employers will want to do both.

Classic Content Validity

My recommendation to employers is to simply follow the provisions in the Uniform Guidelines (1978) on classic content validity. This will include adherence to professional standards automatically. The definitions of skills and abilities in the Uniform Guidelines are so restrictive that they simply can be included under classic content validity.

Knowledge Tests: A Special Case

Knowledge tests are different. The domain sampled is a knowledge domain, not a job domain. From the professional perspective, whether the knowledge domain is an appropriate selection requirement is determined by the job analysis. The "operational definitions," required by the Uniform Guidelines (1978), require a showing that the knowledge is "used in" and is "a necessary prerequisite to performance of . . . work behaviors" (Sec. 14C(1)). This presents a problem, because job analyses normally do not include lists of all the work behaviors.

In working with a test publisher on knowledge tests, an approach has evolved that is helpful to those writing the test items and (I believe) satisfies both professional standards and Uniform Guidelines requirements. It is applied on an item-by-item basis and, thus, avoids broad generalizations. Four standards are applied to each item:

1. The knowledge measured by the question is clearly defined. This provides a succinct definition of the knowledge element to be tapped by the item. The list of these elements provides a clear, detailed definition of the knowledge domain that is sampled by the test. This information also can be used to eliminate items if a particular job does not require the knowledge that the item represents.
2. The way that the question represents the knowledge is clearly explained. This provides information on the relationship between the fact required by the question and the knowledge as defined in the prior standard.
3. How and when the knowledge is used in various work behavior(s) is clearly explained. This defines the work behaviors in which the knowledge is used. It is the first part of the required operational definition.
4. A clear explanation of why the knowledge is a necessary prerequisite to successful performance on the job is provided. This is the second part of the operational definition. It provides extremely important information on the general issue of job relatedness that, in some ways, goes beyond the Uniform Guidelines.

The use of these standards changes the focus from just writing items to a more direct concern with what the job behaviors require. The resulting test items tend to be more straightforward.

A Practical Rule of Thumb

The first consideration in deciding to use content validity evidence to support a job-relatedness claim is to apply the "same as" criterion: the test content must be the same as the job domain or, for a knowledge test, the knowledge domain. Otherwise, empirical evidence must be added.

As a final step in deciding whether using a test can be supported by content validity you might apply my rule-of-thumb — if you could use the test as part of an incumbent's performance evaluation, then it is probably content valid. For example, if the job description for a typist sets an expected typing speed, then administering a typing test as a performance measure might be justified but administering a mental ability test would not be appropriate.

REFERENCES

Anastasi, A. (1988). *Psychological testing* (p. 136). New York: Macmillan.
Goldstein, I. L., Zedeck, S., & Schneider, B. (1993). An exploration of the job analysis-content validity process. In N. Schmitt & W. C. Borman (Eds.), *Personnel selection in organizations* (pp. 3–34). San Francisco, CA: Jossey-Bass.

Schmitt, N., & Landy, F. J. (1993). The concept of validity. In N. Schmitt & W. C. Borman (Eds.), *Personnel selection in organizations* (pp. 275–309). San Francisco, CA: Jossey-Bass.
Uniform guidelines on employee selection procedures., 29 C.F.R. 1607 (1978).

6

Content Validation Form

Richard S. Barrett

The Content Validation Form is a guide for analyzing the content validity and appropriateness of employment tests, particularly multiple-choice tests. It comprises questions with options for indicating that the test or an item meets the standard in question and for indicating the way in which it is deficient. It is divided into two parts, Test as a Whole and an Item-by-item Analysis. Test as a Whole is concerned with the relevance of the test, the adequacy of the job description, the proportion of the job covered, and other issues. Item-by-item Analysis presents questions relevant to each item or portion of the test, including correctness of the scoring key, linkage with the job, need for the knowledge called for by the item, preparation of the applicants, and other points. Many of the questions can be adapted for evaluating simulations, work samples, interviews, or any aspect of a selection procedure that is designed to be content valid. The questions that are the core of the Content Validation Form are discussed below.

It is designed to evaluate and improve multiple-choice tests while they are being developed. Its use can help to head off criticism if the test is challenged, and, of course, it can be used by third parties to evaluate a test.

The Content Validation Form is best used by subject matter experts working under the guidance of a test expert. In working with subject matter experts, it is important to have a large enough group, about six to eight, so that there will be a diversity of opinion.

TEST AS A WHOLE

Before deciding on the nature of the test, the test developers should address several questions.

Is the Test Relevant to the Employer's Needs?

Before and during the job analysis, the test developers should address the objective of the selection procedure of which the test is a part. This analysis should include consideration of the need to identify deficiencies and strengths in the personnel, the training and development program, the labor market, and future needs so they can integrate the testing program into the rest of their human resource program. For example, if clerks have trouble learning their jobs, a clerical aptitude test may be in order; if the problem is careless work, absenteeism, or turnover, a test may not help.

Is the Test Subject to Content Validation?

Content validation is appropriate when performance on the test is similar to the performance required on the job or measures what the Uniform Guidelines on Employee Selection Procedures (1978, hereafter Uniform Guidelines) redundantly call, "necessary prerequisite knowledge, skills, or abilities." The Uniform Guidelines, Section 16D, defines content validity as "demonstrated by data showing that the content of a selection procedure is representative of important aspects of performance on the job."

The issue is complicated by the provision in the Uniform Guidelines (1978) that it also is possible to demonstrate the job relatedness of a selection procedure through construct validity. Section 16E states that construct validity is "demonstrated by data showing that the selection procedure measures the degree to which candidates have identifiable characteristics which have been determined to be important for successful job performance." Constructs are more general than job content. Their validation requires an accumulation of data that demonstrates that the selection procedure measures the construct and that the possession of the construct as measured is, indeed, related to success. This demonstration requires the accumulation of a body of empirical evidence derived from criterion-related validity studies.

Content and constructs blend into each other. It is important to determine whether a test is a measure of content or of a construct, because the two validation strategies are so different. (Nothing says that both strategies cannot be applied to one testing program, but it is rare to do so.)

The content-construct scale, which runs from (virtually) pure measures of content to measures of constructs, illustrates the issue:

Content-construct Scale — Content

Electronic simulators
    Flight training simulators
    Simulator of nuclear power plant operations

Performance on all or part of job
    Probation period
    Promotion or transfer to a job with common elements

Simulations
    Interactive role playing
    Photographic or video presentations
    Paper-and-pencil, etc.

Prerequisite knowledge, skill, or ability

Peripheral knowledge, skill, or ability

Theoretical knowledge

Classical constructs
    Emotional stability, "personality," "attitude, etc."
    Intelligence, aptitude

Content-construct Scale — Construct

Electronic Simulator

A case can be made that some simulators are more content valid than performance on the job itself. For example, electronic simulators of the operation of an aircraft or of a nuclear power plant can test reactions to emergency situations that the pilots or operators may never encounter on the job but that they must be able to perform.

Performance on All or Part of Job

Performance on all or part of the job can be used in the probationary period or in promotion or transfer to jobs with common elements. Adequate measures of elements shared by a test or performance on present and future jobs clearly falls into the domain of content validity.

Simulations

Simulations of aspects of the job may be suitable for validation by content validation strategies. Content validity revolves around the issue of how closely the performance in the simulation approaches the performance on the job.

Prerequisite Knowledge, Skill, or Ability

Prerequisite knowledge, skill, or ability (KSAs) are explicitly included in the description of content validity in the Uniform Guidelines (1978).

Peripheral Knowledge, Skill, or Ability

Peripheral KSA does not form the basis for a claim of content validity for an item or a test. It might be nice for the typist to know the history of the typewriter or to be able to type and talk at the same time, but if the knowledge and skill are not necessary for performance on the job, they cannot properly be used in a test that is justified on the basis of its content validity.

The determination of whether knowledge is truly a necessary prerequisite or is peripheral is a prime topic in the item-by-item section of the Content Validation Form.

Theoretical Knowledge

Theoretical knowledge has great appeal, but many attempts to measure it fail to meet reasonable standards for content validity. Despite the fundamental conviction that those who understand the reasons behind their actions perform better than those who do not, asking theoretical questions may be of limited value, because applicants are unlikely to do well consistently on a truly content-valid test without understanding what they are doing. If they perform properly, they are demonstrating their mastery of the content of the job. Further, it is difficult to evaluate failure to give a reason; applicants who know the reason for the right action may not be able to articulate it.

Classical Constructs

Classical constructs, such as emotional stability, personality, attitude, and ambition as measured by the traditional personality test and employment interview, are so far removed from the job that there is no way they can be said to measure job content. Empirical verification of their value is required.

Is the Job Description Adequate?

See Chapter 3 for a discussion of the standards. The Uniform Guidelines (1978) require that the job behaviors or outcomes and their level of complexity be described. It further requires that there be a measure of the importance of the major elements of the job for use in developing and evaluating the test.

Is an Adequate Portion of the Job Covered by the Test?

The job description provides the basis on which the content of the test can be judged, as specified in Section 15C(5) of the Uniform Guidelines (1978), which requires the user to identify the work behavior(s) that each item or part of the selection procedure is intended to sample or measure (see Chapter 5).

Is the Passing Score Set at the Appropriate Level?

The passing score is critical when it forces the decision to eliminate the candidate from further consideration. It merits careful consideration lest too many potentially competent performers are eliminated or too many incompetents are permitted to clog the subsequent parts of the selection procedure.

Does the Test Meet Empirical Standards?

Item analysis programs produce a variety of data on the items in a multiple-choice test.

ITEM-BY-ITEM ANALYSIS

Once it is determined that the type of test is appropriate, each item or exercise can be analyzed by answering the questions on the Content Validation Form. Unless there is an affirmative answer to each of the following questions, the item or exercise is, to some extent, deficient. Whether the deficiency is fatal depends on the circumstances; no test is expected to be perfect.

Is the Wanted Answer Correct?

This question is so obvious that I am (almost) ashamed to ask it. It is important to establish that the items use up-to-date information that reflects the current procedures as they are actually followed in the organization. All too often, item writers rely on obsolete texts or write items about rules or procedures that are violated without penalty.

Are the Distractors Appropriate?

We now come to one of the fundamental difficulties in the writing of multiple-choice items. Almost anyone can eliminate distractors that are wildly incorrect on the basis of general, not job-related, knowledge and, thus, improve their chances of guessing correctly. To avoid the use of this strategy by test-wise applicants, item writers sometimes write distractors so subtly different from the wanted answer that they may be just as correct, or very nearly so, under some reasonable circumstances.

A classic procedure for writing multiple-choice questions in a field in which there are definitely right and wrong answers, such as mathematics, is to base the distractors on the free responses of a sample similar to the expected applicants. This procedure works poorly in complex judgments or interpersonal relations, in which there may be several satisfactory ways of handling a situation.

Is There a Clear Link between the Information Needed to Respond to the Item and Work Performance?

It is central to the concept of content validity to test for knowledge that applies to the job. Nurses should know the appropriate dosages of dangerous drugs so they can apply the knowledge to avoid serious errors. However, items often are unrelated to work performance. The wanted answer for an item that asks a potential teacher if it is important to motivate the pupil may be selected, but choosing a correct answer does not prove that the applicant would know how to go about it.

Is It Reasonable to Expect that an Applicant, if Appointed, Can and Will Act in Conformity with the Response?

In many circumstances, it is safe to assume that performance will follow knowledge. The nurse who knows that there is an error in a prescription will probably seek a correction. However, all police officers know that they should not sit at a bar in uniform pouring down drinks cadged from the bartender, but some do. Every teacher knows that patience is a virtue, but some are impatient. Most supervisors know that they should organize their work day, but many never learn how.

Is the Knowledge Required to Respond to the Item Needed by the Applicant to Perform the Work?

Police sergeants do not need to know who appoints the commissioner, even if it would be nice to be able to answer questions from friends or the public on that topic. (One thing is certain: sergeants do not know.) A favorite form of testing is to ask for detailed information on personnel policies or other rules that can be easily looked up or obtained from a specialist without interfering with the flow of work.

Have the Applicants Had Access to Education, Training, or Experience Necessary to Prepare Them to Respond to the Item?

Applicants are not expected to arrive at the employment office totally ignorant. Everyone should have acquired some relevant information and skills that are available to them in public education, such as language and arithmetic, by the time they apply. Applicants for jobs for which they are expected to be already trained or experienced, for example, as typists, journeymen pipe fitters, or first-line supervisors, could reasonably be tested to determine the level of their possession of the relevant information and abilities that they claim.

A content-valid test is appropriate when the applicants can be expected to have acquired the necessary KSAs. Some applicants for promotion work so closely with their supervisors that they have an ample opportunity to observe performance on many important supervisory functions; others do not. Sometimes, they even take over in an acting capacity or receive training relevant to the job they are seeking. For them, it is reasonable to test for KSAs they have observed or have been trained to use.

In other situations, they may never observe or participate in a function that is an important part of the job for which they are applying, and may receive all their training, if any, after their promotions.

How Serious Are the Consequences if the Incumbent Does Not Have the Knowledge, Skill, or Ability Needed to Respond to the Item?

The knowledge of how to fight fires is basic to the work of fire lieutenants. No matter how knowledgeable or effective the lieutenants are in other areas, such as filling out forms, if they do not know how to attack fires, the citizens are placed at an unacceptable risk. A simulation that taps this knowledge in a realistic way and that meets other standards gets at important information.

Some information that is superficially job related is really trivial. There is no simple way to determine whether the consequences of ignorance are important, but in many cases, it is obvious that the decrement to performance would be inconsequential.

Is the Information in the Description of a Simulated Situation Adequate to Be the Basis for a Response?

In this context, simulations include the hypothetical situations found in many multiple-choice tests as well as the more elaborate simulations of assessment centers. Item writers often try to bring the realities of the job to the test by describing a situation and asking the applicants how they would respond. Unfortunately, complex situations cannot be described in the few lines available for a multiple-choice test. As a consequence, the applicants must guess at relevant detail before they frame their answers. If they guess wrong, they may miss or distort the point of the question as perceived by its author.

INDICATIONS OF QUALITY

The following questions deal with problems that may not be fundamental but that give an indication of the usefulness of the test. Consistent negative responses would call the item or test into question.

Would Potentially Competent Applicants Probably Respond Correctly?

Experienced lawyers are fond of saying that they could not presently pass the bar examination because they have forgotten material learned in law school that they have never used. If many competent attorneys would, indeed, flunk the bar examination, there is something wrong with it, because the bar examination is supposed to protect the public, not to test one's recollection of information that is irrelevant to that goal.

Would a Person with Inadequate Training or Experience Be Likely to Respond Incorrectly?

If a test is content valid and it deals with important information specific to performance on the job in question, someone who is not knowledgeable about the job should fail the test. However, in preparing a review of the multistate bar examination, I took 51 items as if I were a candidate and got 62 percent correct, a passing rate in most jurisdictions (National Conference of Bar Examiners, 1987), but I am not a lawyer, and no sensible person would seriously consider using me to write a contract or even to deal with a speeding ticket.

Would the Employer Benefit from Teaching the Applicants How to Take the Test?

Teaching clerks to take a typing test by instruction in typing is obviously a benefit to the employer who needs typists, but teaching test-taking skills or obscure historical anecdotes is not.

Does the Item Require a Constructed Response?

Generally, multiple-choice tests require only that the applicant recognize the wanted answer. To be sure, some questions require calculations or interpretation of a chart before the answer is chosen, but they are the exceptions. Although there is a correlation between constructed response and recognition, the two abilities are not the same.

Recognition is passive, but creating a response is an active process. It is difficult to think of situations in which recognition alone is enough. English teachers must recognize bad usage in their students' writing, but the job also requires teachers to instruct the students in good usage. Auditors must recognize errors in entries, but they also must understand their significance and take action.

Is the Response to the Item Free of Influence of Test Wiseness, Complexity of Language, Length and Difficulty of Reading Passages, Writing Ability, and So On?

It is difficult, or impossible, to coach applicants to take some tests. When placed in a realistic simulation of interpersonal relations in an assessment center, most applicants soon begin to behave in the only way they know how, that is, they are themselves. When confronted with well-planned mathematical questions or questions about the interpretation of charts and tables, applicants must be able to solve the problem before selecting an answer. Coaching and test wiseness do not help.

Is the Test Free of Bias against Any Ethnic or Racial Group or Either Sex?

Blatant racism and sexism have been eliminated from most tests, but subtle problems remain. Constant use of "he," "his," and "him" and reference to male-oriented activities and interests in reading passages make tests more difficult for women. Physical tests can be biased against women by overemphasizing upper body strength or against women and some minorities by emphasizing height.

The problems of eliminating such bias are complex and need continuing attention. For the present, probably the best rule is to make the test as job related as possible, with an emphasis on simulating the desired job performance rather than on dealing with verbal abstractions about job performance.

CONCLUSION

Establishing job relatedness through content validity is not as simple as it may seem to those outside the testing profession. There are many tough questions that need to be answered affirmatively before the test can be accepted. Once the test is given, there are standard statistical tests of item difficulty, impact, and reliability that I do not go into here.

REFERENCES

Multi-state Bar Examination. (1987). National Conference of Bar Examiners.
Uniform guidelines on employee selection procedures, 29 C.F.R. 1607 (1978).

7

Multiple-choice Tests

Richard S. Barrett

Multiple-choice tests are used to identify applicants for hiring or promotion who have acquired the knowledge, skills, or abilities to perform on the job. They generally are justified on the basis of content validity, which means that performance on the test is clearly linked to performance on the job. Unfortunately, the linkage between test performance and work performance often is weak.

Multiple-choice testing is most appropriate when it is important to establish whether the applicant has mastered and retained certain factual information and can apply it on the job. When there is a need to know if the applicant understands the rules governing the job or the vocabulary and grammar of the job, multiple-choice tests can be useful. Knowledge often can be tested adequately with multiple-choice tests.

Multiple-choice tests are less appropriate when it comes to implementing the knowledge. Communicating a point to a class, advising a client on which stock to buy, and editing manuscripts generally are too complicated for multiple-choice testing.

I illustrate the points I want to make with items taken from tests that I have encountered during litigation. Similar items can be found in countless other tests.

The following item was designed for applicants who are not required to have had any training or experience in police work. Imagine that you are an applicant who has been instructed to select the best and worst actions to take in the situation described in this paragraph:

You are a trooper. You stop a car for speeding. As you are obtaining the license and registration from the motorist, another car, with six occupants, two of whom are children, pulls up behind the first car and stops. Three of the adults from this car run from the car and assault you, knocking you to the ground. They take your revolver and begin to kick you repeatedly.

1. When a passing motorist stops, ask him to come to your rescue.
2. Yell at passing motorists to call the station for help.
3. Remain silent on the ground and pretend you are unconscious.
4. Ask the motorist whom you originally stopped to help you fight them.
5. Yell at passing motorists to stop and help.
6. When a passing motorist stops, ask him to call for help.
7. When a passing motorist stops, yell to him to go on because they have your gun.

The item was defended under the principle that it simulated a real situation to which a police officer may have to respond because it is based on an incident that actually happened. This item illustrates many characteristics of multiple-choice tests that need to be considered in deciding on the applicability of the technique.

RECOGNITION OF CORRECT RESPONSE PROVIDED BY THE TEST

Rarely does life provide the answers to the problems it poses, but the multiple-choice test format requires that the correct answer (often more appropriately called the "wanted answer") be presented along with distractors designed to mislead an applicant who does not know the wanted answer. Life seldom treats you or me that kindly; there is no homunculus sitting on our shoulders saying, "Here is a list of things you can do; one is the best, another is the worst." We have to construct the solution or dig it out of some source, evaluate it, decide what to do, and do it.

ASKING FOR THE WORST THING TO DO

Frequently, questions ask the applicant to identify the least effective action. No one spends time while being kicked by a bunch of psychopaths to conjure up the most stupid thing to do, but the applicants earned as much credit for selecting the "worst" answer as the "best."

HIDDEN ASSUMPTIONS

Compressing even a simple issue into the few words that are required by the multiple-choice format requires that much relevant material be left out. In this item, the applicant must make many assumptions, for example, that a passing motorist will stop or, if one does not, that the police officer's shouts can be heard by a passing motorist.

INTERPERSONAL SKILLS

Candidates for social worker were asked to select the first thing to do with a pregnant teenager. The wanted answer was to win her confidence. True enough, but there is nothing in the question that would demonstrate that the applicant knows what to do and that, even if the social worker performed in the desired fashion, the teenager would be won over.

CAN DO

Some questions are framed in terms of a desired outcome, without any reference to how the goal is to be accomplished. In the illustration above, there is no guarantee that the applicant could "Remain silent on the ground and pretend you are unconscious."

ABSTRACT SIMULATIONS OF
REAL WORLD ACTIVITIES

Many jobs require the application of knowledge in real situations and the solving of real problems. Many jobs require face-to-face interactions or physical activities that are not understandable on the basis of verbal descriptions alone. Reading about an event is not the same as living through it; even the best written account of an experience does not reproduce its complexity.

Sometimes the reverse happens. Information is included in the item that is not found in real life. For example, the chemical composition of air and temperatures in a room involved in a fire were given in a question, but the information is not available to the firefighter. What was simulated was not the fire but a textbook representation of the fire.

SINGLE CORRECT ANSWER

Generally, the test taker is expected to identify the correct answer, all other answers being wrong. Even in astronomy, statistics, accounting, law, and grammar, there are shadings of correctness, based in part on our imperfect knowledge, and several answers may be reasonable.

NO CORRECT ANSWER OFFERED

In conjunction with a professor of law and a former assistant district attorney, I once examined an item from a police promotion examination based on a five-to-four Supreme Court decision in which the justices wrote seven separate opinions. Furthermore, the issue was so distorted in the question that the attorneys believed that the Supreme Court would probably have disagreed with the wanted answer. The obvious action, to call the district attorney for advice, was not an option.

TELEGRAPHING THE ANSWER

Part of the nature of these tests is that they may present an answer of which the applicant might not have thought, but, once it is presented, it is obviously the wanted answer. One question on an examination for lawyers asked whether certain evidence was admissible. Those who guessed incorrectly that it was inadmissible knew that they had made a mistake when the next question asked about cross-examination on the evidence. One does not need a degree in law to know that there is no cross-examination on inadmissible evidence.

TRIVIA

Because of the effort to have unarguably right and wrong answers, item writers often adapt a sentence from a text, breaking the sentence into the stem and the wanted answer and then inventing the distractors. The more narrow the concept, the less is the argument from disgruntled test takers — hence, the trivia that is found in many multiple-choice tests.

Perhaps the all-time record for trivia was set by a test for principal of elementary school that asked, of the well-known nursery rhyme, "Who killed Cock Robin?" In case you have forgotten, or never knew, the poem contains the line, "'I' said the sparrow, 'with my little bow and arrow, I killed Cock Robin.'"

FACE VALIDITY

Face validity is the superficial appearance of content validity (see Chapter 5).

TIME PRESSURE

Typically, applicants have one and one-half to two minutes to answer each item. Some can be answered very quickly, so one may be able to ponder over more puzzling items for four or five minutes. Meaningful analyses and decisions may take hours or days, with continuing iterations and reiterations, integrations and consolidations, and false starts before the resolution. Multiple-choice tests cannot cope with such problems.

INAPPROPRIATE LANGUAGE

Some test builders rely on reading formulas to determine that their tests do not exceed the presumed educational level required by the job. Reading formulas, which depend on length of sentences, rarity of words, and other quantifiable measures, basically were designed for evaluating reading materials for children. They do not work very well at that level, but they are singularly inappropriate for evaluating the language requirements of multiple-choice tests, in which the wording is honed to compress as much information into as few sentences as possible and each word is scrutinized by the item writer and senior staff to avoid ambiguity. The test then may be administered to applicants who have graduated with average grades from average high schools and who never have been taught to read with the level of precision required to understand the nuances of the multiple-choice test.

FORMAT

Multiple-choice tests present information and ask questions in ways that are unfamiliar except for the multiple-choice tests pupils have taken in school. Many people are unfamiliar with the format, the answer sheet, and the whole testing process. The following is an example of an item that covers a complex issue in its own right and presents it in a way that challenges the test-taking skills more than most:

Below are four examples of adolescent behavior that might possibly be considered "normal":

1. Masturbation.
2. Sodomy.
3. Vocal abuse of police officials.
4. Claiming to hate their parents.

Which one of the following choices lists all of the above that are considered normal behavior and none that are not?

(A) 1, 2, 3, and 4 are all normal adolescent behavior.

(B) 1 and 3 are normal but 2 and 4 are not.

(C) 1, 3, and 4 are considered normal adolescent behavior but 2 is not.

(D) 3 and 4 are considered normal adolescent behavior but 1 and 2 are not.

The format adds unnecessary complications to a question of doubtful validity.

RELIANCE ON TEXTBOOK ANSWERS

Because multiple-choice tests require that there be a definite right answer to each question, item writers often make questions out of statements in reference books. One witness justified a response regarding the procedures for determining the value of stolen property by quoting a sentence out of a thick manual. The court remarked, "I have been on the bench for 17 years and I still don't know how to place a fair value on stolen property."

CORRECTNESS OF WANTED ANSWERS

A chronic problem with multiple-choice tests is the determination that the correct answer is correct and that the others are incorrect. One expert justified the finding that 13 percent of the items in a test were found to be defective by an appeals panel by claiming that it is not unusual to reject or rekey that many answers. When one takes into account the fact that the decision was made by the test-making authority and that the applicants might not have recognized all of the items that had flaws, there are likely to be more defective items than 13 percent.

USE AN APPROPRIATE LEVEL OF DIFFICULTY

There is no point in asking about skills that are far beyond those required by the job. Some item writers are afraid that, if the questions are too easy, everyone will get such high scores that there is no way to differentiate among the applicants. This fear leads to some absurd extremes, such as an item that posed this problem: "A messenger boy was sent to the storeroom to get exactly 13 pints of a solution to be used in developing photographs. He was given a nine-pint jar and a five-pint jar." The question asked how to get exactly 13 pints in only 5 steps.

The applicant for this low level job was tested on the ability to work out this solution:

1. Fill the nine-pint jar.
2. Pour five pints into the five-pint jar, leaving four pints in the nine-pint jar.
3. Empty the five-pint jar into the supply tank.
4. Empty the four pints left in the nine-pint jar into the five-pint jar.
5. Refill the nine-pint jar.
6. Result, 9 + 4 = 13.

RATIONAL PASSING SCORE

Passing score on a certification test should be set at a point where there is best trade-off between passing the incompetent and rejecting the competent, but sometimes, the passing scores obviously are used to control the number entering the profession.

For civil service employment or promotion tests, the passing score should be based on consideration of subsequent selection procedures, adverse impact, and number of openings. There is never a demonstration that the passing score distinguishes between competent and incompetent candidates. In reality, the passing scores often are set solely on the basis of administrative convenience, that is, to reduce the field to make it easier to handle those who remain. If the scores are set high enough to cut down substantially on the number of applicants, there is a considerable risk of eliminating applicants who would have scored high enough on the later parts of the battery to be in contention for the job.

TEST WISENESS

Test-wise applicants resort to all sorts of strategies to identify the wanted answer without actually knowing the subject, including eliminating obviously wrong responses, favoring the longer responses on the ground that it takes more words to qualify the wanted answer than to write an option that is clearly wrong, skipping difficult questions or those that involve computation for later consideration if time permits, using specific determiners, such as discarding alternatives that do not flow grammatically, and being alert to absolutes, such as "always" or "never."

TRAINING IN TAKING TESTS

Programs to train applicants to take tests are effective, despite years of claims to the contrary by some advocates of multiple-choice tests. Except that the training may help to redress the balance caused by inferior education, it is a waste of time, because no one makes a career out of taking multiple-choice tests. Training in the content of the job would improve test-taking and job skills to the benefit of both the applicant and the employer.

ADDITIONAL PROBLEMS

Adverse Impact

Afro-Americans generally score approximately one standard deviation below whites, and Hispanics score between them. This difference in test scores is not necessarily reflected in the measures of performance of Afro-Americans, which are generally only one-half standard deviation below those of whites. Strategies for reducing adverse impact are discussed elsewhere in this book.

Studies spanning 30 years have shown that, for no clearly ascertainable reasons, Afro-Americans perform more poorly on multiple-choice tests when they believe that the results are important than when they are convinced that they are not. Afro-American subjects asked to take a test to provide data on how well it works do better than those who are told that it is a direct measure of intelligence. They score higher when the examiners are of the same race or when there is at least one other Afro-American in the room. Whites do not show the equivalent effect. Because there are few situations more threatening than taking an employment test, the effect can be devastating.

Misuse of Tests

Tests are being used increasingly for purposes beyond selection and certification. They are used to determine pay and continued employment of teachers, even though test publishers themselves reject this use of tests.

CONCLUSION

Multiple-choice tests will continue to be used. It is not the purpose of this chapter to eliminate them but, rather, to point out some limitations on their use. The commitment to an employee who will be on the job for 20 or more years can run into hundreds of thousands of dollars. The investment in selection, particularly on those jobs protected by civil service or union contracts, in which it is virtually impossible to discharge or even to effectively discipline the ineffective employees, is small compared with its benefits.

At most, multiple-choice tests should be used in conjunction with other methods, some of which are discussed elsewhere in this book, so that each kind of information contributes to the most accurate selection.

III

EMPIRICAL VALIDITY

8

Criterion-related Validity

Richard S. Barrett

Criterion-related validity is defined in the Uniform Guidelines on Employee Selection Procedures (1978, hereafter Uniform Guidelines) as being, "Demonstrated by empirical data showing that the selection procedure is predictive of or significantly correlated with important elements of work behavior" (Sec. 16[F]). Although criterion-related validity is the subject of many texts and articles, it is used relatively rarely in the defense of selection procedures. Rather than rehash material that is readily available elsewhere, I will concentrate on issues that are prominent in fair employment.

JOB IDENTIFICATION AND DESCRIPTION

The Uniform Guidelines (1978) specify that there should be enough information about the job to justify the choice of the criterion and to assure that the jobs that are included are homogeneous. However, the job description does not need to be as detailed as the one required for a content validity study.

The Uniform Guidelines (1978) discuss criterion measures in two sections. Section 14B(2), Analysis of the Job, states: "There should be a review of job information to determine measures of work behavior(s) or performance that are relevant to the job or group of jobs in question. These measures or criteria are relevant to the extent that they represent critical or important job duties, work behaviors or work outcomes as developed from the review of job information."

Section 14B(3), Criterion Measures, cautions that "supervisory rating techniques and instructions to raters should be carefully developed" to assure that the measures are free "from factors which would unfairly alter the scores of members of any group. The relevance of criteria and their freedom from bias are of particular concern when there are significant differences in measures of job performance for different groups."

Section 14B(3), Criterion Measures, also warns that, "Proper safeguards should be taken to insure that scores on selection procedures do not enter into any judgments of employee adequacy that are used as criterion measures."

Success in Training

The use of scores on grades in training as criteria for validation studies is tempting but suspect. Predicting the scores on one test with scores on another is one of the easiest tasks in psychology. Using multiple-choice tests as the criterion for validating a multiple-choice test leads to a spurious correlation based on method variance, that is, measuring the ability to take multiple-choice tests regardless of their content. Section 14B(3), Criterion Measures, pointedly admonishes: "Success in training should be properly measured and the relevance of the training should be shown either through a comparison of the content of the training program with the critical or important work behavior(s) of the job(s) or the relationship between measures of performance in training and measures of job performance. . . . Criterion measures consisting of paper and pencil tests will be closely scrutinized for job relevance."

Experimental Ratings

As a general rule, administrative ratings are useless because they are subject to so many pressures and are used to communicate information that is not relevant to the selection process. For example, a loyal employee with long service may be rated inordinately high to get him or her an overdue raise.

STATISTICAL ANALYSIS

The relationship between the scores on the selection procedure and the criterion generally is measured using the correlation coefficient. This simple-appearing statistic is open to frequent misinterpretation. Consider the Correlation Diagrams that appear in Chapter 9. These diagrams show the idealized frequencies derived from the mathematical model of the correlation and are much more smoothly distributed than real data. A brief explanation of how they are constructed is in order.

Each individual has two scores, one on the selection procedure (which is displayed on the horizontal axis, or abscissa) and the criterion measure (which is displayed on the vertical axis, or ordinate). The two scores are represented by a dot at the intersection of a line drawn vertically from the test score on the abscissa and another line drawn horizontally from the point on the ordinate representing the criterion measure. This process is continued until each person is represented by a dot, the location of which is determined jointly by the scores on the test and on the criterion.

With a large number of cases, some dots would fall on top of one another and, therefore, be lost. To avoid this problem, the dots are connected into circles, the areas of which are proportional to the number of persons whose dots fall in a given cell.

To provide a consistent visual impression of the relationship, the scale of the Correlation Diagrams is in standard scores, with the average set at 0.00 and the standard deviation set at 1.00. This procedure solves the problem that would be caused by showing the correlation between height and weight when measured in inches and pounds in contrast to the diagram that would result using the same information recorded in centimeters and kilograms.

The Correlation Diagrams are presented for each 0.10 step from 0.00 to 1.00. There are several points to note. First, because the data are based on the familiar bell-shaped curve of the normal distribution, there is a concentration of scores in the center of the diagram and a dramatic trailing off of frequencies beyond one standard deviation from the mean. Second, even with relatively high correlations, there is a substantial spread of criterion scores associated with a given test score. The diagrams illustrate the size and frequency of the errors in prediction.

Selective Efficiency

Figure 9.12 in Chapter 9 illustrates the principle that the correlation coefficient measures the value of the prediction directly. The value of prediction for a correlation of 0.40 is 40 percent of the value that would be obtained if it were possible to select applicants on the basis of the criterion rather than the test.

Percent of Variance

In statistics books, the squared correlation equals the amount of variance shared between the predictor and the criterion. Using this interpretation, the value of the test in our example would be 0.40^2, or 16 percent, which is not as impressive as 40 percent. This interpretation is mathematically correct, but it is useless if the reader does not know what variance is. Variance is mentioned in passing in elementary statistics texts, but no one really understands it without an intermediate course on analysis of variance. So, although the statement is mathematically correct, it does not contribute to the understanding of the general public.

Some statisticians beg the question by saying that the correlation squared measures the "shared variability." This is misleading, understates the value of the coefficient, and is dead wrong. Everyone who reads this book has some concept of variability based on the normal curve. You recognize that, the wider the curve, the greater the variability. You probably are familiar with some of the more common measures of variability, and when you try to conceptualize shared variability, you most certainly have in mind points somewhere along the normal curve.

One such measure is the range. The evening weather report announces the highs and lows for that date. The difference is a measure of variability, the range, which includes almost 100 percent of the scores, but the range is not the variance.

Another measure of variability is the semi-interquartile range, the boundaries of the middle 50 percent of the scores, but that also is not variance.

The best measure of variability is the standard deviation. About 68 percent of the scores fall between the limits of one standard deviation on either side of the mean, but it is not variance. (In fact, variance is the square of the standard deviation, but there is no way to locate variance on the diagram of the normal curve.)

The statement that the squared correlation equals the proportion of "squared variability" is, therefore, not just wrong, it is meaningless, because there are many measures of variability. Furthermore, it understates the value of the tests.

Corrections

Two corrections are used to give a more accurate picture of the relationship between the predictor and the criterion than is provided by the uncorrected correlation. The first, correction for restriction of range, is appropriate when the predictor is used as part of the screening process, eliminating from the research population those who score low. This correction is based on the reasonable assumption that those who were eliminated bear the same relationship between predictor and criterion as those who were chosen. In other words, there is assumed to be a straight line regression curve, which does not unaccountably bend up or down at the lower score levels.

The second is a correction for unreliability in the criterion. It is based on the principle that it is unfair to penalize the test because the raters cannot agree on their ratings. The result is to predict the core of their agreement and to ignore the random errors in the ratings. This correction should not be applied to the selection procedure, because the unreliability of the test, which degrades the correlation between predictor and criterion, is, nevertheless, an integral part of it.

It is inappropriate to correct for unreliability in the predictor, because the reliability is an integral part of the selection procedure.

SUMMARY

This brief overview of criterion-related validity helps test users and critics to understand the sometimes arcane concepts of the topic; it is no substitute for professional training and experience. It should alert them to ask questions that will enhance their understanding of the empirical standards for testing and fair employment. Special attention is directed toward five basic points.

Job Identification and Description

There needs to be enough detail in the description so that the reader knows what work is done, whether the jobs are homogeneous enough to warrant their being included in the same sample, and that the criterion measure is relevant to the needs of the employer.

Selection Procedures

Although the emphasis is on tests, many of which are presented in the multiple-choice format, all selection procedures are potentially subject to criterion-related validation, because there is always the possibility of assigning numerical values to the performance of the applicants. The list includes interviews, systematically scored information from application blanks, assessment centers, ratings of performance on the lower level job, work samples, and probation.

Criterion Measures

The whole process hinges on the adequacy of the criteria, which should provide accurate, unbiased measures of important aspects of work performance.

Sample

The sample should reflect the characteristics of the applicants who will be chosen on the basis of their scores on the selection procedure. Substantial differences between the sample and the population may dilute the meaning of the outcome.

Statistical Analysis and Interpretation

It is possible to discuss only some of the more important issues and to give the reader the basis for evaluating the reports of research projects. There is no substitute for the services of a competent statistician who is familiar with the issues of employment testing encountered in this specialized application of esoteric mathematics.

SELECTION IMPROVEMENT

There are three basic ways to improve selection, as illustrated in Figure 9.12, Chapter 9.

Recruit More Candidates

If it is possible to recruit more candidates whose potential performance is at least as good as the performance of the pool of candidates in the illustration, the employer can set a higher passing score, which would move the line representing the passing score to the right. As a consequence, the horizontal line representing floor on the performance of the selected candidates would move up and, with it, the average performance of the better applicants.

Recruit Better Candidates

The value to the employer of the whole candidate pool would be greater, so the top quality performance would be better.

Use the Most Valid Selection Procedures

Applying the same analysis to Figures 9.1 through 9.11 in Chapter 9 clearly shows the improved performance to be expected with higher validity.

REFERENCES

Uniform guidelines on employee selection procedures, 29 C.F.R. 1607 (1978).

9

Interpreting the Correlation Coefficient

Richard S. Barrett

The correlation diagrams presented in Figures 9.1 through 9.11 illustrate the correlation coefficient in steps of 0.10 from a correlation of 0.00 to 1.00. The area of each dot is proportional to the number of scores that fall in each cell of a mathematically derived diagram, based on tables prepared by Pearson (1931).

The scatter plots present the data in standard score form, putting both sets of data on the same basis. (The standard score is computed by subtracting the mean from each score and dividing the result by the standard deviation.) This procedure avoids the distortions inherent in using raw scores. A plot of height versus weight in inches and pounds would look different from the same data presented in centimeters and kilograms, but the data would look the same when they were converted to standard score form.

The diagonal lines (horizontal when $r = 0.00$) are regression lines. Customarily, test scores are arrayed along the abscissa (horizontal axis) and the criterion scores along the ordinate (vertical axis). To predict the criterion performance to be expected from an applicant at any test score, draw a vertical line from that score up to the regression line and then move horizontally to read the predicted criterion standard score.

Figure 9.12 illustrates the interpretation of the correlation as an index of selective efficiency (Brogden, 1946). In this article, Brogden shows that the correlation coefficient is related directly to the value of the selection procedure in improving selection. In the example that shows $r = 0.40$, the employer would derive 40 percent of the value of a perfect test, that is,

FIGURE 9.1
Correlation Diagram

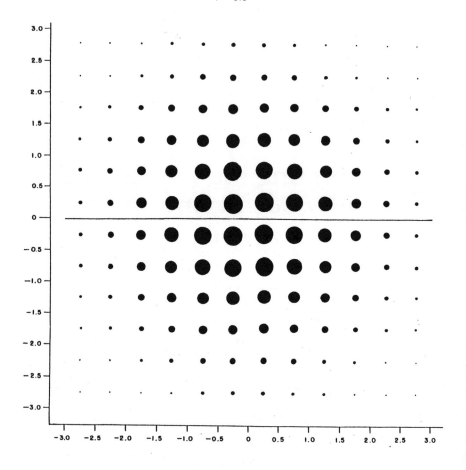

FIGURE 9.2
Correlation Diagram

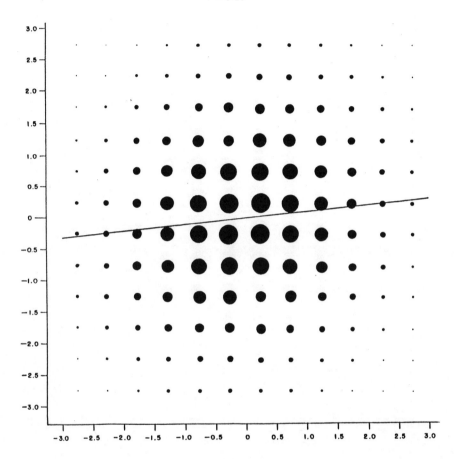

$r = 0.10$

FIGURE 9.3
Correlation Diagram

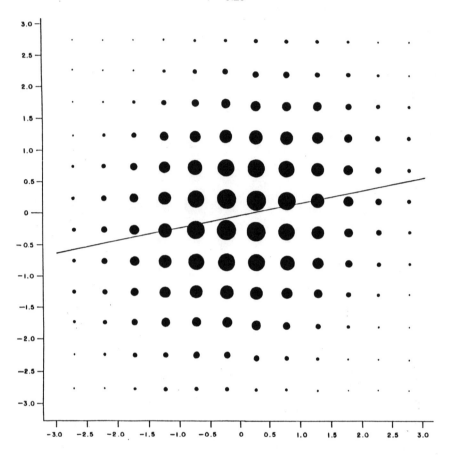

$r = 0.20$

FIGURE 9.4
Correlation Diagram

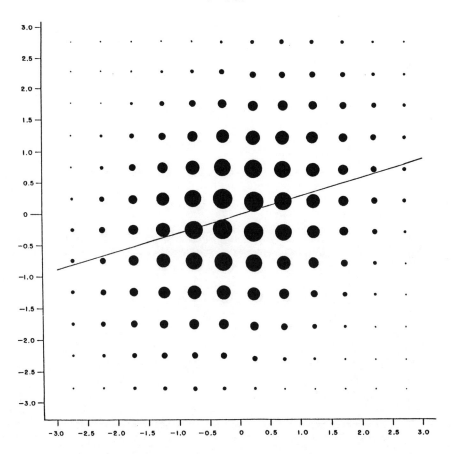

$r = 0.30$

FIGURE 9.5
Correlation Diagram

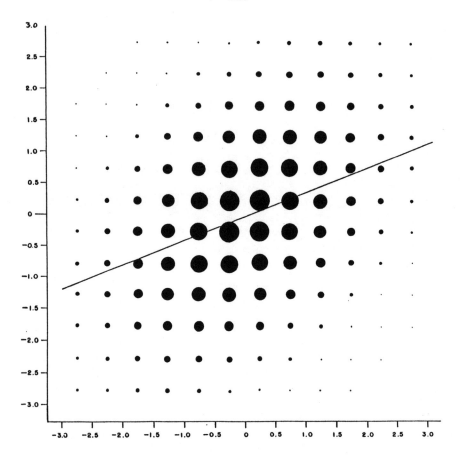

$r = 0.40$

FIGURE 9.6
Correlation Diagram

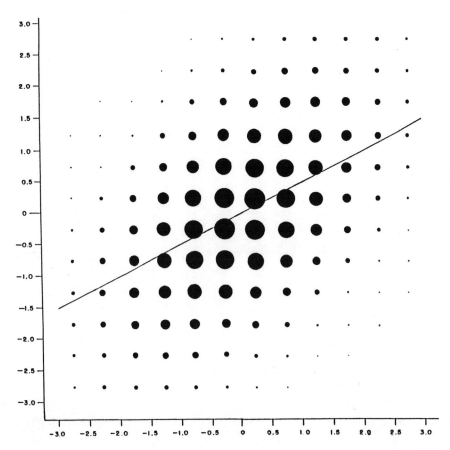

$r = 0.50$

FIGURE 9.7
Correlation Diagram

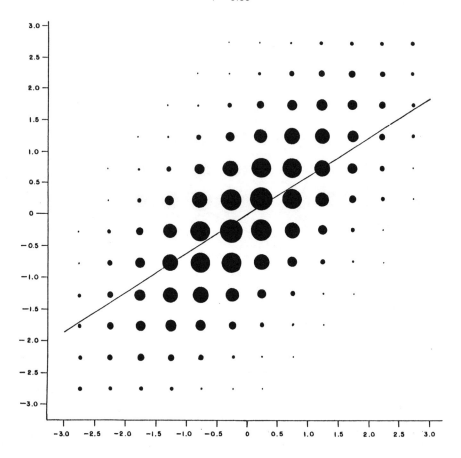

$r = 0.60$

FIGURE 9.8
Correlation Diagram

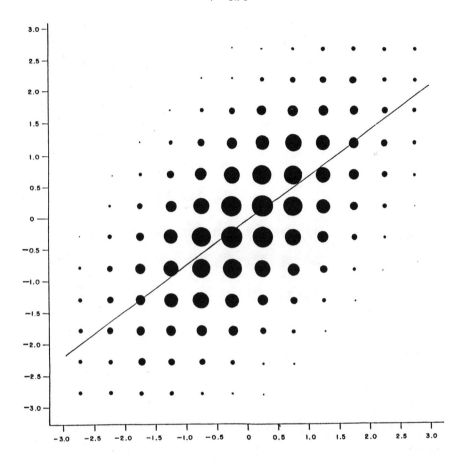

$r = 0.70$

FIGURE 9.9
Correlation Diagram

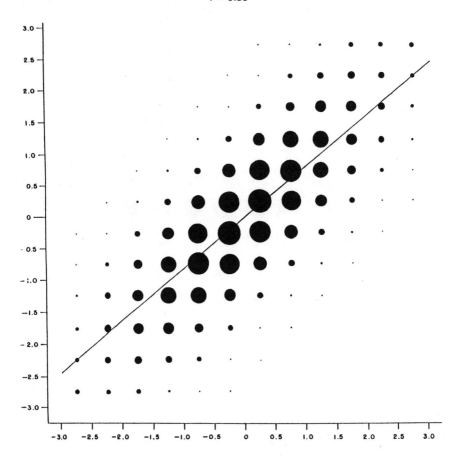

$r = 0.80$

FIGURE 9.10
Correlation Diagram

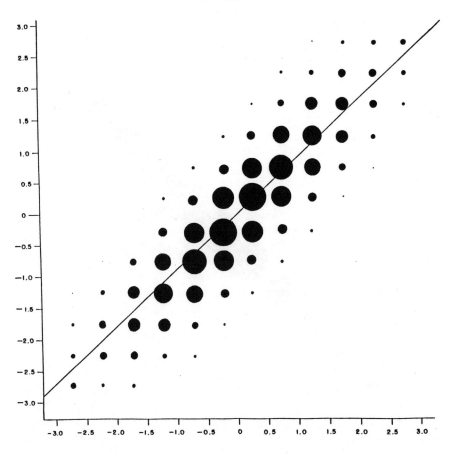

$r = 0.90$

FIGURE 9.11
Correlation Diagram

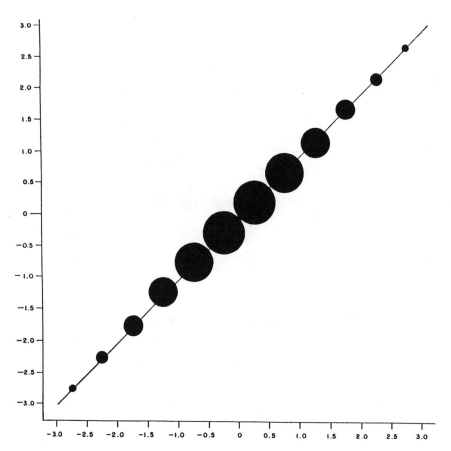

one that would make it possible to select only the best performers from the applicant pool.

In this illustration, approximately 16 percent of the applicants are hired. They are presumed to have passed all of the preliminary screens. The question remaining is how much benefit the employer would derive from using the test. There are several steps to making this determination.

1. Determine the value by intuition or, preferably, by economic analysis of selecting from the applicant pool without the test. After all, many employers do not use tests, and they survive, so there is value in the other parts of the selection process. The value of the applicants hired without using the test is represented by 0.00 on the ordinate.

2. The benefit of improving the selection over chance is determined as part of the same intuitive or economic analysis. Let us assume that an employee who is one standard deviation above the mean of the applicants is worth an additional $100,000 to the employer above the value of the average applicant. The value of selecting only the (potentially) best performers, those whose performance would fall above the horizontal line, is represented by the distance **A**. In this case, the average of their performance would be approximately 1.6 standard deviations above the mean, which would be worth $160,000 to the employer for each applicant who is selected.

3. The best the employer can do is to select those with the highest scores, that is, those whose scores fall to the right of the vertical line. Their value is shown by the distance **B**, approximately 0.64 standard deviations above the average applicant. It is worth $64,000, 40 percent of $160,000.

The scatter plot in Figure 9.12 illustrates an interpretation of a correlation coefficient developed by Brogden (1946). This discussion requires an understanding of the selection ratio, which is computed by dividing the number of persons hired by the number who apply. Figure 9.12 shows the results of employing 16 percent of the applicants.

The first step in using this analysis is to determine the value to the employer of selecting the applicants at random. The average performance on the criterion measure of those who are hired is equal to the average performance of the applicant pool, represented by 0.00 on the scatter plots.

Next, one must determine the value to the employer of selecting only the best performers on the measure that is used as a criterion for the selection study. Figure 9.12 shows that, with a selection ratio of 0.16, the average performance of those who perform best on the criterion measure is approximately 1.60. The improvement that could be gained if only the best performers could be selected is represented on each scatter plot

FIGURE 9.12
Predictive Efficiency

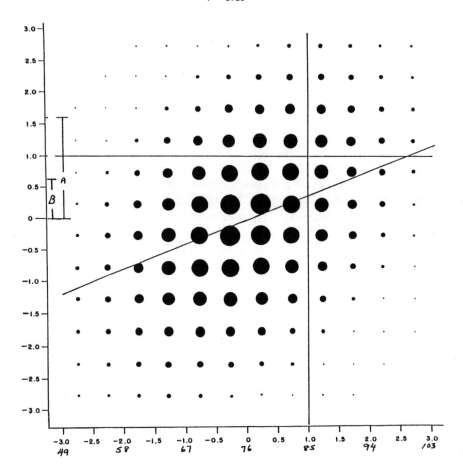

$r = 0.40$

by the line labeled "A" running from the mean (0.00) to the average performance level of the best performers.

Because it is not possible to select the applicants on the basis of their work performance, which is unknown at the time, the employer may use a test which, in this example, has a validity of 0.40, choosing the 16 percent of the candidates who scored highest. The improvement in performance over a random selection, shown comparing the length of the line marked "B" with the length of "A," is directly proportional to the correlation coefficient. The improvement over chance, in this example, is 40 percent. Had the correlation been 0.30, the improvement would have been 30 percent of the maximum, and so on.

REFERENCES

Brogden, H. (1946). On the interpretation of the correlation coefficient as a measure of predictive efficiency. *Journal of Educational Psychology, 37*, 65–76.

Pearson, K. (1931). *Tables for statisticians and biometricians: Part 2* (pp. 78–109). London: Biometric Laboratory, University College.

10

How Much Does a Test Validation Study Cost?

Lance W. Seberhagen

In *Watson v. Fort Worth Bank and Trust* (1988) and *Wards Cove Packing Co. v. Atonio* (1989), why did the Supreme Court say that evidence other than "formal validation studies" may be used to justify employee selection procedures that have adverse impact? The main reason is that certain employer groups convinced the Supreme Court that validation studies were so complicated, time-consuming, and expensive that such studies were impractical for most employers, leaving them no choice but to use quota hiring to ensure that there was no adverse impact.

WHO IS QUALIFIED TO CONDUCT A VALIDATION STUDY?

In an amicus brief submitted to the Supreme Court in *Watson*, the Equal Employment Advisory Council argued that there were currently only 1,500 people in the United States who were qualified to conduct a validation study (Williams, McDowell, Potter, & Dodge, 1987, note 15). These were the 1,500 members of the American Psychological Association (APA) who were members of *both* APA Division 5 (Evaluation, Measurement, and Statistics) and APA Division 14 (Society for Industrial and Organizational Psychology). The Equal Employment Advisory Council estimated that the Uniform Guidelines on Employee Selection Procedures (U.S. Equal Employment Opportunity Commission, Civil Service Commission, Department of Labor, & Department of Justice, 1978, hereafter Uniform Guidelines) covered about 666,000 employers and

49,000 different job classifications. Therefore, the 1,500 qualified psychologists would have an impossible workload if the court required "scientific validation" whenever a selection procedure had an adverse impact against some group. The amicus brief submitted by the American Society for Personnel Administration, the International Personnel Management Association, and the Employment Management Association (Lorber & Kirk, 1987) made similar arguments in the same case.

The numbers quoted by the employer groups in their amicus briefs were devilish exaggerations. Only the largest employers, probably no more than the top 10,000 (not 666,000), are likely to select enough employees into any one job per year to have a chance of finding reliable adverse impact that would require a validation study under the Uniform Guidelines. Similarly, the *Dictionary of Occupational Titles* (U.S. Department of Labor, 1991) contains only about 13,000 occupations (not 49,000), and relatively few of these occupations are likely to have enough selection activity by an employer to permit a finding of reliable adverse impact that would require a validation study.

The employer groups also exaggerated the minimum qualifications needed to conduct a validation study. A Ph.D. degree, APA membership, and membership in both APA Divisions 5 and 14 are not necessary. More reasonable minimum qualifications would be four courses in test development, covering job analysis, employee selection, psychological measurement, and psychological testing; two courses in statistical analysis; and two years of work experience in employment testing, preferably under the supervision of a qualified testing specialist. A person with this background probably would have a master's degree in industrial and organizational psychology, but the degree is not necessary for test validation. Memberships in APA and in APA Divisions 5 and 14 are also desirable but not necessary qualifications.

A basic testing specialist would be able to perform 90 percent of the validation studies needed by most organizations, leaving the most complex studies to higher level experts. For maximum efficiency, the testing specialist should supervise a research team and delegate various tasks (e.g., job analysis, test item writing, test administration, statistical analysis) to research assistants or to other specialists (e.g., statisticians, testing experts).

HOW MUCH DOES A VALIDATION STUDY COST?

In their *Watson* amicus briefs, employer groups (Lorber & Kirk, 1987; Williams et al., 1987) and the Reagan administration (Fried et al., 1987) told the Supreme Court that an employer cannot conduct a validation study for less than several hundred thousand dollars and more than one year of effort. To support this argument, the amicus briefs cited the findings of Gwartney, Asher, Haworth, and Haworth (1979), Lerner (1980), and Outerbridge (1979).

Gwartney and colleagues (1979) estimated that a validation study would cost from $120,000 to $600,000 (about $240,000 to $1,192,984 in 1995 dollars, based on the U.S. Consumer Price Index of May 1995). However, Gwartney and colleagues did not explain how they arrived at their cost estimates.

Lerner (1980) quoted William Gorham, former director of Personnel Research and Development at the U.S. Civil Service Commission (now U.S. Office of Personnel Management), in a 1978 speech to the Personnel Testing Council of Metropolitan Washington, as saying that an adequate criterion-related validation study would cost from $100,000 to $400,000 (about $225,000 to $900,000 in 1995 dollars) and take about two years to complete.

Outerbridge's 1979 survey of test validation study costs compiled cost data from 21 validation studies conducted from 1972 to 1979. Outerbridge found that the median cost of a criterion-related validation study was $178,000 (about $458,000 in 1995 dollars), while the median cost of a content validation study was $364,000 (about $1,070,000 in 1995 dollars). Of the 21 studies, 71 percent required more than one year to complete, and 62 percent required more than two years to complete. Outerbridge noted that she did not identify the typical costs of test validation because her survey was based on a small, unrepresentative sample of available data. Nevertheless, the amicus briefs presented her findings to the Supreme Court as typical costs.

The cost data in three reports cited by the amicus briefs were difficult to interpret because the cost data came from different years, creating dollar variation because of inflation as well as variations in the cost of test validation. Conversion of all dollar amounts to current, inflation-adjusted dollars using the Consumer Price Index provides more consistent data. Many of the validation studies in Outerbridge's 1979 survey also included more than one job or organization, making "total study cost" a false indicator of the cost that an employer would pay to conduct a validation study for one job. "Unit Cost" (i.e., cost per job per organization) gives a more precise basis for planning and policy making. If Outerbridge had presented unit costs, the median cost of a criterion-related validation study would have been $84,000 (about $227,000 in 1995 dollars), and the median cost of a content validation study would have been $8,000 (about $23,000 in 1995 dollars).

Based on my 25 years of test validation experience, I think acceptable criterion-related validation studies can be done for under $25,000 and acceptable content validation studies can be done for under $15,000 (in 1995 dollars). Acceptable test transportability studies would cost even less. Moreover, all three types of studies can be completed within about one to three months, if time is short. Organizations can minimize test validation costs if they employ an in-house testing specialist, have an ongoing test research and development program, maintain reasonably homogeneous job classifications, develop selection procedures that are relevant to more than one job, participate in cooperative validation studies with other organizations, and seek competitive bids when hiring consultants.

Cost data from other sources confirm that the cost estimates in the amicus briefs were too high. A 1975 survey of 1,339 employers by Prentice-Hall and the American Society for Personnel Administration, cited by Friedman and Williams (1982), found that the unit cost of a typical validation study was less than $5,000 (about $14,000 in 1995 dollars). Of course, the real issue is the *minimum* cost of performing an acceptable validation study, not the cost of a typical study, a superior study, or a wasteful study.

I know of several examples of high quality, low cost validation studies. In four multiorganization studies, sophisticated test batteries were developed by criterion-related validation at a unit cost of about $3,900 to $13,900 in 1995 dollars. In two single-organization studies, content-valid tests were developed for job families at a unit cost of about $2,900 and $3,900 in 1995 dollars. The world record for the least expensive validation study goes to Hunter (1983a) for his meta-analytic, validity generalization study in which he validated the General Aptitude Test Battery for 12,000 jobs at a unit cost of only $0.42 (about $0.63 in 1995 dollars). The $0.42 per job does not include the cost of the 515 validation studies used in the meta-analysis, but those costs were paid long before Hunter's study, and Hunter extended the validity of the test to 12,000 new jobs.

Another practical consideration is that employment tests do not necessarily have to be validated every year but only when there is a meaningful change in job requirements. Most employment tests have a useful life of at least four to five years before another validation study should be done (Lefkowitz & Gebbia, in press). Therefore, the cost of each test validation study can be budgeted over several years.

Most discussions of testing cost also fail to note that good testing is normally an investment, not an expense, because the selection of better employees will result in higher efficiency and productivity for the organization. Even small improvements in productivity because of test validation can have a big payoff. For example, assume that a new employment test improved the production value of each new hire by only $1,000 per year and the employer used the same test to hire 50 new employees per year for five years. If those 250 new hires stayed with the employer for an average of ten years, the dollar gain in productivity would be $2,500,000 from using the new test, which is probably more than 50–100 times the cost of test validation. As another example, Hunter

(1983b) estimated that the U.S. Employment Service could increase work force productivity by $79.36 billion per year (about $119.47 billion in 1995 dollars) if it made optimal use of the General Aptitude Test Battery for placing 4 million employees per year.

The record shows that validation studies are practical to conduct for most employers, and I hope that the Supreme Court will get better advice from its friends the next time the court decides to hear a case on employment testing.

REFERENCES

Fried, C., Reynolds, W. B., Ayer, D. B., Clegg, R., Nager, G. D., Flynn, D. K., & Shanor, C. A. (1987). *Brief for the United States as amicus curiae supporting respondent* (U.S. Supreme Court: *Watson v. Fort Worth Bank and Trust*). Washington, DC: U.S. Government Printing Office.

Friedman, T., & Williams, E. B. (1982). Current use of tests for employment. In A. K. Wigdor & W. R. Garner (Eds.), *Ability testing: Uses, consequences, and controversies: Part II.* Washington, DC: National Academy Press.

Gwartney, J., Asher, E., Haworth, C., & Haworth, J. (1979). Statistics, the law and Title VII: An economist's view. *Notre Dame Lawyer, 54,* 633–660.

Hunter, J. E. (1983a). *Test validation for 12,000 jobs: An application of job classification and validity generalization analysis to the General Aptitude Test Battery* (USES Test Research Report No. 45). Washington, DC: U.S. Department of Labor.

Hunter, J. E. (1983b). *The economic benefits of personnel selection using ability tests: A state of the art review including a detailed analysis of the dollar benefit of U.S. Employment Service placements and a critique of the low-cutoff method of test use* (USES Test Research Report No. 47). Washington, DC: U.S. Department of Labor.

Lefkowitz, J., & Gebbia, M. (in press). The "shelflife" of a test validation study: A survey of expert opinion. *Journal of Business and Psychology.*

Lerner, B. (1980). Employment discrimination, adverse impact, validity, and equality. In P. B. Kurland & G. Casper (Eds.), *Supreme court review, 1979.* Chicago, IL: University of Chicago Press.

Lorber, L. Z., & Kirk, J. R. (1987). *Brief for the American Society for Personnel Administration, the International Personnel Management Association, and the Employment Management Association as amici curiae supporting the respondent* (U.S. Supreme Court: *Watson v. Fort Worth Bank and Trust*). Washington, DC: Breed, Abbott, & Morgan.

Outerbridge, A. N. (1979). *A survey of test validation study costs* (Technical Memorandum 79-18). Washington, DC: U.S. Office of Personnel Management.

U.S. Department of Labor. (1991). *Dictionary of occupational titles* (4th ed.). Washington, DC: U.S. Government Printing Office.

Uniform guidelines on employee selection procedures, 29 C.F.R. 1607 (1978).

Wards Cove Packing Co., Inc. v. Atonio. 109 S. Ct. 2115 (U.S. Supreme Court 1989).

Watson v. Fort Worth Bank and Trust. 108 S. Ct. 2777 (U.S. Supreme Court 1988).

Williams, R. E., McDowell, D. S., Potter, E. E., & Dodge, G. E. (1987). *Brief amicus curiae of the Equal Employment Advisory Council in support of the respondent* (U.S. Supreme Court: *Watson v. Fort Worth Bank and Trust*). Washington, DC: McGuiness & Williams.

11

Validity Generalization

Neal Schmitt

DEFINITION AND HISTORY

The term "validity generalization" refers to the extent to which a research-based conclusion that test scores provide valid inferences about job performance in one organization or context implies that the same test (or other measures of the same psychological construct) is valid in another, similar situation. This seemingly simple notion (that validity of tests generalizes across situations) did not seem to be supported by early criterion-related validation research.

Perhaps the most comprehensive reviews of the use of tests in personnel selection until the introduction of meta-analytic techniques (a statistical means of data summary and aggregation used to support validity generalization) were conducted by Ghiselli (1966, 1973). Ghiselli summarized the existent research for a wide variety of tests used in the employment context to predict both training and job performance criteria. Ghiselli's research generally was taken as evidence that test validity was specific to a given situation. This situational specificity notion was taken as evidence that the use of a test, even a thoroughly researched test, must be supported by a new validation study whenever the test is used in a different situation or by a different employer.

However, beginning in 1977, Schmidt and Hunter (1977) attacked this situational specificity hypothesis, arguing that true validity does generalize across situations and that differences in observed validity coefficients are because of statistical artifacts in the original validity studies, such as differences in the range of abilities and performance in the study sample, differences in the quality of the performance criterion used in the validation study, and simple sampling error. Schmidt and Hunter and their colleagues (1981) began a program of research that led them to conclude that ability tests (including tests of verbal, quantitative, and spatial ability, deductive and inductive reasoning, and mechanical comprehension) are valid predictors of performance on the job and in training for all jobs in all settings. However, Hunter and Hunter (1984) have indicated that validities of cognitive ability tests will vary as a function of the complexity of the jobs performed by study participants.

The last two sentences in the previous paragraph point to the fact that validity generalization has taken on two different meanings in the literature over the past 20 years. The notion that all variability in validity coefficients is accounted for by various artifacts and that there is a single true validity is a very strong version of validity generalization. A second version that specifies that a researcher can expect to find nonzero (positive) validity in all situations that are similar to those in which the original validation research was conducted but that validities may vary as a function of some situation, study, or sample characteristic is a weaker statement of validity generalization. The Hunter and Hunter (1984) paper is an example of the latter type of finding, namely, that validity of the subscales of the General Aptitude Test Battery varied as a function of the complexity of the jobs performed by study participants but that one could expect some validity for these tests in most, if not all, situations.

Even if the Schmidt and Hunter (1981) claim that cognitive ability tests are valid for all jobs in all situations is correct, the possibility of differences across situations for other constructs remains. The Hunter and Hunter (1984) research indicates that the validity of a cognitive ability test (although likely never zero) may vary. The aims of this chapter are to describe briefly the basics of the meta-analytic approach (for a complete description of the complexities of meta-analysis and validity generalization, see Hunter & Schmidt, 1990) used by Schmidt and Hunter to support their validity generalization claims and then to describe the type of information I believe necessary to support a validity generalization defense of selection procedures.

STATISTICAL ARTIFACTS IN VALIDATION RESEARCH AND HOW THEY ARE CORRECTED

The conceptual approach outlined by Schmidt and Hunter (1981) in testing whether the variation in validity within job-test combinations is really zero begins with the location of the available validity research. The average and variance of these validity coefficients weighted by the sample sizes of the studies that generated the validity coefficients are computed. From the variance of these validity coefficients is subtracted the variability that would result from various statistical artifacts. Schmidt and Hunter proposed the following potential statistical artifacts: small sample sizes, computational and typographical errors, differences between studies in test reliability, differences in factor structure of tests representing the same construct, differences between studies in criterion reliability, differences between studies in criterion contamination and deficiency, and differences between studies in range restriction (variability among study participants in test and job performance measures). If the variance remaining after the subtraction of variance because of these artifacts is close to zero, then a conclusion of validity generalization (of the strong version referred to above) is warranted. The average validity coefficient is taken as the true validity coefficient. If a sizable portion of the variance in validities is unexplained by these arti- facts, then further examination of study characteristics sometimes is undertaken to identify the variables along which true validity varies. The literature refers to the latter variables as "moderator variables," that is, variables that moderate or explain differences in validity across studies or situations. Job complexity was a moderator of the General Aptitude Test Battery validities summarized by Hunter and Hunter (1984).

In most subsequent validity generalization research, corrections to the original variance have been made for sampling error (i.e., small sample sizes), differences in criterion reliability, and differences in range restric- tion. Information on the other artifacts is usually, if not always, unavail- able and must be assumed.

The fact that it has been necessary to use these assumed distributions as the basis of corrections proves not to be that critical, because in many validity generalization studies, the variance because of sampling error alone has accounted for the great bulk of the variability in observed validity coefficients. A so-called bare-bones model that includes only corrections for sampling error often accounts for 75 percent or more of the observed variance in validities (Schmidt & Hunter, 1981). The fact that the amount of the variance in validities is accounted for by sampling error is partly a function of the sample sizes of the studies that form the data base. When sample sizes are larger, then the variance accounted for by sampling error will not be as large (see Schmitt, Gooding, Noe, & Kirsch, 1984) and the importance of other artifacts usually will be correspond- ingly greater.

The steps one takes in a validity generalization study, then, are:

1.   Gather the relevant studies, both published and unpublished.
2.   Code the relevant data from these studies (i.e., validity, sample size, any information about other potential artifacts, characteristics of the study that might affect the validity).

3. Calculate the desired descriptive statistics across studies (e.g., the average validity coefficient).

4. Calculate the variability of the validity coefficients.

5. Calculate the variability because of sampling error and the variability of any artifacts if data on the latter exist. With appropriate justification, assumed artifact distributions may be used.

6. Subtract variability because of artifacts (5 above) from the observed variability in validities (4 above).

7. Assess the degree to which meaningful variation remains after correction for artifacts. Often, credibility intervals are placed around the mean validity (corrected for range restriction and criterion unreliability). These intervals specify the range of validity coefficients one might expect if a study of the ability performance relationship were replicated. A percentage (75 percent is often used as a criterion) of validity variance accounted for also is used as a basis to decide if the evidence that validity is generalizable is sufficient.

8. If the conclusion is that a great deal of variability in validities remains after correction for artifacts, then use the coded study characteristics to assess the degree to which moderator variables exist.

An example of hypothetical data constructed by the author to illustrate these steps is depicted in Table 11.1. The first five columns in this table are data that might be compiled from ten different studies of a test–job performance relationship. The person doing this meta-analysis hypothesized that the design of the criterion-related study might affect the size of the validity coefficients, so this person coded whether the study was predictive or concurrent. After the data were coded, the experimenter computed the average sample-size weighted validity coefficient. This value is equal to the sum of the column labeled "Nr" (833.99) divided by the sum of the column labeled "N" (2,191) across all ten studies. Following step 4 above, the experimenter next computed the variability of the validity coefficients obtained by dividing the sum of the last column (16.77) by the sum of the column labeled "N" (2,191). In step 5, variability because of sampling error, which is the only artifact evaluated in this simple study, was computed using the formula:

$$\sigma_c^2 = [(1 - \bar{r}^2)^2 \, K] \, / \, \Sigma N_i$$

where K is the number of studies (10 in this case), $\bar{r}$ equals the average validity, and the sum of N_i is the total N across all studies. In step 6, the variability because of sampling error (0.0033) is subtracted from the observed variability in validity coefficients (0.0076).

Because the variance accounted for by sampling error is only about 40 percent of the total observed variance in validities, a researcher might pursue the possibility that a moderator accounts for the differences in

TABLE 11.1
An Application of Meta-analytic Formulas to the Test–Job Performance Relationship

Study	Year	Type of Validation Study	N	r	Nr	$r_i - \bar{r}$	$N_i(r - \bar{r})^2$
1	1952	Predictive	57	0.38	21.66	0.00	0.00
2	1971	Concurrent	72	0.19	13.68	-0.19	2.60
3	1968	Concurrent	98	0.23	22.54	-0.15	2.21
4	1973	Predictive	212	0.41	86.92	0.03	0.19
5	1958	Concurrent	70	0.23	16.10	-0.15	1.58
6	1984	Predictive	580	0.39	226.20	0.01	0.06
7	1979	Predictive	320	0.50	160.00	0.12	4.61
8	1956	Concurrent	79	0.26	20.54	-0.12	1.14
9	1981	Concurrent	412	0.31	129.58	-0.07	2.02
10	1983	Predictive	291	0.47	136.77	0.09	2.36
Totals			2,191		833.99		16.77

$\bar{r} = (833.99) / 2{,}191 = 0.38$
$\sigma_r^2 = 16.77 / 2{,}191 = 0.0076$
$\sigma_e^2 = 7.3 / 2{,}191 = 0.0033$

Source: Compiled by the author.

validity coefficients. In this instance, that appears to be the case, because validities generated from predictive criterion-related studies exceed those obtained from concurrent studies. Specific and systematic approaches to the assessment of moderator effects are contained in various validity generalization articles cited below as well as the text on meta-analysis by Hunter and Schmidt (1990). Another possibility, namely, that other uncorrected artifacts account for some of this variance, was not evaluated for this set of data.

What I have just presented are the basic steps in a meta-analysis. These steps are complicated by an increasingly large set of "refinements" to the statistical procedures, many of which are outlined in the Hunter and Schmidt volume (1990). In addition, this literature is still developing, as evidenced by many recent journal articles, including those of Schmidt, Hunter, and their colleagues (e.g., Law, Schmidt, & Hunter, 1994). The users of validity generalization analyses must continue to be informed by this literature if they are to use the results of such analyses appropriately and, particularly, if they are to perform their own meta-analyses for purposes of defending selection procedures using validity generalization arguments. Although these refinements have contributed significantly to the complexities of meta-analysis, they have not changed the substantive conclusions of the Schmidt-Hunter work in that, in most studies, there is reasonably convincing evidence that validities generalize across similar situations and subject populations, at least in terms of the second or weaker version of validity generalization referred to above.

Finally, in addition to paying special attention to the quantitative details underlying a meta-analysis, there are a number of other factors that contribute to the quality of a meta-analytic study. The following is a version of a list of such factors proposed by Bullock and Syvantek (1985). The list is revised so that it applies more directly to the case of validity generalization.

1.   The nature of the hypothesized ability and performance constructs about which one is aggregating data should be clearly stated. What measures of the ability construct are included in the data base, and what criteria are used in assessing the ability-performance relationship?

2.   The study should include all the publicly available studies in the defined content domain, not just those that are readily available or published. If there is reason to believe that some studies may not be available, methods are available to estimate what effect this "file drawer" problem might have on the conclusions of the meta-analysis. See Hunter and Schmidt (1991, pp. 510–514) for a review of these procedures.

3.   Studies should not be selected on the basis of their methodological rigor, time of publication, or publication status. Rather, if the researcher suspects that these factors may influence the estimate of the ability-

performance relationship, they should be recorded and evaluated as potential moderator variables.

4.　The final list of studies used in the analysis should be available, as should the data that are coded from these studies.

5.　Variables characterizing the research or studies should be selected or coded based on a priori or theoretical grounds rather than just because they are available in the papers reviewed.

6.　Documentation of the coding scheme(s) used to summarize the studies should be available. The manner in which problems in the application of this coding were resolved should be detailed, including the way missing data problems were treated.

7.　Multiple raters should be asked to apply the coding scheme, and the interrater agreement and reliability of these raters should be assessed.

8.　All variables that are analyzed should be reported (particularly if a series of moderator analyses are employed) to allow other investigators the opportunity to evaluate the degree to which chance variations in the relationships in a subset of studies might have accounted for the obtained results.

9.　The study characteristics should be reported in as much detail as is possible to allow for an assessment of the nature of appropriate generalizations. Of particular importance in validity generalization research would be the nature of the jobs performed by the study participants.

In the next section of this chapter, I provide brief summaries of some of the many meta-analytic studies that are relevant to concerns about validity generalization.

RESULTS OF REPRESENTATIVE
VALIDITY GENERALIZATION WORK

Two meta-analytic summaries of a variety of ability-performance relationships have been conducted (Hunter & Hunter, 1984; Schmitt et al., 1984). In both of these efforts, the researchers reported relatively high and generalizable validities for cognitive ability, work sample measures, biodata, and assessment centers, while generally low validities were reported for interviews, personality tests, and measures of training, experience, and education. In addition, validities of these measures evaluated against work samples and training success exceeded those in which performance ratings served as the criterion.

Specialized validity generalization analyses have been conducted for a wide variety of different measures and constructs by Barrick and Mount (1991); Gaugler, Rosenthal, Thornton, and Bentson (1987); Hirsh, Northrop, and Schmidt (1986); McDaniel and Schmidt (1985); Pearlman, Schmidt, and Hunter (1980); Rothstein, Schmidt, Erwin, Owens, and

Sparks (1990); Schmidt, Gast-Rosenberg, and Hunter (1980); Schmidt, Hunter, and Caplan (1981); and Tett, Jackson, and Rothstein (1991). In most of these studies, particularly those involving cognitive ability measures, the conclusion has been that the validities do generalize and that various sources of error account for large portions of the variance in observed validities. In some of these studies, most of the validity variance was accounted for by sampling error alone. Even in those studies in which there was evidence that sampling error and other artifacts did not account for sizable portions of the validity variance, credibility intervals placed around the estimate of population validity usually indicated that one could have a reasonable expectation that validity in a new situation would not be zero. Again, this latter finding is consistent with the second and weaker version of validity generalization referred to above.

USING VALIDITY GENERALIZATION TO SUPPORT THE USE OF SELECTION PROCEDURES

The Society for Industrial and Organization Psychology's *Principles for the Validation and Use of Personnel Selection Procedures* (1987) outlines what would be required of an organization interested in supporting the use of their selection procedures on the basis of validity generalization work. They describe the manner in which the literature review should be done. Assuming that this evidence indicates generalizability of validity for a procedure for particular kinds of jobs or job families, then two additional conditions should be met: the researcher or user should be able to show that the proposed measure is a measure of the same construct or trait as was measured in the meta-analytic data base, and there must be convincing evidence that the job in the new setting is similar to the jobs or job family from which the existing data were derived.

The *Principles* goes on to point out that the cumulative evidence from validity generalization studies is more reliable and accurate than the evidence from any single study. Also relevant is the observation that validity generalization evidence may not be helpful in deciding how to optimally combine different predictors, presumably because we often do not know what the meta-analytic intercorrelation between predictors might be.

VALIDITY GENERALIZATION IN THE GUIDELINES

The Uniform Guidelines on Employee Selection Procedures (hereafter Uniform Guidelines) were published in 1978, only shortly after the first application of validity generalization. The concept of generalizing the results of criterion-related validation research across situations preceded the development of statistical tools (i.e., meta-analysis) that provided the means by which to analyze the degree to which such generalization was feasible. Hence, a number of statements in the Uniform Guidelines are applicable to the use of validity generalization.

In Section 15E(1)(e), the Uniform Guidelines state that all reasonably accessible studies that constitute the body of evidence regarding the validity of a measure should be included in the bibliography and that the studies included should be reasonably current and apply current methods of research. The population and the sample drawn from it as well as the performance measures or job behavior studied must be sufficiently similar to permit generalization (Section 15E(1)(a), (b), and (c) and Sections 7B(2), 7D, and 8B). The Uniform Guidelines also state that there should be evidence that the selection procedures are fair and valid for different demographic groups (Sections 7B(1), 7B(3), 7C, and 15E). Further, the degree to which work behaviors across the research studies and the situation of interest are similar must be established and the means by which similarity is established must be described (Section 14D(4)(b) and Section 15E(1)). Finally, the sources and nature of any unpublished data should be adequately described, and if possible, reports on these data should be provided (Section 15E(1)(e)).

These principles clearly are consistent with our description of validity generalization work except insofar as they require the examination of bias across different groups. This issue certainly can be examined if data on subgroup membership are available in the original research reports and if the variance in validities after correction for various statistical artifacts suggests that moderators of the validity coefficients may exist. It is obvious from the statements in the Uniform Guidelines that expert professional judgment serves as the basis for a validity generalization argument. Judgments are made about the similarity of the constructs measured, the job behaviors required of workers, and the nature of the samples studied. Although the possibility that these judgments are subjective or erroneous certainly should be of concern, it should not be of any greater concern than it is when a researcher makes judgments about the relevance of a criterion in a criterion-related validation study, the degree to which a content domain is adequately sampled in a content validity study, or the hypotheses used in assessing construct validity.

SUMMARY

Use of validity generalization is a viable, and often desirable, means of selecting and justifying a selection procedure. To use validity generalization, one must have available a data base regarding the particular ability-performance relationship of interest. Appropriate steps must be taken to access and aggregate this data base, to analyze the available data in a competent manner, and to draw appropriate conclusions about the true validity and the manner and situations to which this validity can be generalized. In assessing the possibility of generalization to a particular set of job applicants, one must be concerned that the same construct is measured and that the job behaviors (or required knowledge, skills, and abilities) are the same as those that were the focus of the studies summarized in the validity generalization data base. If appropriately conducted, a validity generalization study should be of greater value than any single criterion-related validation study.

REFERENCES

Barrick, M. R., & Mount, M. K. (1991). The Big Five personality dimensions and job performance: A meta-analysis. *Personnel Psychology, 44,* 1–26.

Bullock, R. J., & Syvantek, D. J. (1985). Analyzing meta-analysis: Potential problems, an unsuccessful replication, and evaluation criteria. *Journal of Applied Psychology, 70,* 108–115.

Gaugler, B. B., Rosenthal, D. B., Thornton, G. C., III, & Bentson, C. (1987). Meta-analysis assessment center validity. *Journal of Applied Psychology, 72,* 493–511.

Ghiselli, E. E. (1973). The validity of aptitude tests in personnel selection. *Personnel Psychology, 26,* 461–477.

Ghiselli, E. E. (1966). *The validity of occupational aptitude tests.* New York: Wiley.

Hirsh, H. R., Northrop, L. C., & Schmidt, F. L. (1986). Validity generalization results for law enforcement occupations. *Personnel Psychology, 39,* 399–420.

Hunter, J. E., & Hunter, R. F. (1984). Validity and utility of alternative predictors of job performance. *Psychological Bulletin, 96,* 72–78.

Hunter, J. E., & Schmidt, F. L. (1990). *Methods of meta-analysis.* Newbury Park, CA: Sage.

Law, K. S., Schmidt, F. L., & Hunter, J. E. (1994). A test of two refinements in procedures for meta-analysis. *Journal of Applied Psychology, 79,* 978–986.

McDaniel, M. A., & Schmidt, F. L. (1985). *A meta-analysis of the validity of training and experience ratings in personnel selection.* Paper presented at the 93rd annual convention of the American Psychological Association, Los Angeles, CA.

Pearlman, K., Schmidt, F. L., & Hunter, J. E. (1980). Validity generalization results for tests used to predict job proficiency and training success in clerical occupations. *Journal of Applied Psychology, 65,* 373–406.

Rothstein, H. R., Schmidt, F. L., Erwin, F. W., Owens, W. A., & Sparks, C. P. (1990). Biographical data in employment selection: Can validities be made generalizable? *Journal of Applied Psychology, 75,* 175–184.

Schmidt, F. L., Gast-Rosenberg, I., & Hunter, J. E. (1980). Validity generalization results for computer programmers. *Journal of Applied Psychology, 65,* 643–661.

Schmidt, F. L., & Hunter, J. E. (1981). Employment testing: Old theories and new research findings. *American Psychologist, 36,* 1128–1137.

Schmidt, F. L., & Hunter, J. E. (1977). Development of a general solution to the problem of validity generalization. *Journal of Applied Psychology, 62,* 529–540.

Schmidt, F. L., Hunter, J. E., & Caplan, J. R. (1981). Validity generalization results for two jobs in the petroleum industry. *Journal of Applied Psychology, 66,* 261–273.

Schmitt, N., Gooding, R. Z., Noe, R. A., & Kirsch, M. (1984). Meta-analyses of validity studies published between 1964 and 1982 and the investigation of study characteristics. *Personnel Psychology, 37,* 407–422.

Society for Industrial and Organizational Psychology, Inc. (1987). *Principles for the validation and use of personnel selection procedures* (3rd ed.). College Park, MD: Author.

Tett, R. P., Jackson, D. N., & Rothstein, M. (1991). Personality measures as predictors of job performance: A meta-analytic review. *Personnel Psychology, 44,* 703–742.

Uniform guidelines on employee selection procedures, 29 C.F.R. 1607 (1978).

IV

SELECTION PROCEDURES

12

Simulations

Richard S. Barrett

One route to content validity is to simulate the activities required by the job. Paper and pencil simulations are popular because they are generally cheaper than more elaborate electronic simulators. The Fire Scene Simulation Test is an example of such a simulation. It is described in the instructions to Firefighters seeking promotion to Company Officer, as:

A test of how well you can direct a crew in its initial response to a fire. In this test you will assume that you are a Fire Company Officer who has been newly assigned to your company. You are to describe the actions that you, as a Company Officer, would take and what orders you would give to your crew at the scene. The test has several parts:

Assignments to trucks and pumpers, including the sizes of the crews, and the equipment on the vehicles that may be used in fighting the fire.

Photographs of buildings with a simulated fire.

Street diagram showing a bird's eye view of the building and its environs.

List of equipment used in fighting fires.

Conditions, such as a description of occupants and their whereabouts, time of day, and weather conditions.

Test questions to which the applicants respond.

DEVELOPMENT OF FIRE SCENE SIMULATION

The Fire Scene Simulation is prepared individually for each jurisdiction since they differ in many relevant characteristics. Equipment that works in flat Miami may be useless in hilly San Francisco. The development of the test follows these steps:

Job Description

The traditional job description is augmented by specific information needed to prepare the test, such as the nature and geography of the city, size of crews, and the equipment.

Selection of Problems

Three simulated fires make an adequate test. A test using three scenes would probably include two pumpers (engines) and one truck (hook-and-ladder), since there are roughly twice as many pumpers as trucks. With three fires, it is possible to have a range from a simple fire in a single family dwelling to a complex fire in an office building or apartment.

Photographs

Local photographs are taken, in part to enhance face validity, but primarily to reflect differences in terrain, architecture, and building codes that impinge on fire fighting. Color photographs in which an artist has drawn in realistic smoke and flames are preferred to drawings because they more accurately portray the scene.

Street Diagram

A plan view is prepared of the building, neighboring buildings, and streets. Conventional symbols are provided to show the location of parked vehicles, hydrants, and other particulars. Some of the symbols are used by the applicant to show the placement of the vehicle, the deployment of ladders and hoses, and the location of other activities.

List of Equipment

A list of equipment carried on the vehicles used in the test is compiled locally because the equipment varies within the department, and between departments. What is called a deck cannon in one city is called a multiversal in another. This list is edited to eliminate equipment that is not part of the test, such as blankets and splints.

Conditions

The time of day and day of the week are specified, since, when coupled with information about the residents, such as their work or school schedules, they influence the attack on the fire. Information about precipitation, temperature, and other conditions that are not adequately shown in the photograph but that would be observable by a person on the scene is included.

Test Questions

A set of questions is used to elicit responses about the planned attack on the fire. Questions are answered in writing in a test booklet, and the placement of equipment and location of activities are shown on the Street Diagram. Typical questions are:

Where do you position your vehicle?

Where do you order each member of your crew to go?

What do you order each crew member to do?

What equipment would you order each crew member to carry?

Review with SMEs in Fire Fighting

A review by experienced fire fighters is essential to avoid errors such as showing smoke pouring out an impermeable stone facade.

Preparation of Applicants

Since it is likely that the applicants are unfamiliar with the Fire Scene Simulation, they are allowed to participate in a dry run in which they are given a sample test with at least one problem on a truck and one on a pumper. Answering the same questions that will be part of the test and reviewing sample answers trains the applicants in taking the Fire Scene Simulation.

Administration

Since the applicants have had experience with the dry run, they need minimal further instruction at the time of the test.

Scoring

The scoring key is developed after the test has been administered to avoid any possibility of a compromise of security. A *Scoring Key Development Committee* comprising the senior officials of Fire Department who are concerned with fire suppression or training develops anchors for five points for each question. The key is applied by the *Scoring Committee,* which is generally made up of several pairs of Battalion Chiefs and others who are knowledgeable about fire fighting. Disagreements of more than one point within a pair are settled by the Scoring Key Development Committee or its deputy.

ISSUES

Critics of the Fire Scene Simulation have made several points related to its use. The more common ones are commented on below:

Would Not Oral Responses Be Better, since the Company Officer Issues Orders Orally?

Written answers are preferred over oral responses for several reasons. The applicants appear to accept the assurance that their answers will be graded on their content, and that spelling, grammar, and penmanship are not evaluated. The logistics of recording and grading oral responses are awkward and time consuming. Overt or unconscious bias that may result from conclusions based on the vocal range and accent is eliminated; no one can tell from written responses the sex or race of the applicant.

In one case, the written notes made by the applicants as they prepared for the oral presentations were scored using the same scoring key. The scores were almost identical, probably because most applicants read their written notes into the record.

Would It Not Be Better to Have a Dynamic Rather Than Static Test with a Sequence of Questions in Which the Responses to Subsequent Questions Depend on the Effects of the Prior Decisions?

Inclusion of the development of the fire after the initial attack is beyond the scope of the Company Officer's responsibilities because the Battalion Commander generally takes command soon after the initial attack on the fire. The initial attack is complicated enough to generate wide variability in the quality of the responses. In any case, developing second or third steps and scoring keys to go with them would be inordinately complicated because there are so many options open to the Company Officer.

Doesn't the Lack of Time Pressure and the Sense of Danger Invalidate the Test?

The Fire Scene Simulation cannot produce the stress of time pressure or the tension caused by the knowledge that fires spread rapidly and errors can be serious, even fatal. There is no way to introduce these stresses in a test. Applicants who cannot decide what to do in the less threatening setting of the test are considered to be unlikely to make correct decisions under pressure.

Since Applicants Perform Many of the Same Duties as Their Company Officers, Who Are Really Working Foremen, Why Not Include Ratings of Their Performance?

Fortunately, there are so few fires that the applicants who had worked in the quieter sections of even the most arson prone cities would have little opportunity to show their skills. Further, since Fire Fighters mostly do as they are told, there is little occasion to observe their decision making ability.

CONCLUSION

Thus far, the Fire Scene Simulation has either not been challenged in Court, or has survived challenges on the basis that it is content valid in accordance with the Uniform Guidelines. It costs more to score than the multiple-choice test, but it is cheaper to administer and score than an Assessment Center, but it does have some limitations. The primary limitation of this kind of test is that it depends on problems that can be represented by a picture.

The job of Company Officer makes it amenable to this kind of test. It is more complex than that of the usual working foreman or foreman, but not too complex to simulate. The objectives of the job are clear; the enemy is the fire, and the objective is to put it out while saving lives and property.

13

Person-environment Congruence

Richard S. Barrett

Person-environment congruence is the fit between the subordinate's perceptions of the requirements of the job and the requirements of the supervisor or of the organization. Selection procedures based on person-environment are based on the principle that applicants who are otherwise qualified are more likely to succeed on a job if their performance style fits the culture of the organization and of their immediate supervisors. The Performance Priority Survey (PPS) is a forced distribution procedure (Q-Sort) with which supervisors and subordinates (or applicants) indicate the priority they perceive for behaviors required by the subordinate's job or, in the case of applicants, the jobs they are seeking. The sample PPS presented below is made up of ten statements to be assigned to one of the five categories of importance from "least important" through "neither most nor least important" to "most important" in accordance with the frequencies shown at the head of the columns. The forced distribution of the Q-Sort approximates a normal distribution.

Typical instructions read:

Read all of the statements in this *Performance Priority Survey*, and decide on their relative importance to the work on the job under consideration. Mark each statement with an X in the box under the heading that indicates the importance of the work behavior it describes relative to the other behaviors. Be sure to mark the

Adapted with permission from Barrett, R. S. (1995). *Employee selection with the Performance Priority Survey. Personnel Psychology, 45,* 653–662.

number of Xs shown above the boxes opposite "Number of statements at each level of importance."

The sample statements are from different versions of the PPS. Some are specific to fighting fires; others are more general:

L e a s t	N e x t	N e i t h e r	N e x t	M o s t	< Relative Importance
1	2	4	2	1	Number of statements at each level of importance
1	2	3	4	5	*Scale Value*
☐	☐	☐	☐	☐	Discipline subordinates for rule infractions
☐	☐	☐	☐	☐	Work hard
☐	☐	☐	☐	☐	Counsel Fire Fighters on family and personal problems
☐	☐	☐	☐	☐	Know procedures for fighting fires
☐	☐	☐	☐	☐	Accept extra work without complaint
☐	☐	☐	☐	☐	Fight for what you believe in
☐	☐	☐	☐	☐	Stand by your decisions
☐	☐	☐	☐	☐	Follow instructions to the letter
☐	☐	☐	☐	☐	Keep up-to-date in your field
☐	☐	☐	☐	☐	Make tactful critique of instructions

The PPS may be tailored to a specific job (as in the study of promotions in the fire department cited below) or may be more generally applied to a broad range of jobs with common characteristics, such as those in middle management, sales, or secretarial work. In all applications, the individual statements refer to activities relevant to the job or are closely associated with performance. There are several different types:

Statements from job descriptions, such as "Discipline subordinates for rule infractions."

Behaviors that are relevant to the job but that are not included in the typical job description, such as "Work hard."

Activities that are not part of the job but that some subordinates may mistakenly perform, such as "Counsel Fire Fighters on family and personal problems." (Company officers are instructed to refer those needing counseling to professionals retained by the fire department.)

Statements that do not refer directly to behavior but are closely associated with it, such as "Know procedures for fighting fires."

Statements about behaviors that reflect personality traits, for example, "Accept extra work without complaint" would be used instead of the generalized personality trait of "Willingness."

A Q-Sort is used because the forced distribution avoids the influence of response set by requiring the respondents to make the five discriminations from most to least important, rather than rating all the more attractive statements near the top of the scale. The PPS should comprise about 40 independent statements that cover the major job behaviors.

AGREEMENT SCORE

The degree of congruence between pairs of reports is determined by an Agreement Score, which is a Pearson product-moment correlation between the scale values assigned by the pairs of respondents to all of the items in the PPS. There are two major kinds of pairings, which are the subject of the studies described below.

Applicants and Supervisors

High agreement between an applicant and his or her prospective supervisor leads to the prediction that the supervisor would find the applicant to be a satisfactory employee.

Applicants and Organizational Climate

High agreement between the applicant and the organizational climate leads to the prediction that the applicant would fit the organization. Organizational climate may be measured in two ways. First, the PPS reports of the supervisors in a relatively homogeneous portion of an organization may be averaged. Second, organizational climate may be inferred from the use of a policy-capturing study in which the statements are scored on the basis of how the choices are related to performance, similar to the procedure for scoring biodata.

VALIDITY OF THE PERFORMANCE PRIORITY SURVEY

The studies described below illustrate the use of the PPS in three different settings.

Supervisor-subordinate Fit

Supervisor-subordinate pairs from different organizations independently prioritized 40 statements of a PPS of their subordinate position. The incumbents were middle managers and professionals performing different jobs in different organizations. The supervisors reported on a Likert scale how satisfied they were with the performance of their subordinates. The correlations of the Agreement Score with the ratings of the subordinates by their supervisors is 0.57 ($p < 0.01$).

Person-organization Fit I

Applicants for positions of first-line supervisor in an auto-assembly plant that was under construction filled out a specially designed PPS as part of their application procedure. After the plant had been in operation about 18 months, the second-level supervisors recorded their priorities for the jobs of the first-line supervisors under their direction. The organizational climate was determined by averaging the second-level supervisors' responses to each statement. Agreement Scores were computed between the organizational climate and the priorities reported by each of the applicants for the job of first-level supervisor. The correlation of the Agreement Scores with the second-level supervisors' summary performance ratings of the first-line supervisors resulted in a predictive validity of $r = 0.42$, ($n = 145, p < .0001$).

Person-organization Fit II

The PPS was studied in a large metropolitan fire department. Organizational climate was determined by averaging the priorities for the job of firefighter assigned by the second-level supervisors (battalion chiefs) on the PPS. The Agreement Scores between the organizational climate and the priorities assigned by the applicants correlated with summary rankings of overall competence provided by their battalion commanders, $r = 0.21$ ($n = 156, p < 0.01$).

An additional analysis was performed using the standard empirical technique of scoring each item on the basis of the differences in the priorities assigned by high and low ranked subordinates ($n = 104$). The resulting key was then cross-validated on a holdout sample, yielding a correlation $r = 0.38$ ($n = 52, p < 0.01$).

The variation in the perceptions of priorities can be shown by the item with the highest item-test correlation. The responses to "Know procedures for fighting fires" correlate $r = 0.37$ ($p < 0.01$) with the ranking.

ADVERSE IMPACT

The difference in scores on the traditional multiple-choice test between African-Americans and whites in the fire department study was 1.05 standard deviations. The difference on the PPS was 0.39 standard deviations, which means that use of the PPS would produce less adverse impact than the cognitive test.

DISCUSSION

Selection

Applicants could be screened on the basis of the congruence of their priorities with those of the organization to which they are applying. Those applicants whose priorities are markedly at variance with the priorities of the organization are less likely to succeed, and they may have low morale if the organization imposes on them an alien mold that they do not fit.

Placement

Applicants who have the education and experience necessary for the job and who pass the first screen of the PPS could be directed to prospective supervisors on the basis of the level of their agreement on priorities. Discussion of their priorities could form part of the preemployment interview.

Privacy

Because the PPS asks the respondent to evaluate different aspects of work behavior, it includes no items that could be construed as an invasion of privacy.

Face Validity

The PPS asks sensible questions about work behaviors. The importance of the task of setting priorities is clear to the applicants.

Faking

The applicants in studies reported in Person-organization Fit I and Person-organization Fit II had every reason to try to "fake good," but the PPS was valid nonetheless. It is difficult to fake, because applicants do not know the employer well enough to anticipate the organizational climate. It is even more difficult to anticipate the priorities of the prospective supervisor whom they may never have met.

Selection of Whyte's Organizational Man

Criterion-related validation is open to the charge that it rewards conformity by selecting people who are like those who have been successful in the past. The PPS can help to avoid this trap by including items like "Fight for what you believe in" or "Stand by your decisions," which are not characteristic of the organization man or woman. Furthermore, a low rating on statements like "Follow instructions to the letter" is symptomatic of an independent spirit, which is sought by some employers.

SUMMARY

Person-environment congruence as measured by the PPS has been correlated with performance ratings in several different settings. Subjects ranged from firefighters seeking promotion through first-line foremen to middle managers and professionals. The Agreement Scores derived from generic PPS forms and versions developed for specific jobs were valid. Concurrent validity was obtained when Agreement Scores were computed between individual supervisors and their subordinates. Predictive validity occurred under circumstances that made it impossible for the applicants to know the organization, as well as when the applicants knew the job intimately.

The adverse impact in the fire department study was substantially less than that of the traditional multiple-choice test of job knowledge. Further work is necessary to determine whether the PPS serves the user's legitimate interest in efficient and trustworthy workmanship, is substantially equally valid with other selection procedures, and has less adverse impact, thus, meeting the standard set forth in Section 3B, Consideration of Suitable Alternative Selection Procedures, of the Uniform Guidelines on Employee Selection Procedures (1978).

REFERENCE

Uniform guidelines on employee selection procedures, 29 C.F.R. 1607 (1978).

14

Situational Judgment Tests

Mary Ann Hanson and Robert A. Ramos

Situational judgment tests have been used as employee selection tools for several decades, but in recent years, this approach has become increasingly popular. These tests present applicants with realistic, job-related situations, usually described in writing. Applicants are asked what should be done to handle each situation effectively. These tests are typically multiple-choice, that is, applicants are asked to choose among several possible responses or courses of action for each situation. Table 14.1 shows an example of a situational judgment test item.

A few situational judgment tests have employed a video format. In these tests, applicants are asked to watch a videotaped scenario of actors portraying an evolving situation. The screen freezes at the point in the situation at which the applicant must make a decision. Then, the applicant is asked to choose from a series of either written or videotaped responses. Although research is not available comparing video and written formats for situational judgment tests, the ability of the video format to portray the often subtle and complex nature of interpersonal situations at work offers exciting possibilities.

The most common use of situational judgment tests is for selecting managers and supervisors. However, situational judgment tests also have been developed to predict success in other types of jobs, including insurance agents, police work, and sales positions. This sort of test has become increasingly popular for selecting employees to work in customer service positions. Most of the available research shows that these tests can be valid and useful for selecting candidates who are more likely to

TABLE 14.1
Example of a Situational Judgment Test Item

You and someone from another department are jointly responsible for coordinating a project involving both departments. This other person is not carrying his or her share of the responsibilities. You should . . .

_____ Most Effective   _____ Least Effective

a. Discuss the situation with your manager and ask your manager to take it up with the other person's manager.

b. Remind the coworker that you need help and that the project won't be completed effectively without a full team effort from both of you.

c. Tell your coworker that he or she is not doing a share of the work, that you will not do it all yourself, and that if your coworker doesn't start doing more, you'll be forced to take the matter to management.

d. Try to find out why your coworker is not doing his or her share, and explain that this creates more work for you and makes it harder to finish the project.

e. Get someone else from the other department to help with the project.

Source: Compiled by the author.

succeed (see Hanson, 1994, for a complete review of this literature). Situational judgment test scores predict job performance ratings satisfactorily. Scores on situational judgment tests also have been shown to be related to other organizationally important criteria, such as salary, promotion rate, and tenure. Although the actual content of situational judgment tests differs across the various applications, they all appear to focus on interpersonal and problem-solving situations and the skills needed to handle these situations effectively.

A few situational judgment tests are available "off the shelf," but much of the information available concerning the usefulness of these tests is related to situational judgment tests developed for a particular company and for a particular job or group of jobs.

Situational judgment tests typically are developed by first identifying the job-relevant situations to be used as item stems. Situations appropriate for this purpose occasionally have been found in available training materials or job analysis results. However, situations most often are obtained from job incumbents or other job experts by asking them to describe difficult situations that they have encountered or observed on the job.

Second, response options sometimes are developed by presenting these situations to job incumbents or other job experts and asking them to generate lists of possible actions, some that would be effective and some that would be ineffective in handling the problems described in the situation. Another approach is to present the situations to individuals unfamiliar with the job and ask them what they would do to handle each situation. This latter approach results not only in responses that represent a wide range of effectiveness levels but also in incorrect responses that applicants are likely to choose (i.e., good distractors).

The third step in situational judgment test development is to develop scoring procedures. This generally involves collecting additional information from job experts, although a few researchers have developed keys based solely on their own judgment. Most often, the development of scoring procedures involves either asking job experts for their judgments concerning the effectiveness of the various response options or asking them to complete the test. When the latter approach is used, scoring procedures then are developed empirically based on some external criterion, such as the job performance or the tenure of these job experts, that is, responses chosen most often by those with better performance or more experience are assigned higher scores. In some cases, preliminary versions of the situational judgment test are administered to both job experts (incumbents) and novices (applicants); situational judgment test items and response options then can be chosen to optimally differentiate between these two groups.

Scoring situational judgment tests is not as straightforward as scoring more traditional multiple-choice tests. Interpersonal situations are complex, and often, there is not one answer that is clearly "correct," while the rest are clearly "wrong." Rather, the possible actions in response to the sort of difficult, job-related situations included in most situational judgment tests vary along a continuum of effectiveness, ranging from very effective to very ineffective. Judgments obtained from job experts concerning the effectiveness of each possible action or response option can be used to assign item-level scores, that is, applicants are assigned the average effectiveness rating of the response they choose as their item-level score. This gives applicants more credit for choosing wrong answers that are relatively effective than for choosing wrong answers that are very ineffective. These item-level scores then can be averaged to generate an overall test score. Research has shown that this type of effectiveness weighting can result in more reliable situational judgment test scores than simple number correct scoring (Hanson, 1994) and, thus, scores with more potential for usefulness. Situational judgment tests often are not very long; some contain as few as 20 items, but most contain about 50 items. This is, at least partly, because a fair amount of reading is required to complete each item. Thus, maximizing score reliability is an important concern for situational judgment tests.

Some situational judgment tests present a situation and then ask applicants to answer several different questions about that one situation, but most of these tests present a new situation for each question, that is, each item is a different situation. One particularly promising approach is to ask applicants to identify both the most *and* the least effective response for a situation (Motowidlo, Dunnette, & Carter, 1990). In addition to providing twice as much information about the applicant, this approach could be viewed as tapping both the ability to perform effectively (i.e., correctly identify the most effective responses) and the ability to avoid serious mistakes (i.e., correctly identify the least effective responses). Still other situational judgment tests ask applicants what would most likely happen next as a result of the actions taken by the target individual in the situation.

One important concern is the extent to which situational judgment tests tap general mental ability or, conversely, the extent to which these tests can contribute to the prediction of job performance and other important criteria above and beyond those obtained using general mental ability tests alone. The available research suggests that the relationships between situational judgment tests and measures of both verbal ability and general mental ability are moderately large. However, in studies that have included both types of measures, situational judgment tests have been shown to have stronger relationships with measures of job performance than do these other tests. Thus, it appears that situational judgment tests go beyond simply measuring general mental ability. Perhaps these tests tap the affective or personality-related aspects of interpersonal or managerial skill. This point of view is supported by studies that have found relationships between situational judgment test scores and certain personality traits (e.g., dominance — Hanson, 1994) and supervisory style (e.g., a democratic style — Mowry, 1957).

Prediction of success in managerial and leadership positions is a difficult problem with which researchers and managers have struggled for years. Thus, the potential that the situational judgment test approach has shown for predicting success in managerial and supervisory positions is particularly exciting. In addition to showing the potential for improved prediction of managerial success, situational judgment tests are also economical to administer because of their paper and pencil, multiple-choice format. Other approaches to managerial selection, such as assessment centers, can be time-consuming and costly to administer. In addition, situational judgment tests seem to be related to the interpersonal aspects of personality (e.g., dominance). Thus, these tests have the potential for tapping important personality characteristics while avoiding the response distortion or faking problems associated with traditional personality inventories.

Whites tend to score slightly higher than blacks on situational judgment tests, but the differences are much smaller than those typically found for tests of general mental ability. Females score slightly higher than males on situational judgment tests, although in most of the available research, the differences between males and females are not statistically significant. Thus, situational judgment tests show some promise for minimizing or even avoiding the social and legal problems that plague the use of many ability tests in employee selection.

Situational judgment tests can be viewed as low-fidelity simulations. These tests use depictions of actual job situations as a selection tool. This provides some additional advantages. First, situational judgment tests have high face validity, that is, the test items have the appearance of being relevant for the jobs they are used to select into. Face validity can be important for obtaining user acceptance, on the part of both applicants and managers responsible for the selection of employees. Second, a situational judgment test may provide a realistic job preview to the applicants. Applicants completing these tests become familiar with the types of situations they are likely to encounter on the job if they are hired. This could provide them with an opportunity to turn down the job if they are not well-suited and may better prepare them for the job should they choose to accept it.

Based on all of these advantages, one might wonder why anyone would not choose to use a situational judgment test for selection. There are probably two main reasons why this sort of test is not appropriate for all selection problems. First, the usefulness of these tests has been demonstrated only for jobs that have large interpersonal components, especially managerial jobs. It could be that the situational judgment format is not as effective for other types of jobs or other content areas. For example, this type of test may not be useful for a job in which the job requirements are primarily technical. Further research is needed to determine in which settings these tests are not useful and for which applications they are likely to be the most useful.

Second, situational judgment tests are relatively expensive to develop. Ability tests can be purchased off the shelf, but a substantial investment of organizational resources is required to customize a situational judgment test for a particular selection purpose. Not a great deal of evidence is available concerning the extent to which a situational judgment test developed in one organization is likely to be useful in another. The evidence that does exist is, for the most part, negative. Situational judgment tests appear to be the most valid and useful for the jobs and organizations for which they are originally developed. Even though similar job-related situations are likely to occur in different organizations, different scoring keys may be needed to reflect differences in organizational goals, values, or emphases. Research concerning the generalizability of situational judgment tests across organizations or purposes would make a great contribution toward making this technology more widely available. If existing tests could be revised, rather than starting from scratch for each purpose, the cost to an organization of using such a test could be reduced greatly.

In summary, situational judgment tests generally have been developed to measure interpersonal and problem-solving skills. Scores on these tests have been shown to be useful in selecting employees for a variety of jobs, particularly those with large interpersonal components. These tests also seem to show less adverse impact against protected groups than do standard ability tests. Back in 1961, Rosen argued that even if How Supervise? (which is a situational judgment-type test) did not add anything to the prediction of success beyond that obtained with intelligence tests and biographical data, "it can be argued that . . . the instrument's high face validity makes it more desirable to use than some others" (p. 97). Since that time, research has shown that situational judgment tests can contribute to the prediction of success beyond tests of general mental ability alone; thus, the rationale for using these tests is even stronger today.

REFERENCES

Hanson, M. A. (1994). *Development and construct validation of a situational judgment test of supervisory effectiveness for first-line supervisors in the U.S. Army.* Unpublished doctoral dissertation, University of Minnesota, Minneapolis.

Mowry, H. W. (1957). A measure of supervisory quality. *Journal of Applied Psychology, 41,* 405–408.

Motowidlo, S. J., Dunnette, M. D., & Carter, G. W. (1990). An alternative selection procedure: The low fidelity simulation. *Journal of Applied Psychology, 75,* 640–647.

Rosen, N. A. (1961). How Supervise? — 1943–1960. *Personnel Psychology, 14,* 87–99.

15

Assessment Centers

Sarah E. Henry

This chapter examines some of the current issues relating to the strategy, design, and implementation of assessment centers, with "best practice" examples to illustrate practical ways to deal with the issues. Issues of interest include diagnosis and job analysis, methods and design, scoring systems, policy determination, implementation (operations planning, assessor selection, training and assignment, data retention), and validity.

DEFINITION

The 1989 "Guidelines and Ethical Considerations for Assessment Center Operations" (hereafter Guidelines and Considerations) defines an assessment center as a standardized evaluation of behavior based upon multiple inputs, with multiple trained observers and techniques used. Judgments about behavior are made, at least partially, from assessment simulations. The judgments are pooled in an assessor meeting or by a statistical integration process using comprehensive accounts or ratings of behavior. The pooling results in evaluations of the performance of the assessees on the dimensions or other variables that the assessment center is designed to measure. There are ten elements essential to an assessment center:

job analysis,

a classification system for behavioral observations,

information for evaluating dimensions determined by job analysis,

multiple assessment techniques,

job-related simulations,

multiple assessors for each assessee,

assessor training and performance guidelines,

systematic procedure to record behaviors,

assessor-prepared reports and records, and

information integration.

OVERVIEW

Since the early 1950s, assessment centers have been a popular method for selecting and promoting managerial and other professional-level personnel. Though the technique has been used largely for management, supervisory, and professional positions, applications have been extended to other employees, such as production line workers and supervisors and customer service representatives. Part of the popularity and acceptance of assessment centers is their moderate to high predictive validity and a perception of fairness. Assessment centers are at least as valid as standardized tests and have less adverse impact than tests. Some benefits ascribed to assessment centers include improvements in selection and promotion hit rates, development focus, quality and productivity, employee return on investment, employee motivation and commitment, and defensibility, as well as better-integrated business strategies and human resource systems.

As an example of current practices, the development and administration of the assessment center designed for Diamond-Star Motors is used throughout the rest of this chapter. The company was a 50-50 joint venture between Chrysler and Mitsubishi Motors Corporation. The company built a new auto assembly plant to produce 240,000 cars per year.

Job Analysis

The first step in designing the assessment center was an intensive multimethod job analysis conducted by teams of psychologists and consultants. Jobs that did not yet exist were developed, and the closest approximation to these jobs was selected for analysis. The Japanese management emphasized *kaizen*, a group effort to improve quality and safety and to reduce costs.

Dimension Information from Job Analysis

Critical dimensions for production worker performance and assessment included cognitive ability, basic skills (high-school reading, simple arithmetic, manual dexterity), technical skills, mechanical aptitude, willingness to perform varied jobs, values and work style congruence, teamwork, interpersonal skills, *kaizen* and problem-solving skills, oral communication skills, and ability to detect errors for quality inspection. Critical dimensions for supervisor performance and assessment include those listed for production workers plus leadership; planning, organizing, and decision making; training and continuous learning; counseling and consulting; writing; and presentation skills.

Multiple Assessment Techniques and Job-related Simulations

The selection procedure employed five hurdles that the applicant had to pass before selection. In addition to the assessment center, there were screens based on an evaluation of experience, the scores on the General Aptitude Test Battery and Bennett Mechanical Comprehension test, a medical examination, a panel interview, and self-selection based on a realistic job preview. The assessment center included two team exercises to measure *kaizen*, teamwork, and interpersonal and oral communication skills and an inspection simulation. Supervisor candidates additionally completed an "in basket" exercise to measure planning, organizing, and decision-making skills, a team exercise to measure leadership, role-playing to measure training and counseling skills, and individual exercises to measure writing and presentation skills.

Systematic Recording Procedures, Behavioral Classification Systems, Assessor-prepared Reports, and Information Integration

Scoring and rating processes were developed for each exercise, and cutoff scores were selected when appropriate and when norms were available. A behavior observation form with standard note coding was developed so assessors could record the behavior of up to three applicants during an exercise. Immediately after each exercise, assessors completed a behavior observation checklist for each assigned assessee on each assessed dimension to record the frequency of a specific behavior on a three-point scale ("never occurred," "occurred once or twice," "occurred more than twice"). For example, the checklist for the *kaizen* dimension included the following behaviors:

made a suggestion that generated group discussion,

offered *kaizen* suggestions that were implemented,

suggested improvements to assembly process,

pointed out deficiencies or problems in assembly process,

explained an integrated and systematic approach for completing a task,

did not actively participate in *kaizen*,

implemented improvements during process,

accepted ideas of others,

improved upon others' suggestions,

checked assembly to be sure it met specifications, and

offered incorrect solutions to problems.

Assessors then rated the degree to which the applicant met requirements on a five-point scale.

Each scale was behaviorally anchored for specific exercises to provide rating standards for assessors. Finally, assessors chose an independent overall exercise rating, with the five-point scale, used only for research and assessor feedback, for each assigned assessee. Statistical models were used to produce final overall scores for both supervisors and production workers and to choose the best functional placement for production workers. Policies for candidate feedback were developed, and teams were trained to conduct feedback and development planning sessions with each person hired.

Assessor Training and Performance Guidelines

Assessors completed 16 hours of training, nine full-day practice sessions with live assessees, and assignment to an experienced mentor, with retraining every six months. Assessors participated in peer review sessions and received weekly statistical reports to compare their individual rating policy with the desired rating policy; counseling was provided if individual policies deviated. Assessors participated in end of day and regularly scheduled *kaizen* sessions to suggest improvements for any aspect of the assessment process, as well as to design parallel exercises.

Results

Most applicants who passed all the hurdles were hired. Turnover was in the single digits in an industry accustomed to much lower retention. Product quality exceeded Japanese standards achieved in Japan; team and individual performance and productivity were excellent. No significant legal challenges arose, despite the massive applicant pool. No adverse impact was found, and results indicated fairness. Behavior checklists improved convergent and discriminant validity. The shrunken corrected validity of the entire selection process for production workers was $r = 0.35$ ($n = 1,628$) and for supervisors $r = 0.54$ ($n = 145$). Utility analysis indicated a net cost benefit per employee of \$3,161–\$12,645 for production workers and \$4,273–\$17,093 for supervisors when the analysis was performed in 1990.

ISSUES

Issues of interest for the strategy, design, and implementation of assessment centers include diagnosis and job analysis, methods and design, scoring systems, policy determination, implementation, and validity. Though the issues overlap, each will be examined separately against the backdrop of the 1989 Guidelines and Considerations and the practical example of Diamond-Star Motors.

Diagnosis and Job Analysis

Increasingly, a job does not exist to analyze, and because job analysis is the cornerstone of establishing content and construct validity and validity generalization and providing information for exercise and simulation design, future jobs must be designed. In today's organizations, a job incumbent is expected to fulfill several roles simultaneously and flexibly; thus, common and specific role behaviors provide the analytic framework for identifying assessment dimensions.

Methods and Design

New methods for assessment are quickly becoming available because of new technology. Other disciplines, such as education, have established validity of methods, such as portfolio assessment, in which an assessee prepares a portfolio of work samples, skills, and other information for assessment. Self-assessment, using structured assessment tools, is valid, especially for personality-based (rather than ability-based) attributes; self-assessments are significantly related to superior and peer evaluations and are less affected by halo error, despite the well-reported high degree of leniency. Other sources of assessment information might be collected from bosses, peers, subordinates, customers, and suppliers in a 360 degree or "surround" assessment format. Assessment design can incorporate information from job analyses so that exercises become actual work samples that produce actual business output usable for the organization, such as development of business plans or new product ideas. The optimal number of assessment dimensions is not known, but it appears that assessors reduce large numbers of dimensions to several to manage high cognitive demands.

Scoring Systems

An issue receiving a great deal of attention in the literature is that of rating and scoring systems, including cutoff scores. Suggestions for decreasing assessor rating error and increasing reliability and validity have, in the past, focused upon type and quality of assessor training as well as upon behavioral definitions of relevant performance dimensions. Even so, assessors still must make inferential leaps from observed behaviors to quantitative performance dimension ratings. Many rating errors still can occur, because raters must recognize and attend to relevant information about candidates, organize and store the information for later access, recall the information when ratings are made, and integrate information about the candidate into summary overall judgments.

One way to reduce cognitive demands upon assessors is to specify a prototype with operational behaviors organized into dimensions, based upon the job analysis, such as the checklists used for Diamond-Star. Critical behaviors can be identified and refined with retranslation techniques; a maximum of 12 behaviors is needed for stable dimensional ratings. Thus, assessors simply record frequency of observed behaviors during assessment. Statistical behavioral policies can be created to convert behavior frequencies to ratings, or frequency sums can be substituted for dimensional ratings, reducing the scoring of assessment performance to a nearly objective level. Exercises can be designed to elicit optimal numbers of desired behaviors. Checklists provide reductionistic coding strategies and serve as retrieval cues to guide accurate recall.

Another way to reduce cognitive demands is to use recording and scoring methods such as behavioral checklists that eliminate the need for time-consuming, expensive, and only slightly valid consensus discussions, in which assessors arrive at a consensus rating for each dimension across exercises. The purpose of the consensus discussion is judgmental pooling and data integration, and a statistical integration model, such as that used for Diamond-Star, is superior to a subjective consensual model.

Policy capturing, a method of statistically weighted individual (or group) decision factors and assessment dimensions, increases the predictive validity between scores and performance. Models with equal factor weight outperform differentially weighted models and produce greater criterion prediction than nonstatistical methods (natural and rational). Content scoring schemes (simple counts of decisions made, memos completed for an in basket) outperform more subjective schemes such as individual or panel ratings of a participant's performance.

Policy Determination

The Guidelines and Considerations suggest that, prior to the introduction of a center, a policy statement should be prepared and approved by the organization. The policy statement should address assessment objectives, the assessment population (and methods for selecting assessees from the population, notification, assessment policy), the assessor population and use of assessors, use of data, qualifications of consultant(s) or assessment center developer(s), and validation strategies and models, along with appropriate documentation of the relationship of job content to dimensions and exercises with evidence of reliability in observation and rating of behavior. Other useful notes would be to include how assessment information will be used to integrate other parts of the human resource system, such as individual development, training, career development, promotion, succession, and so on.

Implementation

Particularly for massive assessment efforts, implementation issues are critical, beginning with a well-developed operations plan that details resource requirements (staff, materials, facilities, technology, costs, time, and so on), schedules, responsibilities, and progress reporting. The operations plan also should outline the results and benefits expected from the assessment center, as well as plans for utility analysis if appropriate. The operations plan also needs to include plans for data retention and analysis and any required research, such as reliability, validity, adverse impact, fairness, and so on.

Because of the high cost of assessment, efforts to streamline assessment efforts are underway. A "disassembled" assessment center may be used in which candidate performance is videotaped and later observed and scored by independent off-site assessors with statistical ratings combination. Though the Guidelines and Considerations indicate that multiple assessors must be used for each assessee, they do not suggest that multiple assessors must rate the same dimensions in each exercise; an alternate model might be multiple raters randomly assigned across methods and dimensions. Independent multiple ratings could be statistically combined to produce overall dimensional and exercise scores. Other ways to streamline assessment are reductionistic strategies following predictive validity studies, as previously outlined for Diamond-Star. Streamlining can be accomplished by careful reengineering of manual, labor-intensive processes to utilize automation effectively, including statistical scoring wherever practicable. One simple streamline for Diamond-Star was premailing of information packets, employment forms, and questionnaires for applicant completion at home prior to assessment attendance.

Assessor Selection, Training, and Assignment

Though these issues receive much attention in the Guidelines and Considerations, most centers expend most resources upon design and validation. We know that diverse assessors (sex, ethnic background, age) are important. Psychologists are better assessors than managers.

Most assessors receive one or two days of training; at minimum, the training includes reducing rater error or bias and developing skill in observing and evaluating assessee behaviors. The Guidelines and Considerations suggest that training should include thorough knowledge and understanding of the organization and job being assessed; the assessment techniques and relevant dimensions; evaluation and rating procedures, including data integration; assessment policies and practices of the organization; feedback procedures when appropriate; and demonstrated ability to record and classify behavior, to give accurate oral and written feedback when required, and to play objectively and consistently the role called for in interactive exercises.

Also suggested is that length may vary because of a variety of considerations: trainer and instructional design considerations, assessor considerations, and assessment program considerations. The Guidelines and Considerations require clearly stated minimal performance guidelines for assessors, including the ability to administer an exercise (if required); to recognize, observe, and report the behaviors measured in the center; to classify behaviors into the appropriate dimensions; and to rate behavior in a standardized fashion. Also suggested is measurement of assessor performance through rating performance, report critiques, and observation. The longest time that should elapse between training and assessor service is six months, and refresher courses are recommended for assessors with less than two centers in two consecutive years.

Typical assessor training is not as extensive as that suggested by the Guidelines and Considerations. The Diamond-Star example provides a practical version of more extensive training efforts, highlighted by true-score practice training and nine-session apprenticeship with a mentor to build skills in evaluating multiple candidates (one assessee for the first three sessions, two for the next three sessions, three for the final three sessions); mentors "certify" their apprentice's skills at the end of the nine sessions and recommend additional sessions as needed. Another highlight of the Diamond-Star training was the provision of statistical judgment models with deviations from the desired judgment policy for continued accuracy and reliability.

Typically, assessors observe two to three assessees for all dimensions simultaneously. Cognitive overload is common. In addition to the previously mentioned methods for reducing cognitive overload, assessors could be assigned to observe one or two dimensions across exercises, observing all assessees simultaneously. Even better, assessors could be assigned portions of a behavior checklist, observing and recording only that portion for all assessees. Independent assessor ratings would streamline assessor assignment.

Validity

Issues of content, construct, and predictive validity are covered elsewhere in this book. Issues related to content validity of assessment centers include the need to clearly operationalize (with behaviors or actions) assessment dimensions and to clearly link information from job analysis to choice and definition of dimensions and to exercise and work sample design, as well as to scoring systems. Some suggestions for improving construct validity include standardization of assessment development and administration, proper categorization of behavior, improved assessor training techniques, and combination of performance across exercises with a multiple cutoff decision model as opposed to a compensatory decision model. Using behavior checklists improves dimension construct validity by reducing the cognitive demands placed upon raters.

Business validity is critical for the continued usage of assessment centers. They are expensive, and costs relate to up-front purchase and development, administration, candidate and assessor time, the potential cost of adverse impact and limited validity and defensibility for less valid selection methods, the cost of not making the highest percentage of correct decisions, and other obvious costs. Utility analysis can help make a business case for assessment, and return on human investment models also offers a structure for predicting both "revenue" and cost benefits that can relate assessment to business strategy and ability to effect desired strategies.

REFERENCE

Task Force on Assessment Center Guidelines. (1989). Guidelines and Ethical Considerations for Assessment Center Operations. *Public Personnel Management, 18*, 457–470.

16

A Legally Defensible Interview for Selecting the Best

Gary P. Latham and Christina Sue-Chan

After the decision in *Griggs v. Duke Power* (1971), many employers abandoned tests, thinking that this act would protect them from the provisions of Title VII of the Civil Rights Act. The Uniform Guidelines on Employee Selection Procedures (1978, hereafter Uniform Guidelines), however, state explicitly that any procedure that is used to determine who is hired or promoted must be examined against the same criteria as are pencil and paper tests (e.g., a measure of aptitudes or interests) or a job simulation (e.g., an assessment center).

A seminal book by Thorndike (1949) listed four psychometric criteria for evaluating selection tests, namely, validity, reliability, freedom from bias, and practicality. Because of the relative ease with which interviews are conducted, the interview is perceived by most practitioners to be highly practical. Thus, the interview is used more than any other procedure for making hiring decisions. This is true despite the fact that the interview has long been known within the scientific community typically to be very poor on the remaining three criteria, because it usually is unstructured, that is, different interviewees often are asked different types of questions. When they are asked the same questions, the questions frequently are not job related. When the questions are job related, the answers usually are transparent to the interviewees. When the correct answers are not obvious to the interviewees, what constitutes correct or acceptable answers often is not agreed upon by different interviewers within the organization. Hence, the interobserver reliability and the criterion-related validity of the interview are low. The interview data generally reflect nothing more than the idiosyncratic biases of different interviewers. Interviewers, unlike pencil and paper tests, are prone to such decision-making biases as the similar-to-me error, stereotyping, contrast effects, and anchoring.

A meta-analysis (Hunter & Hunter, 1984) revealed that the validity of the typical interview is only 0.14. A second meta-analysis (Weisner & Cronshaw, 1988), however, revealed that interviews that are structured, are based on a job analysis, and are conducted by a panel minimize the above problems. A third meta-analysis (McDaniel, Whetzel, Schmidt, & Maurer, 1994) revealed that the structured interview that is the most effective in this regard is the situational interview.

DEVELOPING THE INTERVIEW

The situational interview is grounded firmly in theory, namely, goal setting (Locke & Latham, 1990). This theory states that intentions predict behavior. The purpose of the interviewer, therefore, is to discover the applicant's intentions with regard to the various situations that will be encountered in the organization. The interview questions focus on skills (e.g., interpersonal, technical) as well as organizational fit (alignment with the organization's values).

Consistent with legal requirements in both Canada and the United States, the questions asked in a situational interview are based on a job analysis conducted within the organization. The job analysis procedure used is the critical incident technique (Flanagan, 1954). It identifies the critical dimensions or core competencies of a job in the organization.

The steps followed in developing a situational interview are shown in Table 16.1. An example of a critical incident from a job analysis that was conducted by the authors is as follows: The company emphasizes the importance of its ethics policy. The policy stipulates that employees are not to accept gifts from suppliers. A high level manager accepted a wrist-watch from a good friend who was also a supplier. The manager was terminated by the vice president because of the signal that it would have sent throughout the company if senior management had not followed the ethics policy.

Inherent in each situational interview question is a dilemma that forces applicants to state their true intentions rather than merely respond with what they believe the interviewer wants to hear (i.e., a socially desirable response). Jargon indigenous to the company is eliminated from the dilemma to ensure that applicants from within the company do not have an unfair advantage over those people outside the company who are seeking employment. The interview question derived from the above incident regarding ethics is as follows:

Your boss has emphasized to you the necessity of having a strong financial fourth quarter. You have heard rumors from people whom you trust that a customer who contributes at least 15 percent to your bottom line may be taking her business to a competitor. As you sit contemplating whether to discuss this issue with this customer, she contacts you by telephone. She invites you and your subordinates to attend a fishing trip hosted at her organization's retreat. Your company's written policy on such matters states that you are to say no, but this policy is seldom discussed by anyone. You even know of cases where it has been overlooked in the past. You can tell that the customer sounds impatient on the phone. She wants an answer immediately. Your boss is away on vacation. Accepting this invitation may be your best chance for salvaging this business relationship. Given the necessity for a strong fourth quarter, what would you do in this situation?

Contributing to the structure of the situational interview is the development of a scoring guide for each interview question by the interviewers prior to conducting the interview. This is done to facilitate interobserver reliability and, hence, validity when the interview is conducted and to minimize bias regarding the interviewee's age, race, sex, color, national origin, physical handicap, and so on. The development of this scoring guide is, in many ways, a team-building exercise for the

TABLE 16.1
Steps for Developing a Situational Interview

---

1. Perform a job analysis, using the critical incident technique.
2. Develop an appraisal instrument based on the job analysis.
3. Select one or more incidents that were used to develop each performance criterion or core competency.
4. Transform the critical incident into a "what would you do if . . ." question.
   a. Use literary license.
   b. Remove jargon indigenous to the hiring organization.
5. Develop a scoring guide to facilitate agreement among interviewers on what constitutes a good (5), acceptable (3), or unacceptable (1) response to each question. Attempt to develop 2 and 4 anchors if feasible.
6. Review the questions for comprehensiveness of coverage of the core competencies identified in the job analysis and listed on the performance appraisal instrument.
7. Perform a pilot study to eliminate questions for which interviewees give the same answers or interviewers cannot agree on the scoring.
8. Conduct a criterion-related validity study if feasible to do so.

Source: Compiled by the author.

organizational incumbents in that they are forced to confront and resolve differences in their values as to what constitutes an outstanding, an acceptable, or an unacceptable answer prior to interviewing candidates.

The scoring guide for each situational question typically consists of a five-point scale. Each scale contains at least three behavioral benchmarks or illustrations for a 5, a 3, and a 1 answer. These illustrations are determined by organizational incumbents in the following way: Without mentioning names, think of an employee who you have observed to be outstanding on this dimension. What would that person say in response to this question?

The same question is repeated with regard to a person who is unacceptable (a 1 benchmark) or minimally acceptable (a 3 benchmark). Through discussion of the answers to these questions, incumbents choose an illustration from the cited examples. Thus, at least three benchmarks are developed prior to conducting the interview to assist interviewers in their evaluation of interviewee responses.

Before the interview is used to make selection decisions, a pilot test is conducted to determine whether there is variability in the answers to the interview questions and whether the interviewers can agree on the scoring of each answer. If nearly everyone is given the same score, the question is deleted; if the scoring guide does not result in interobserver reliability, either the scoring guide is modified or the question is discarded.

Two or more people usually conduct a situational interview. These people include job incumbents with whom the applicant, if hired, will work plus a member from the human resources department. Sample questions that are not scored are posed to the applicant to orient the person to this interview approach. When the interview begins, one person asks the questions and all people on the interview panel record the answers. This minimizes the likelihood that important information contained in the applicant's answers will be lost.

The answers to the interview questions are not evaluated against the scoring guide until the interview is completed. An interviewee does not have to state literally what is listed as an illustration of a 5 answer to receive a grade of 5 from the interviewers. A behavioral illustration is only a guide to help ensure that interviewers use the same value system in reaching a decision regarding the suitability of an applicant's answers. Thus, what constitutes a 5 answer in one company may constitute only a 2 answer in another organization. For example, a high score in many companies to the situational question presented above is to accept the invitation from the customer because little harm is done in doing so and the financial payoff for the company may be great. At Weyerhaeuser, where adherence to the company's ethics is used as a competitive advantage, that same answer would receive a low rating. The scoring guide reflects the values or culture of the organization that is using the interview.

Another purpose of the pilot study is to determine whether the wording of each question is unambiguous to the interviewee. If an applicant doing the actual interview asks for clarification of a question, the interviewer offers to repeat the question and asks the interviewee to state his or her assumptions regarding the meaning of the question. To do otherwise is to depart from the interview's structure and increase the likelihood that, in obtaining additional information from the interviewer, some applicants will have an unfair advantage over others. Thus, the situational interview ensures that every applicant is asked the same questions, every question is job related, the answers to the questions are not transparent to applicants, and a scoring guide provides a frame of reference for ascertaining whether an interviewee's response is outstanding, minimally acceptable, or unacceptable in a particular organization.

Because the situational interview is so structured, it can be administered by computer or written questionnaire. There is a danger, however, in doing so. Virtually everyone wants to talk to (interview) an applicant before making a selection decision. The person or persons who do well on the questionnaire, be it pencil and paper or via a computer, are, thus, likely to be interviewed ("So, tell me about yourself."). All the problems that the situational interview is designed to overcome are likely to reappear as soon as it becomes a situational questionnaire that is followed by unstructured communication between the interviewer and the interviewee.

PSYCHOMETRIC CRITERIA

Reliability and Validity

The reliability and criterion-related validity of the situational interview have been investigated for a variety of jobs, including office clerical employees, clerical and administrative employees in the British financial services sector, school custodians, sawmill workers, pulp mill workers, newsprint mill workers, retail sales personnel, factory service technicians, correctional officers, front-line supervisors, public health supervisors and managers, and university faculty. In a review of the literature on the situational interview, Latham (1989) reported interobserver reliability estimates ranging from 0.76 to 0.96, concurrent validity coefficients ranging from 0.30 to 0.50, and predictive validity coefficients ranging from 0.14 to 0.45. The 0.14 coefficient was obtained when the interviewers ignored the scoring guide.

The performance criteria in these studies include supervisory ratings of job performance, hard criterion measures, and peer assessments of organizational citizenship behavior. As noted earlier, a meta-analysis of the situational interview reported the mean validity, when correlated with job performance, is 0.50 (McDaniel et al., 1994). A meta-analysis that corrected for predictor and criterion unreliability and range restriction reported a validity coefficient of 0.61 (Perry & Latham, 1994).

Bias

Three sources of interviewer bias are anchoring, the similar-to-me error, and contrast effects. When people process complex information, there is a tendency to use heuristics or rules of thumb to simplify a judgmental task. Anchoring is one such information-processing shortcut that often is used unconsciously by people when they estimate an uncertain value such as the quality of an interviewee's responses. Anchoring can have a deleterious effect on an interviewer's judgment if the selection decision is biased in the direction of an initial estimate of the candidate's performance.

Typically, interviewers examine a candidate's resume and job application. This initial rating serves as an anchor for the interviewer. It can have a deleterious effect during the interview if the interviewee's performance is substantially different from what the initial screening devices suggested. For example, if the resume indicates that the applicant is a marginal candidate but the subsequent interview performance is excellent, the interviewer's evaluation of the candidate's performance is likely to be biased in the direction of the initial evaluation.

Kataoka, Latham, and Whyte (1994) found that the situational interview was more resistant to anchoring effects than either the conventional structured interview or the patterned behavior description interview. In the conventional structured interview, applicants are asked questions regarding job responsibilities, duties, and knowledge as well as achievements on previous jobs. The questions are not necessarily based on a job analysis, and there is no scoring guide (Maurer & Fay, 1988). The patterned behavior description interview is based on the premise that past behavior predicts future behavior. Thus, the patterned behavior description interview focuses on what the individual has accomplished (or failed to accomplish) in the past and how the person went about doing it. The patterned behavior description interview asks the applicant "what did you do WHEN . . ." (Janz, 1989). In addition, the patterned behavior description interview allows interviewers to probe applicants. Finally, all applicants are asked to provide the name of the person who can confirm that the reported event occurred. Similar to the conventional structured interview, the patterned behavior description interview does not have a scoring guide. It is likely that the behavioral anchors provided by the situational interview's scoring guide counteracted the initially misleading anchor that was available to the interviewers prior to the interview.

The similar- or dissimilar-to-me error explains in part why interviewers are prone to race, ethnicity, gender, and age biases. People demonstrate this bias by selecting applicants whose values and characteristics are similar to their own in the context in which they function. The bias occurs because people have a tendency to understand others in terms of their own experiences. Interviewers, for example, may view an interaction with an applicant to be rewarding if the applicant, by demonstrating similarity to the interviewer in some way, validates the interviewer's self-image. Hence, the interviewer is predisposed to feeling positively toward the applicant and may penalize another applicant who has the same job knowledge, skill, and abilities as the former individual but who is dissimilar to the interviewer on factors irrelevant to the job, such as race, sex, age, or ethnicity.

Latham and Skarlicki (1994) examined this interviewer error in terms of cultural bias on the part of Canadian Francophone managers in Quebec. The situational interview was resistant to this error: the Francophone managers rated an interviewee whom they presumed was an Anglophone identical to the way the same interviewee was rated by another group of managers who presumed that the very same interviewee was a Francophone. However, managers who used the conventional structured interview rated the same applicant much lower when he or she was presumed to be an Anglophone rather than a Francophone.

Lin, Dobbins, and Farh (1992) examined the effects of interviewer-interviewee race and age similarity on interview outcomes using the situational interview and the conventional structured interview. They found strong same-race as well as age effects with the conventional structured interview relative to the situational interview. Thus, it is not surprising that the situational interview is a valid predictor of job performance for both blacks and whites, as well as for both males and females (Latham, Saari, Pursell, & Campion, 1980).

Contrast effects have been shown in numerous studies to be a problematic source of decision-making bias in rating interviewees. They occur when people are rated against one another rather than against the requirements of the job. Maurer and Lee (1994), in a study of police officers, found that the situational interview minimizes the contrast error.

Practicality

Latham and Finnegan (1993) examined the practicality of the situational interview, the patterned interview, and the unstructured interview from the viewpoint of managers who had used all three interview formats, managers who had used only the patterned and the unstructured format, student applicants, and attorneys who specialize in Title VII litigation in the United States. Managers defined practicality in terms of the extent to which an interview enabled them to legally defend an interview decision, hire or reject an applicant solely on job-related reasons, compare applicants on an objective basis, determine whether an applicant has the ability to perform the job, and appear organized and prepared to the applicant. The attorneys defined practicality in terms of the ease of defending a client in court, the extent to which the questions in the interview were a representative sample of the types of occurrences that the applicant would encounter on the job, freedom from bias in the evaluation of the applicant, whether the questions were based on a job analysis, and whether all applicants were asked the same questions. Applicants viewed practicality as the extent to which the interview allowed them to present their qualifications in the best possible light, resulted in fair decisions about their suitability based on their qualifications for the job, and enabled them to learn enough about the job to decide if they wanted it.

Of the three interview methods, all of the managers (even the ones who had never used the situational interview prior to the study) and the attorneys perceived the situational interview to be more practical than the patterned and the unstructured interviews. However, the results were reversed for the students who were applying for jobs. They preferred the unstructured interview over the patterned behavior description interview and the situational interview because they were optimistic about winning a lawsuit if they did not receive an offer of employment.

DISCUSSION

As globalization influences the way organizations do business, organizations need to acknowledge the role that cultural differences play in business decision making, especially the hiring and promoting of employees. Moreover, with growing diversity in the North American work force, the effect that demographic diversity has on human resource decisions must be examined. Employment decision-making practices that adversely impact people on the basis of their age, race, sex, religion, color, national origin, or disability are not tolerated by the courts in either Canada or the United States. Yet, managers wish to hire people who will enhance the competitiveness of their respective organizations. The situational interview satisfies these concerns in that it has relatively high reliability and validity, it minimizes interviewer biases, and it is viewed as practical by both interviewers and the attorneys who may have to defend an interview decision in the courtroom.

REFERENCES

Flanagan, J. C. (1954). The critical incident technique. *Psychological Bulletin, 51,* 327–358.

Griggs v. Duke Power Co. 401 U.S. 424 (1971).

Hunter, J. E., & Hunter, R. F. (1984). The validity and utility of alternative predictors of job performance. *Psychological Bulletin, 96,* 72–98.

Janz, T. (1989). Patterned behavior description interviews. In G. Ferris & R. Eder (Eds.), *The employment interview: Theory, method, and practice* (pp. 158–168). Newbury Park, CA: Sage.

Kataoka, H. C., Latham, G. P., & Whyte, G. (1994, June). *The relative resistance of the situational, patterned behavior, and conventional structured interviews to anchoring effects.* Paper presented at the annual conference of the Administrative Sciences Association of Canada, Halifax, Nova Scotia.

Latham, G. P. (1989). The reliability, validity, and practicality of the situational interview. In G. Ferris & R. Eder (Eds.), *The employment interview: Theory, method, and practice* (pp. 169–182). Newbury Park, CA: Sage.

Latham, G. P., & Finnegan, B. (1993). Perceived practicality of unstructured, patterned, and situational interviews. In H. Schuler, J. Farr, & M. Smith (Eds.), *Personnel selection and assessment: Individual and organizational perspectives* (pp. 41–55). Hillsdale, NJ: Erlbaum.

Latham, G. P, Saari, L. M., Pursell, E. D., & Campion, M. A. (1980). The situational interview. *Journal of Applied Psychology, 65,* 422–427.

Latham, G. P., & Skarlicki, D. P. (1994, May). *The relative effectiveness of the situational and patterned behavior description interviews in minimizing the similar-to-me bias of Canadian Francophone managers.* Paper presented at the annual meeting of the Society for Industrial and Organizational Psychology, Nashville, Tennessee.

Lin, T., Dobbins, G. H., & Farh, J. (1992). A field study of race and age similarity effects on interview ratings in conventional and situational interviews. *Journal of Applied Psychology, 77,* 363–371.

Locke, E. A., & Latham, G. P. (1990). *A theory of goal setting and task performance.* Englewood Cliffs, NJ: Prentice-Hall.

Maurer, S. D., & Fay, C. (1988). Effect of situational interviews, conventional structured interviews, and training on interview rating agreement: An experimental analysis. *Personnel Psychology, 41,* 320–344.

Maurer, S. D., & Lee, T. W. (1994). Towards a resolution of contrast error in the employment interview: A test of the situational interview. In D. P. Moore (Ed.), *Academy of Management best papers proceedings.* Dallas, TX: Academy of Management.

McDaniel, M. A., Whetzel, D. L., Schmidt, F. L., & Maurer, S. D. (1994). The validity of employment interviews: A comprehensive review and meta-analysis. *Journal of Applied Psychology, 79,* 599–616.

Perry, B., & Latham, G. P. (1994). *A meta-analysis of the situational interview.* Unpublished manuscript, University of Toronto.

Thorndike, R. L. (1949). *Personnel selection.* New York: Riley.

Weisner, W. H., & Cronshaw, S. F. (1988). The moderating impact of interview format and degree of structure on the validity of the employment interview. *Journal of Occupational Psychology, 61*, 275–290.

17

Personality Assessment

Robert Hogan

The conventional wisdom of industrial/organizational (I/O) psychology, at least since World War II, has been that personality measures are not valid predictors of job performance (Guion & Gottier, 1965). There are probably two reasons for this belief, one ideological, the other empirical.

With regard to the ideological reason, U.S. psychology historically has been strongly influenced by behaviorism; despite the current enthusiasm for cognitive psychology, behaviorist themes pervade industrial psychology — consider, for example, the constant reference to "job behaviors" in the Equal Employment Opportunity Commission (EEOC) guidelines for test validation. Behaviorism largely is critical of the concept of personality, arguing that what people do depends on where, not who, they are, that is, on circumstances rather than on character. Behaviorism also tends to overlook individual differences because, as a research activity, behaviorism involves the search for general laws. Thus, to the degree that a person embraces behaviorist principles — and that includes a surprising portion of modern psychology — that person will be skeptical about the concept of personality.

The empirical reasons for the widespread skepticism about the validity of personality measures are the facts that there are so many bad ones around — there are hundreds of flawed personality measures in the published literature and more in the pipeline — and that much of the early research was poorly done. The typical study in the I/O literature consisted of a researcher choosing one of these measures, often on the basis of convenience, asking a sample of incumbents to complete it, and then correlating scores on the personality measure of convenience with a criterion measure of convenience (usually a supervisor's rating). This process was repeated over and over, and the result was empirical literature filled with insignificant or contradictory findings.

Starting sometime in the early 1980s, the climate of opinion slowly began to change such that, today, most knowledgeable observers believe that well-constructed personality measures are an important part of any valid preemployment screening process. I believe there are at least four reasons for this change of mind. The first is the so-called cognitive revolution; research by social learning theorists shows that people can learn simply by watching others, without being reinforced, and peoples' expectancies — cognitive variables — influence their reactions to events. Both of these conclusions serve powerfully to undermine traditional behaviorism and to legitimize the notion of individual differences.

The second reason for the change is the increasing popularity and acceptance of the Five Factor model (Wiggins, 1995). The Five Factor model makes three primary claims. First, normal personality can be described in terms of five broad factors, called Surgency (Extraversion), Emotional Stability, Agreeableness, Conscientiousness, and Intellect. Second, and more importantly, all existing measures of personality assess, with more or less efficiency, some or all of these five dimensions. Third, and most importantly, if you want to measure personality, then you must assess at least these five dimensions. Because earlier research did not systematically sample all five dimensions, that research was, necessarily, an inadequate evaluation of the links between personality and occupational performance.

A third reason for the increasing popularity of personality measures in employment selection is that a series of meta-analyses support the notion that they are valid. For example, Barrick and Mount (1991) studied the relationship between the Big Five personality dimensions and job criteria across five occupational groups and concluded that, at the least, measures of conscientiousness reliably predict job proficiency and turnover. Tett, Jackson, and Rothstein (1991) concluded that, if tests are chosen on the basis of job analysis and if researchers conduct confirmatory rather than exploratory analyses and study incumbents with reasonable job tenure, then they find larger validity coefficients than those reported by Barrick and Mount. Other important reviews substantiating the validity of personality measures include papers by McHenry, Hough, Toquam, Hanson, and Ashworth (1990); Ones, Viswesvaran, and Schmidt (1993); and McDaniel and Frei (1994).

I believe the results of these meta-analyses are lower bound estimates of the validity of personality measures in predicting job performance, because, in conducting the meta-analyses, the researchers combined the results of research based on personality tests that are not equivalent in their construction, their measurement goals, or their underlying theory — the California Psychological Inventory (Gough, 1987) and the Myers-Briggs Type Indicator have nothing in common other than that they are both called personality tests. The researchers also sometimes misclassified scales, which reduced validity coefficients. In addition, they had no systematic basis for classifying the jobs included in the meta-analyses; military recruits were combined with social workers, but the personality variables necessary for effectiveness in the military must be different from the characteristics necessary for effective performance in social work. Finally, these meta-analyses aligned personality scales with job performance criteria in an ad hoc fashion. Consequently, the fact that any results emerged speaks to the robustness of these measures.

A final reason for the increasing popularity of personality measures is a technical issue that people only recently have begun to recognize. The Five Factor model provides a taxonomy of the domain of personality predictors. I/O psychologists increasingly are sensitive to the facts that the criterion space must also have a structure and that a competent investigation of the link between personality and job performance requires aligning predictors and criteria in a rational and systematic way. For example, one might expect measures of extraversion to predict the ability to meet the public well, but one would not expect measures of extraversion to predict performance in training. When predictors are aligned correctly with criteria, better results will emerge.

When thinking about using personality measures to predict job performance, it is useful to be clear about what personality is. This proves to be a bit tricky, because the word "personality" has two definitions. On the one hand, personality refers to hypothetical factors inside people — temperaments, traits, information-processing schemas — that explain why they act as they do. This is the most popular definition of personality. It is also the hardest to study scientifically and, in my judgment, the least important from a practical perspective. On the other hand, personality refers to a person's reputation, to how he or she is perceived and described by the persons with whom he or she interacts. Although this is the less popular definition, it is the easiest to study scientifically and the most important from a practical standpoint.

So far I have outlined the reasons why I/O psychology historically has distrusted personality measures, outlined the reasons why those views are changing, and defined personality. The remainder of this chapter will take up more operational issues in the use of personality measures for preemployment screening. The first of these issues concerns what it is that personality inventories measure. They typically are described as "self-report" measures, but I think this is misleading. The sort of psychological processes that create a person's responses to items on a personality measure are identical to the processes that govern a person's responses to questions during an interview and to questions during social interaction more generally, that is, item responses are self-presentations, not self-reports. People use the responses to tell others how they would like to be regarded — people read an item and very quickly decide whether they are the kind of person who would agree with it. This means that personality inventories sample a person's typical interpersonal style, and it is their typical interpersonal style that creates their reputations. Thus, personality inventories sample, in a somewhat inefficient manner, a person's reputation.

The claim that personality inventories sample a person's reputation is important, because this explains their validity. Personality measures typically are validated by comparing scores on the measures with observers' ratings. What is it that observers rate? A person's reputation. What is it that personality measures sample? Aspects of a person's typical interpersonal style. What is it that creates a person's reputation? His or her interpersonal style. What is the best predictor of future behavior? Past behavior. What is it that creates a person's reputation? His or her past behavior. Thus, reputation is the best single predictor of a person's future behavior, and scores on a well-developed measure of personality are, at least in principle, the second best predictor of a person's future behavior.

The second issue concerns the claim that behavior is more important than personality and that we should be more interested in a person's actual job performance than in his or her personality. This claim reflects the pervasive and often unrecognized behaviorist bias to which I alluded earlier. There are two points to be made here. First, in industrial psychology, jobs normally are described in terms of tasks or required behaviors. Thus, an entry-level manager might "prepare memos," "enforce company policy," "supervise subordinates," and so on. However, this misses the point; the real question concerns what it is that the good — as opposed to the typical — entry-level managers do, and that usually involves "building a team," "being fair," "attending to morale" — issues and activities that cannot be reduced readily to behaviors. It is not what a person does but how he or she does it — respectfully, quietly, persistently — that determines effective performance.

The second point is that people's behavior is a function of who they are — their personalities. We never take behavior at face value; rather, we use behavior to make inferences about the kind of person with whom we are dealing. Behaviors are high fidelity, narrow bandwidth expressions of personality dispositions.

A third issue concerns the often heard comment that people constantly change and that that fact invalidates personality measurement. Beginning about 1980, a series of studies have shown that personality is much more stable than the critics realized. For example, Costa and McCrae (1988) found that correlations between the scales on their measure of the Five

Factor model over a six-year period averaged 0.83, and Helson and Wink (1992) found correlations between scale scores on the California Psychological Inventory and the Adjective Checklist (Gough & Heilbrun, 1980) over ten years averaged about 0.70. However, the best evidence for the stability of personality comes from well-designed longitudinal studies. Conley (1984, 1985) followed up a sample originally studied by Kelly (1955) and found test-retest correlations averaging about 0.34 over 45 years. Comparable results are presented by Finn (1986), Helson and Moane (1987), and Haan, Milsap, and Hartka (1986).

A fourth issue concerns the question of why one would use a personality inventory for employment decisions, other than the fact that they are there. The answer is that, if one conducts a job analysis interview for virtually any job, the incumbents always describe such characteristics as "being loyal," "showing respect," "staying calm under pressure," and "taking initiative" as crucial for effective performance. If one asks incumbents to fill out a job analysis questionnaire, they again list such characteristics as self control, stress tolerance, leadership, and the ability to listen as essential for job performance (Hogan & Stark, 1992). These characteristics are all qualities that well-constructed measures of normal personality are designed to assess.

Similarly, Borman and Motowidlo (1993) draw a distinction between "task performance" and "contextual performance." Evaluations of task performance concern how well an incumbent performs the assigned tasks of his or her job. Contextual performance, in contrast, is unrelated to performance on specific tasks; rather, it concerns a more diffuse orientation to work as reflected in such activities as volunteering, putting in extra effort, cooperating, following rules, and supporting the goals of the organization, all of which are equally important for job performance.

Task performance and contextual performance are relatively independent; job experience predicts task performance, but personality predicts contextual performance. The overall point here is that a behaviorist orientation that focuses on specific task behaviors will minimize the importance of personality, but if one asks about how a job should be done, as well as what it entails, and if one asks about contextual performance, one quickly sees the point of personality measurement as part of the preemployment screening process.

A fifth issue concerns what the alternatives are to using personality inventories for preemployment screening. There are six obvious alternatives, and the first is an assessment center. A well-run assessment center will provide comprehensive and valid information regarding a person's suitability for hiring or promotion. On the other hand, assessment centers are very expensive, and research since World War II indicates that most of the valid variance in an assessment center can be captured with perhaps

90 minutes of psychometric testing, at a fraction of the cost of an assessment center.

A second alternative is an interview. Interviews are a universal part of every personnel selection process and always will be. Nonetheless, the validity of interviews is always in question (Hunter & Hunter, 1984), making them hard to defend in terms of their validity and reliability. In addition, interviews can be used to assess characteristics — race, age, and gender — whose assessment is, in fact, prohibited by the Civil Rights Act of 1964.

A third alternative are cognitive tests — measures of memory and numerical and quantitative ability. Many psychologists believe that cognitive tests can predict performance in every job in every setting (Schmidt & Hunter, 1981, p. 1128), but I doubt that this is true. Cognitive tests predict training performance, but above some minimal cut score, they are not very useful for predicting job performance. All of the validity is at the low end — if a person is dull, he or she will not be very good. However, if a person is bright, all bets are off. Moreover, cognitive tests always have adverse impact on minority job applicants. In the absence of demonstrated validity coefficients, this adverse impact leaves one at risk for a claim of discriminatory hiring practices, even perhaps for intentional discrimination, because employers know in advance how such tests will affect the selection of minority applicants. Finally, cognitive tests tell us what a person can do, not what a person will do, that is, they provide no dispositional information.

A fourth alternative is the Minnesota Multiphasic Personality Inventory (MMPI), which is used almost universally to screen applicants for public safety jobs — police, airline pilots, nuclear power plant personnel. Nonetheless, there is virtually no evidence that MMPI scale scores are related to job performance, and its use is being challenged increasingly on the grounds of invasion of privacy. It is also the case that clinically oriented tests, such as the MMPI, can be construed, under the terms of the Americans with Disabilities Act, as medical exams; if so, then they can be administered only after a person has been given a tentative job offer.

A fifth alternative to measures of normal personality are honesty or integrity tests. Some reviewers believe that these tests predict performance in every job, that, after cognitive tests, they are the single most valid way to forecast job performance. Honesty tests are useful when a job requires compulsive tendencies and attention to detail, but they are negatively related to flexibility, openness to change, and creativity. A mindless use of honesty tests will rob an organization of its creativity and innovativeness.

Finally, there are biographical data measures. These measures usually are valid, and they rarely yield adverse impact — two crucial features of any selection procedure. The problem is that, if you examine their item content, they are essentially crude and unsystematic measures of personality and interests. Moreover, there is no recognized structure to biographical data, which makes the systematic accumulation of knowledge using such measures impossible.

In my view, therefore, there are no alternatives to well-constructed personality inventories if one wants to assess such qualities as leadership, initiative, organizational citizenship, service orientation, creativity, ability to work under pressure, and loyalty, and job analyses routinely show that these characteristics are the most valued qualities in virtually every job.

The final issue to be raised here concerns the degree to which personality measures discriminate against protected classes and violate the terms of the Americans with Disabilities Act. The data on this topic are quite clear — there is no evidence that well-constructed personality inventories systematically discriminate against any ethnic or national group (Hogan & Hogan, 1995). Moreover, persons with disabilities receive, on average, the same scores as nondisabled persons (Hayes, in press). Moreover, persons over 40, as a group, receive slightly higher scores than persons under 40 (Hogan & Hogan, 1995).

The American Psychological Association's Science and Practice Directorates wrote to the chairman of the EEOC to point out that personality tests are not medical examinations when they assess job-relevant abilities or skills and are, therefore, appropriate for preemployment screening purposes (Howell & Newman, 1994).

Finally, the EEOC issuance 915.002, dated March 14, 1995, is intended to clarify the meaning of the term "disability." The issuance (pp. 902–910) notes that such personality traits as poor judgment, irresponsible behavior, and poor impulse control are not disabilities or impairments. Moreover, employers do not have to excuse a person's misconduct, even if it is the result of a disability, if they do not excuse similar misconduct from their other employees — employers may hold all employees, disabled and nondisabled, to the same standards of conduct and performance.

This chapter makes four general points. First, scores on personality measures are relatively stable over time. Second, well-constructed personality measures are valid forecasters of on-the-job performance — especially those aspects known as contextual performance (Borman & Motowidlo, 1993). Third, personality measures are nondiscriminatory, and, therefore, they promote social justice and equal employment opportunity. Finally, well-constructed personality measures have fewer shortcomings than all of their alternatives.

REFERENCES

Barrick, M. R., & Mount, M. K. (1991). The Big-Five personality dimensions in job performance: A meta-analysis. *Personnel Psychology, 44,* 1–26.

Borman, W. C., & Motowidlo, S. J. (1993). Expanding the criterion domain to include elements of contextual performance. In N. Schmitt & W. C. Borman (Eds.), *Personnel selection in organizations* (pp. 71–98). San Francisco, CA: Jossey-Bass.

Conley, J. J. (1985). Longitudinal stability of personality traits: A multitrait-multimethod-multilocation analysis. *Journal of Personality and Social Psychology, 49,* 1266–1282.

Conley, J. J. (1984). Longitudinal consistency of adult personality: Self-reported psychological characteristics across 45 years. *Journal of Personality and Social Psychology, 47,* 1325–1333.

Costa, P. T., Jr., & McCrae, R. R. (1988). Personality in adulthood: A six-year longitudinal study of self-reports and spouse ratings on the NEO personality inventory. *Journal of Personality and Social Psychology, 54,* 853–863.

Finn, S. E. (1986). Stability of personality self-ratings over 30 years: Evidence for an age/cohort interaction. *Journal of Personality and Social Psychology, 50,* 813–818.

Gough, H. G. (1987). *Manual for the California Psychological Inventory.* Palo Alto, CA: Consulting Psychologists Press.

Gough, H. G., & Heilbrun, A. B., Jr. (1980). *The Adjective Checklist manual: 1983 edition.* Palo Alto, CA: Consulting Psychologists Press.

Guion, R. M., & Gottier, R. F. (1965). Validity of personality measures in personnel selection. *Personnel Psychology, 18,* 135–164.

Haan, N., Milsap, R., & Hartka, E. (1986). As time goes by: Change and stability in personality over fifty years. *Psychology and Aging, 1,* 220–232.

Hayes, T. L. (in press). Personality correlates of performance: Does disability make a difference? *Human Performance.*

Helson, R., & Moane, G. (1987). Personality change in women from college to midlife. *Journal of Personality and Social Psychology, 53,* 176–186.

Helson, R., & Wink, P. (1992). Personality change in women from early 40s to early 50s. *Psychology and Aging, 7,* 46–55.

Hogan, R., & Hogan, J. (1995). *Hogan personality inventory manual* (2d ed.). Tulsa, OK: Hogan Assessment Systems.

Hogan, J., & Stark, D. (1992, June). *Using personality measures to select firefighters.* Paper presented at the sixteenth annual meeting of the International Personnel Management Association Assessment Council, Baltimore, Maryland.

Howell, W. C., & Newman, R. (1994, May 11). Personal correspondence to Toney E. Gallegos, Chairman, Equal Employment Opportunity Commission.

Hunter, J. E., & Hunter, R. F. (1984). Validity and utility of alternative predictors of job performance. *Psychological Bulletin, 96,* 72–98.

Kelly, E. L. (1955). Consistency of the adult personality. *American Psychologist, 10,* 659–681.

McDaniel, M. A., & Frei, R. L. (1994). Validity of customer service measures in personnel selection: A review of criterion and construct evidence.

Manuscript submitted for publication.

McHenry, J. J., Hough, L. M., Toquam, J. L., Hanson, M. A., & Ashworth, S. (1990). Project A validity results: The relationship between predictor and criterion domains. *Personnel Psychology, 43,* 335–354.

Ones, D. S., Viswesvaran, C., & Schmidt, F. L. (1993). Comprehensive meta-analysis of integrity test validation: Findings and implications for personnel selection and theories of job performance. *Journal of Applied Psychology, 78,* 679–703.

Schmidt, F. L., & Hunter, J. E. (1981). Employment testing: Old theories and new research findings. *American Psychologist, 36,* 1128–1137.

Tett, R. P., Jackson, D. N., & Rothstein, M. (1991). Personality measures as predictors of job performance: A meta-analytic review. *Personnel Psychology, 44,* 703-742.

Wiggins, J. S. (1995). *The five-factor model of personality: Theoretical perspectives.* New York: Guilford Press.

18

Employment Drug Testing

Stephen D. Salyards and Jacques Normand

Our purpose with this chapter is to address some of the key issues that should be considered before deciding to implement a drug-testing program. We briefly discuss the scope of the drug problem, legal constraints in testing, accuracy of drug test results, and evaluations of program usefulness, economic utility, and fairness. In-depth discussions of these topics can be found in Normand, Lempert, and O'Brien (1994).

MAGNITUDE OF THE DRUG PROBLEM

Findings from two large-scale, ongoing surveys (the High School Senior Surveys and their follow-up components on college-age youth and young adults [Johnston, O'Malley, & Bachman, 1992] and the National Household Survey on Drug Abuse [National Institute on Drug Abuse, 1991]) indicate that illicit drug use has steadily decreased over the past decade after peaking in the late 1970s and early 1980s. Despite these declines, drug use continues to affect sizable portions of the work force and selected industries.

According to a 1990 household survey of employee drug use, 7 percent of full-time and 8 percent of part-time workers ages 18 and over reported current (past month) use of one or more illicit drugs. Among full-time employees ages 18 to 34, rates of illicit drug and heavy alcohol use varied by industry. Rates of illicit drug use were relatively low among male professional, manufacturing, and transportation workers (i.e., past month use of 9.0 percent, 9.7 percent, and 10.5 percent, respectively).

Intermediate levels of illicit drug use were found among male retail trade (16.8 percent), repair services (16.1 percent), and wholesale trade workers (13.8 percent). Of construction workers, 20 percent reported using an illicit drug during the past month. More than 20 percent of men employed full-time in construction (26.4 percent), transportation (20.4 percent), and wholesale trade (20.5 percent) reported heavy alcohol use in the past 30 days. Many of the estimates for women were not reported because of small sample sizes, but the data that were available showed little variability in alcohol or drug use for women across industries.

Illicit drug use was more common among men, younger workers (ages 18 to 25), blacks, residents of large metropolitan areas, and residents of the western United States. Illicit drug use was substantially higher among the unemployed than among full-time or part-time employees, while heavy alcohol use showed little variation by employment status.

Data pertaining to drug use specifically at work showed that alcohol was the most commonly used drug, with 8 percent of the men and 5 percent of the women reporting alcohol use during work hours. Illicit drug use was relatively low, with 6 percent of the men and 2 percent of the women reporting the use of an illicit drug while at work. Marijuana was the most prevalent illicit drug used, with 5 percent of the men and 1 percent of the women reporting marijuana use at work.

LEGAL CONSIDERATIONS

The law both requires and restricts workplace drug testing. Over the past decade, the executive and legislative branches of the federal government have not only authorized drug testing by public and private employers but also mandated or encouraged it in some settings. Their actions provide legal authority for drug testing that overrides all contrary authority except the U.S. Constitution. Limits on what the law can authorize or command have been established by courts in suits challenging the legal authority or constitutionality of employee drug testing.

Executive Order No. 12564 (1986) introduced the concept of a "drug free workplace" and promoted many of the features of workplace drug testing that now have become standard for public and certain private employers. The order required all federal agencies to adopt employee drug-testing programs that included mandatory testing of employees in security and safety sensitive positions, with the scope and rationale for testing left to the discretion of agency heads. It also permitted the testing of employees in other positions when there was reason to suspect illegal drug use, as part of an accident or safety investigation, or as a follow-up to treatment or counseling for illegal drug use. The Supplemental Appropriations Act of 1987 required federal contractors to guarantee a drug-free workplace; although drug testing was not mandated, it was recommended. Subsequent court decisions have eliminated many, but certainly not all, constitutional barriers to government-mandated drug testing.

In the law relating to drug testing, three critical distinctions emerge. The first is the public-private distinction. Drug testing done by a government agency or contractor is subject to Fourth Amendment search-and-seizure constraints that will not hamper a private firm that chooses to test for drugs on its own initiative. The second is the distinction between pre-employment and postemployment drug testing. Generally speaking, both governmental agencies and private businesses face fewer legal constraints in testing job applicants for drug use than current employees. The third turns on the distinction between state and federal law. Drug-testing programs that are sanctioned under federal law may, nevertheless, be prohibited under the law of a particular state. State law will not, however, prevent the federal government from testing its own employees in compliance with federal law, nor can it hinder employers within a state from complying with federally mandated testing.

Although the scope of workplace drug testing is limited by certain state and federal constitutional restrictions, these limits are generous and allow a broad range of employees to be tested using a wide range of reliable methodologies. The emerging judicial consensus in favor of drug testing appears to reflect widely held perceptions that drug abuse is one of our nation's most serious problems; drug users, at least in certain sensitive positions, pose a threat to workplace safety and productivity; drug testing is reliable and accurate; and drug testing can be performed in a manner that minimizes intrusions on privacy and dignity. As long as judges continue to hold these same beliefs, courts are unlikely to tamper with either legally mandated or private drug-testing programs.

TYPES OF DRUG-TESTING PROGRAMS

Workplace drug-testing programs are of three distinct types: preemployment testing of job applicants, incident-driven or for-cause testing of employees (e.g., postaccident, fitness for duty), and postemployment testing without specific cause, often conducted on a random and unannounced basis for employees in targeted (usually sensitive) positions. Approximately 24 million tests are performed annually in the United States at a cost of $1.2 billion. Preemployment testing of applicants is, by far, the most prevalent type of drug-testing program.

In 1988, the Department of Health and Human Services (HHS) issued its "Mandatory Guidelines for Federal Workplace Drug Testing Programs." The HHS guidelines contain many of the quality control standards and procedural safeguards that have served as a model for most programs implemented since 1988. The guidelines require testing urine for five classes of commonly used illegal drugs: marijuana; opiates, such as heroin and morphine; cocaine; amphetamines; and phencyclidine. The Omnibus Transportation Employee Testing Act of 1991 mandated alcohol as well as drug tests for safety sensitive jobs in the transportation industry.

DRUG-TESTING ANALYTICAL METHODS

Several techniques are available for substance abuse screening, but only blood- and urine-based methods have, thus far, achieved widespread acceptance by the forensic sciences community. Urine is the preferred specimen for occupational drug screening: collection is noninvasive and requires no medical training, sufficient amounts are readily obtainable, and drug detection is possible over a longer period than in blood. Urine tests also are less expensive and easier to perform than blood tests. Because workplace drug testing is virtually synonymous with urinalysis, we will limit the focus of the remaining sections to a discussion of urine-based methods of drug use detection.

In all laboratories that support government-regulated programs, a two-stage urinalysis procedure must be followed. The initial screening method must be based on immunoassay, followed by a confirmatory test that must be an acceptable form of gas chromatography–mass spectrometry (GC/MS). Immunoassays use drug-specific antibodies to detect the presence of drugs and their metabolites. When a specimen containing the drug or its metabolite is mixed with these reagents, the antibodies bind with the drug metabolites for which they were prepared. The more drug present, the stronger is the chemical signal.

Chromatography is a process by which a chemical mixture carried by a liquid or gas is separated into components. Once the chemical components in the mixture have been isolated, an analysis of each component's unique molecular properties (mass spectrum) is performed to identify and quantify each drug. The analytical technique of GC/MS is widely recognized by forensic toxicologists as the most conclusive method for confirming positive initial screens. The GC/MS method is so powerful that it is able to identify the "chemical fingerprint" that is unique for each drug.

MEASUREMENT ISSUES RELATED
TO DRUG TEST RESULTS

Now that we have briefly reviewed the technology behind the most commonly used drug-testing methods, we turn to the issue of how effectively these methods do what they were designed to do (i.e., detect drug metabolites in urine). One of the most important factors that affects the use of a measurement procedure is its decision accuracy.

With drug testing, as with other classification methods, decisions can be either correct or incorrect. Correct decisions are of two types: true positive (finding a drug that is present) and true negative (failing to find a drug that is not there). Incorrect decisions can be categorized as false positive (finding a drug that is not there) and false negative (failing to find a drug that is present). Two of the more commonly applied indexes of decision accuracy are referred to as "sensitivity" and "specificity." A test's sensitivity reflects the probability that the test will give a positive result when the drug or one or more of its metabolites is present. Hence, a drug testing procedure with a sensitivity of 0.95 will correctly identify 95 percent of the drug users (true positives) but will yield negative results for the remaining 5 percent (false negatives). A test's specificity reflects the probability that the test will give a negative result when the drug or one or more of its metabolites is absent. Thus, a drug-testing procedure with a specificity of 0.95 will correctly identify 95 percent of the negatives (true negatives) and will incorrectly identify 5 percent of the negatives as positive (false positives).

Within the forensic community, there are well-established professional standards for conducting employment drug testing. Informed professional consensus is that single-procedure methods are not acceptable and that confirmation by a second analytical method based on a different chemical principle is required. The initial test is referred to as the "screening test," and the second test is referred to as the "confirmation test." A confirmation test that relies on different properties of a drug to determine its identity (i.e., a different chemical principle) is essential to ensure that sources of error that are unique to the initial screening test are not simply confirmed by the second test. A drug test result is reported as positive only if *both* the initial screening test and the confirmation test results are positive.

Immunological methods are the most sensitive screening techniques used in mass drug-testing programs, and GC/MS is the most specific commercially available confirmation technique. When these two methods are combined in series, the likelihood of obtaining a false positive result is essentially zero. The advantage of series testing is that the combined specificity of the tests is greater than that of either test alone. As specificity increases, the likelihood of a false positive result decreases accordingly. However, it also is true that the combined sensitivity will be less than that of either test alone, and, thus, a certain number of drug users will be misclassified as negative for drug use. In the context of employment drug testing, this trade-off is considered acceptable because of the greater importance given to minimizing false positives over that of identifying every drug user.

How reliable are employment drug test results as an indicator of recent drug use? Obviously, the answer will depend on the particular features of a given program, such as the stringency of its analytical techniques and quality control procedures. Professional guidelines for certifying laboratories are extremely demanding and are comparable to those established by the HHS for accrediting laboratories. For example, any laboratory wishing to be certified by HHS must participate in a thorough quality control evaluation that covers all aspects of drug testing from collection and analysis to reporting of result. The occurrence of even a *single* false positive test can result in the laboratory having its accreditation denied or revoked. Therefore, the real question is how reliable the results are of a screening test that is performed by an accredited laboratory.

A large-scale evaluation of preemployment drug testing (Normand & Salyards, 1989) included, as part of its research program, a blind proficiency component to assess the reliability of its HHS-accredited laboratory. Five of the 21 validation study sites participated in a quality control study and submitted a total of 250 blind (i.e., without the laboratory's knowledge) proficiency-testing specimens. Of these proficiency-testing specimens, 50 were blanks (i.e., drug free), 92 contained potential cross-reactive agents or drug metabolites that were not included in the initial screening test panel, and 32 were spiked with drug metabolites at concentrations just above the cutoff levels. The overall efficiency across all drug classes was 99.8 percent, with an overall sensitivity of 84 percent and a specificity of 100 percent (i.e., no false positives). The results of this double-blind quality control study indicate that, with use of an accredited laboratory, extremely reliable drug test results can be expected.

SYSTEMATIC ERRORS

Systematic measurement errors are caused by factors that consistently affect an individual's test results but have nothing to do with what the test is trying to measure. Immunoassay tests in particular may be susceptible to systematic sources of error under certain conditions. For example, attempts to adulterate a urine specimen by substantially altering its pH (i.e., acidity or alkalinity) or diluting its concentration can cause immunoassay tests to produce false negative results. A phenomenon referred to as "cross-reactivity" also may pose problems, because some of the antibodies used in the immunoassay tests may bind (cross-react) with chemicals that are structurally similar to the target drug or metabolite. For example, kidney tumors can produce unusually high amounts of certain enzymes in the urine, which, in turn, can cause an immunoassay test to produce a false positive result for cannabinoids.

Because of a higher concentration of melanin and various melanin metabolites in the urine of blacks and Hispanics, some critics have speculated that members of these ethnic groups can erroneously test positive for marijuana. This notion has received a great deal of attention in the media, but the research indicates that it simply has no basis in scientific fact. Even so, this has not prevented some rather unscrupulous critics of drug testing from continuing to claim that melanin cross-reacts with immunoassay tests. It should be emphasized that even substantiated sources of systematic error normally would not present a problem if proper confirmatory tests were performed according to professional standards.

PROGRAM EFFECTIVENESS

Despite the widespread implementation of occupational drug-testing programs, few studies have attempted to evaluate their effectiveness in achieving business objectives. The fundamental issue from a program evaluation perspective is whether the introduction of drug testing empirically relates to important organizational outcomes. With regard to random drug testing, evaluations have mostly involved describing trends in employee drug use patterns following program intervention. For example, studies conducted by the military and nuclear power industry have demonstrated a decrease in positive drug test results after random drug testing was initiated. Such results could be taken to suggest a deterrent effect. However, most organizations with random drug-testing programs also have implemented a wide array of other countermeasures, including work-based prevention and treatment initiatives and even other forms of drug use detection, such as applicant and incident driven drug-testing programs. It has been virtually impossible in most cases to unravel the effects of random drug testing from those of these other organizational initiatives. Decreases in positive drug test results may be because of any one of these efforts acting alone or in combination or may be because of entirely extraneous influences, such as changes in work force demographics or social norms favoring abstinence. Of course, the more important issue of whether the desired changes in drug use levels relate to productivity has yet to be tested using scientific methods.

In the area of for-cause testing, only two studies have, thus far, been reported (Crouch, Webb, Peterson, Buller, & Rollins, 1989; Sheridan & Winkler, 1989). However, the intention of both studies seems to have been to isolate the effects of individual drug use on work behaviors (explanatory analysis) rather than to evaluate the organizational impact of implementing for-cause testing (program evaluation). The two approaches pose different research questions, apply different methodologies in addressing the questions, and come to different conclusions about the types of inferences that can be drawn from the study results. The explanatory analysis attempts to unravel the unique contribution of drug use from other influences in explaining employment outcomes (e.g., accidents, disciplinary problems), whereas the program evaluation approach attempts to assess the validity of making employment decisions (e.g., transfer, fire, promote) based on the operational use of a drug-testing program. Unfortunately, investigations of for-cause testing to date have employed research methods that allowed neither drug effects nor program effectiveness issues to be addressed adequately. The evaluation of for-cause testing as a decision-making tool, therefore, remains largely unexplored.

The most common form of drug testing by far is preemployment testing of job applicants, yet, these types of programs have received only slightly more attention from the research community than random or for-cause testing. Nevertheless, most studies of preemployment drug testing have detected statistically significant relationships between drug test results and one or more employment outcomes. Most notable among these findings have been the relationship between test results and absenteeism, job retention, disciplinary actions, and subsequent problems with drugs and alcohol. The presumed relationship between preemployment drug test results and accidents has been mixed, perhaps because of variations across organizations in the frequency of accidents, administrative reporting procedures, or level of exposure to safety hazards. However, even within the same organization and job, other factors associated with drug use (e.g., absenteeism and on-the-job withdrawal) may have served to reduce exposure to work hazards, thus putting drug users at no greater risk for accidents than other workers.

As an illustrative example of preemployment drug-testing research, we will describe the first, and perhaps most comprehensive, large scale evaluation of this type of program conducted to date (Normand, Salyards, & Mahoney, 1990). The study was initiated in 1987 by the U.S. Postal Service and involved 21 postal installations across the country. Job applicants who successfully completed the initial stages of selection (such as qualifying exams and evaluations of training and experience) were asked to submit urine samples during their medical exams. Specimens were dispatched to a central lab and screened for drugs. The test results played no role in the hiring process and were known only to the research staff. Of the 5,465 applicants tested for drugs, 4,403 were eventually hired after passing background and medical checks.

Absenteeism and turnover trends were monitored over a four-year period. Early reports showed significantly higher levels of absenteeism and involuntary terminations among those who tested positive. The disparities grew over the course of the study. At the four-year mark, those who had tested positive showed, compared with the negative group, significantly higher rates of absenteeism (11.39 percent versus 6.85 percent of scheduled work hours) and involuntary job terminations (23.64 percent versus 13.34 percent). No significant associations were detected between test results and accidents or injuries during this same time period.

Investigators also collected data relating to disciplinary infractions, employee assistance program (EAP) referrals, and medical claims. Employees who had tested positive were more than twice as likely to have been formally disciplined and were three times as likely to have experienced problems requiring EAP intervention compared with other study participants. The medical claims analysis indicated that the average dollar amount of claims filed by the drug-positive group was 83 percent higher than that of the negative group ($486.65 versus $264.81 per year, respectively). Further analysis of the EAP and medical claims data indicated that those who tested positive before employment were at much greater risk for experiencing subsequent problems with drugs and alcohol compared with those who had tested negative. Drug-positive employees were 3.5 times as likely to be referred to the EAP for drinking problems and nearly six times as likely to be referred for drug abuse problems as those who had tested negative. A similar pattern of risk emerged from the medical claims analysis. Drug-positive employees were 3.4 times as likely as their drug-negative peers to file medical claims having an alcohol- or drug-related diagnosis.

Evaluations of program effectiveness require, as a first step, a demonstration that a significant relationship exists between drug-testing programs and work-related outcomes. However, there are other considerations that need to be taken into account when using drug tests to make employment decisions. One such consideration is whether these relationships are moderated by the personal or background characteristics of employees. A moderated relationship may indicate that drug test results predict differently for different subgroups of employees. Under such circumstances, the predictive use of such a procedure could, therefore, affect the accuracy of decisions regarding individuals and raise questions of test fairness. For example, differences are known to exist in the prevalence of illicit drug use among applicant subgroups defined on the basis of such legally protected factors as age, race, and sex. Unless these differences in illicit drug use (as measured by a urine toxicology screen) reflect comparable differences in job performance indicators, the drug test will yield biased predictions. Under current legal guidelines, prediction bias that works to the disadvantage of a minority group (i.e., where predicted performance is lower than measured performance) calls for corrective action on the part of the employer.

The only known fairness analysis of drug testing was reported by the U.S. Postal Service as part of its evaluation of preemployment drug testing. The results indicated that the predictive meaning of drug test results was essentially the same for all subgroups. Applicants who had tested positive for drugs showed a greater risk for absenteeism, involuntary turnover, disciplinary actions, and EAP referrals, regardless of group identity. In the very few instances in which predictive bias was present, the bias always worked to the advantage of the minority group by predicting more favorable outcomes than were actually observed over the course of the study.

Another important consideration involves assessing the practical value or economic utility of drug-testing programs. Only two peer-reviewed studies have reported program-specific information pertaining to the costs and benefits of drug-testing programs (Normand, Salyards, & Mahoney, 1990; Zwerling, Ryan, & Orav, 1992). Both were concerned with preemployment drug testing and were conducted on two different study samples within the Postal Service. Both estimates indicated that substantial costs could be avoided by screening out applicants who test positive for illicit drugs. The utility of drug testing in a particular setting will vary with such factors as the prevalence of drug use among a given population, the cost of testing, and the stringency of the analytical methods employed.

INTERPRETING PROGRAM EVALUATION RESULTS

We offer a comment on interpreting the findings summarized above. It should be kept in mind that the observed associations between drug test results and employment outcomes do not necessarily mean that the relationships are causal in nature. Readers often misconstrue these findings to mean that drug-induced impairment literally caused job absences, disciplinary problems, and degraded performance resulting in termination of employment. Program evaluation results do not provide the type of information needed to support such causal inferences, and explanatory studies of drug effects in the workplace have lacked the methodological rigor to address the issue. From a theoretical standpoint, it is just as plausible to argue that other factors related to both drug use and problematic behaviors have produced these associations. For example, etiological studies of drug involvement indicate that drug use often is one facet of a deviance-prone lifestyle characterized by social nonconformity, rebelliousness, and irresponsibility (Newcomb, 1988). Associations between drug use measures and employment problems may be more because of deviant values and attitudes than drug-induced performance impairment. As a potential explanatory construct, social deviance may have implications beyond merely providing a context for understanding the results of field studies. For example, if disruptive drug use is associated with other counterproductive attitudes and practices, then addressing only the inappropriate drug use will not correct the deviant attitudes that are the actual source of the employee's problems.

SUMMARY

Many considerations are important to developing and implementing a sound drug-testing program. We briefly have reviewed some of the more critical legal, measurement, and program evaluation issues. Drug testing, even when mandated by law, should be viewed as merely one element in an overall plan to reduce the negative impact of drug abuse in an organization. The plan should be narrowly tailored to the needs of the organization. If there is no clear indication of significant drug use at the work site, then a preventive, educational effort may prove to be more beneficial. A carefully thought-out policy will take these and many other considerations into account. The well-being and dignity of employees and the effectiveness of the organization in meeting its business objectives very well may depend on it.

REFERENCES

Crouch, D. J., Webb, D. O., Peterson, L. V., Buller, P. F., & Rollins, D. E. (1989). A critical evaluation of the Utah Power and Light Company's substance abuse management program: Absenteeism, accidents and costs. In S. W. Gust & J. M. Walsh (Eds.), *Drugs in the workplace: Research and evaluation data* (pp. 169–193). Rockville, MD: National Institute on Drug Abuse.

Executive Order No. 12564, 51 Fed. Reg. 32,889–32,893 (1986).

Johnston, L. D., O'Malley, P. M., & Bachman, J. G. (1992). *Smoking, drinking, and illicit drug use among American secondary school students and young adults, 1974–1991* (Vols. 1 and 2). Rockville, MD: National Institute on Drug Abuse.

Mandatory guidelines for federal workplace drug testing programs, 53 Fed. Reg. 11970–11989 (1988).

Omnibus Transportation Employee Testing Act of 1991, Pub. L. No. 102-143, §3.

National Institute on Drug Abuse. (1991). *National household survey on drug abuse: Main findings 1990*. Rockville, MD: Author.

Newcomb, M. D. (1988). *Drug use in the workplace: Risk factors for disruptive substance use among young adults*. Dover, MA: Auburn House.

Normand, J., Lempert, R. O., & O'Brien, C. P. (Eds.). (1994). *Under the influence?: Drugs and the American work force*. Washington, DC: National Academy Press.

Normand, J., & Salyards, S. D. (1989). An empirical evaluation of preemployment drug testing in the U.S. Postal Service: Interim report of findings. In S. W. Gust & J. M. Walsh (Eds.), *Drugs in the workplace: Research and evaluation data* (pp. 111–138). Rockville, MD: National Institute on Drug Abuse.

Normand, J., Salyards, S. D., & Mahoney, J. J. (1990). An evaluation of preemployment drug testing. *Journal of Applied Psychology, 75*, 629–639.

Sheridan, J., & Winkler, H. (1989). An evaluation of drug testing in the workplace. In S. W. Gust & J. M. Walsh (Eds.), *Drugs in the workplace: Research and evaluation data* (pp. 195–216). Rockville, MD: National Institute on Drug Abuse.

Supplemental Appropriations Act of 1987, Pub. L. No. 100-71, §503.

Zwerling, C., Ryan, J., & Orav, E. J. (1992). Costs and benefits of preemployment drug screening. *Journal of the American Medical Association, 267*, 91–93.

19

A Modern Approach to Minimum Qualifications

Lance W. Seberhagen

DEFINITION

For purposes of this chapter, minimum qualifications (MQs) are defined as "pass-fail assessment procedures that can be applied to all job applicants on the basis of information obtained from job application forms." This definition is intended to distinguish MQs from other pass-fail criteria for employment, such as compliance with work rules or the achievement of minimum acceptable scores on selection procedures administered to job applicants after the application process (e.g., written tests, work sample tests, interviews, physical ability tests, medical exams). MQs are a special case of pass-fail criteria and the setting of cutoff scores for employee selection. Examples of traditional MQs include minimum requirements for education, experience, occupational licenses, driver's licenses, citizenship, residency, height, weight, age, and sex.

ROLE IN SELECTION PROCESS

MQs can play an important role as the first step in the selection process (not counting recruitment) by providing a fast and inexpensive way to screen out applicants who obviously are unfit for the job. Applicants who satisfy the MQs then can be subjected to more time-consuming and costly assessment devices to identify the best qualified applicants for the job. MQs are most useful for selecting new hires, because there are large numbers of unknown applicants who must be processed for each job, but

MQs also may be useful for promotion, transfer, and other employment decisions.

The major shortcoming of MQs is that they provide a very crude assessment of an applicant's qualifications. MQs typically are stated in brief, imprecise terms in job descriptions, recruitment ads, and vacancy announcements. Standard application blanks ask a limited number of very general questions and then provide little space for answers. Applicants vary in the understanding, care, and skill with which they complete application blanks. Inconsistent scoring results when raters must use judgment to interpret MQs and have short deadlines to process many applications. Reliable scoring is even more difficult when raters attempt to assess MQs on the basis of unstandardized resumes without requiring all applicants to complete standard application forms.

Thus, it is a good practice to give "benefit of the doubt" to the applicant regarding MQs. After all, the consequences of a borderline decision in favor of an applicant are not great, because it means only that the applicant will be invited to undergo more intensive assessment devices (e.g., written tests, simulation exercises, interviews) in competition with all other applicants who have passed the MQs. Employers should not use MQs as the only basis, or even the primary basis, for making final employment decisions.

INAPPROPRIATE USES

The real controversy over MQs begins when employers are not content to use MQs merely to screen out obviously unfit applicants but set artificially difficult or unnecessary MQs for other purposes, such as to reduce the number of applicants to be processed, justify higher salaries (when MQs are a factor in job evaluation), restrict competition for employment, enhance the prestige of the organization, or discriminate against certain groups (e.g., sex, race, politics). A combination of proper MQ screening and random selection is the best way to reduce the number of applicants to be processed. Misuse of MQs for other purposes will serve only to generate discrimination complaints and other grievances.

WHO SHOULD DEVELOP MINIMUM QUALIFICATIONS

In most organizations, MQs are developed in a rather casual fashion, as a minor aspect of a position classification study or the result of simple negotiation among managers. Sometimes, employee groups and professional associations also will be contacted for their input on MQs. The casual approach is not recommended, because MQs are "employee selection procedures" under legal and psychological standards. Therefore, MQs should be developed by a testing specialist who has appropriate training and experience in psychological measurement, testing, employee selection, job analysis, and statistical analysis.

TECHNICAL STANDARDS

Job Relatedness (Validity)

MQs should not be artificial or arbitrary barriers to employment. MQs should be designed to assess all important knowledges, skills, abilities, and other qualities needed for successful work performance, to the extent possible, without being contaminated by other, irrelevant factors. MQs also should be limited to assessing qualities that are developed primarily *before* employment in the job, as opposed to those developed primarily *after* employment. Content validation is the most practical way to demonstrate job relatedness. Criterion-related validation also is acceptable but usually is not technically feasible. Construct validation is acceptable but is rarely feasible or practical.

No Abstract Traits

MQs should be limited to the assessment of directly observable behavior to facilitate content validation. Assessment of abstract psychological constructs (e.g., intelligence, motivation, leadership, sensitivity) requires the use of criterion-related validation or construct validation, neither of which usually is feasible for MQs.

True Minimums

MQs should be designed to screen out only those applicants who obviously are unfit for the job rather than to attempt to differentiate between best qualified and less qualified applicants or simply to reduce the number of applicants to be processed. MQs normally should be no higher than the qualifications of current job incumbents who are performing acceptable work.

Minimum Adverse Impact

MQs should be designed to maximize utility while minimizing adverse impact by race, sex, age, and other protected classes. One of the best ways to reduce adverse impact is to establish many alternative ways to satisfy the MQs (e.g., combinations of education and experience, substitution of experience for education, acceptance of credit and noncredit courses, acceptance of civilian and military experience, acceptance of paid and unpaid experience).

Objective Scoring

MQs should be written in clear and precise terms to require a minimum of judgment in scoring. Ideally, the MQs should be able to be scored by machine.

Consistency

Jobs that require the same kind and level of worker characteristics should have very similar MQs. Higher level jobs normally should have more demanding MQs than lower level jobs.

Compliance with Psychological Standards

MQs should comply with generally accepted professional standards (e.g., American Educational Research Association, American Psychological Association, & National Council on Measurement in Education, 1985; Society for Industrial and Organizational Psychology, 1987).

Compliance with Legal Standards

Title VII, the Americans with Disabilities Act, and other federal Civil Rights laws prohibit employment discrimination on the basis of race, color, sex, religion, national origin, age, and disability. MQs should comply with the Uniform Guidelines on Employee Selection Procedures (U.S. Equal Employment Opportunity Commission, Civil Service Commission, Department of Labor, andDepartment of Justice, 1978) and other legal standards as appropriate (e.g., U.S. Equal Employment Opportunity Commission, 1992).

MAJOR PROBLEM AREAS

Education Requirements

Some employers require a bachelor's degree, regardless of courses, as the basic MQ for professional and management jobs on the assumption that a college degree shows learning ability, motivation, and discipline. This is a dangerous practice, because degree requirements are likely to have an adverse impact by race, sex, or age, causing a discrimination complaint. Such MQs probably are not defensible, because the employer would have to conduct a criterion-related validation study to justify the assessment of such abstract worker characteristics, and such studies usually are not feasible.

A better approach with education requirements is to use courses, rather than degrees, as the unit of analysis and to justify MQs by showing the logical relationship between the content of courses and the content of the job. For example, instead of a degree in accounting as the basic MQ for accountants, simply require six to eight courses in accounting, which is typical of the required courses for a major in accounting. These six to eight courses can be defended easily on a content validity basis and give the employer essentially the same skills that it would have obtained from requiring a degree in accounting, which would be much more difficult to justify in court.

Occupational Licenses

Many occupational licenses are required by state or local law, but requiring a license may be discriminatory if it causes an adverse impact and the licensing agency does not use validated selection procedures.

Physical Ability

Traditional height and weight requirements are hard to validate and often produce an adverse impact by sex, race, and national origin. Physical performance tests and medical exams normally provide a more valid alternative procedure with less adverse impact. The Americans with Disabilities Act also requires employers to provide individualized assessment and reasonable accommodation to persons with disabilities.

Sex

Employers can claim "sex" as a bona fide occupational qualification only under the most narrow of circumstances, such as for purposes of authenticity (e.g., fashion model, undercover agent, actor). Customer and coworker preferences normally are insufficient to justify sex as a bona fide occupational qualification.

SUPPLEMENTAL APPLICATION BLANKS

Standard application blanks are too limited in size and scope to collect all of the information needed to assess the MQs for every job in an organization. Thus, the modern way to measure MQs is to use a supplemental application blank (SAB) to ask more specific questions for each job or job family. SABs also may be used to provide the basis for training and experience ratings to provide a ranking of candidates above the minimum passing level (further discussion of training and experience ratings is beyond the scope of this chapter).

SABs normally range from one to ten pages and may use a variety of question formats (e.g., yes-no, multiple-choice, short answer, short essay). Objectively scored questions are the most reliable and practical, par-ticularly if one expects to assess a large number of applicants. Machine scoring is recommended if more than 1,000 applicants are expected.

Ideally, SABs should be distributed to applicants when they request a standard application blank, and applicants should submit all completed application forms together in one package. If an applicant submits just the standard application form, the employer will have to give or send the applicant the appropriate SAB, and the process becomes a bit more complicated. Thus, standard application forms and SABs should be designed to provide easy matching of forms by name, social security number, birthdate, or other appropriate data, in the event that an applicant submits the two forms separately.

SAB questions may be designed to assess not only traditional MQs of education and experience but also new types of MQs, such as self-assessment, availability, and interest. Most job applicants have little knowledge about the specific duties, necessary qualifications, and working conditions of the jobs for which they are applying. An SAB can give potential applicants a realistic picture of the work, including the undesirable aspects, so that applicants can withdraw from the process if they do not like what they see. The key is to make sure that all SAB questions focus on important screen-out topics and are phrased in terms of observable behavior. A typical SAB might include 30 to 50 yes-no questions, such as:

Have you graduated from high school or received a General Equivalency Diploma?

Do you have a valid driver's license?

Are you able to count money and make change quickly and accurately?

Are you willing to smile and say "Thank you" to each customer?

Are you willing to wear a uniform at work?

Are you available to work any day of the week (Monday to Sunday)?

Are you willing and able to come to work on time, every day?

SABs are relatively easy to develop and use but can be an effective tool for eliminating obviously unfit applicants. SABs also may provide evidence for terminating employees for poor performance if they agreed to do something on the SAB and then later refused to do it.

REFERENCES

Society for Industrial and Organizational Psychology. (1987). *Principles for the validation and use of personnel selection procedures* (3rd ed.). College Park, MD: Author.

Standards for educational and psychological testing. (1985). Washington, DC: American Psychological Association.

U.S. Equal Employment Opportunity Commission. (1992). *A technical assistance manual on the employment provisions (Title I) of the Americans with Disabilities Act.* Washington, D.C.: U.S. Government.

U.S. Equal Employment Opportunity Commission, Civil Service Commission, Department of Labor, and Department of Justice. (1978). Uniform guidelines on employee selection procedures. *Federal Register, 43,* 38290–38315.

20

Background Data for Personnel Selection

Garnett S. Stokes and Cheryl S. Toth

Background data information (biodata) has been touted as a new frontier in employee selection, but it is a technique that has a long history of use in organizations. As early as 1894, background data were suggested for selection of salespersons. Interest in biodata has grown because of extensive evidence for its validity, particularly incremental validity evidence above that commonly obtained with cognitive ability measures, and its relatively low adverse impact. With its increasing popularity, however, have come increasing concerns with faking, invasion of privacy, perceived lack of job relevance, and issues of "controllability" — the extent to which the event or behavior measured in a background data form is under the control of the individual.

This chapter provides information related to the development, validation, and use of biodata as a selection tool. We will address the issues mentioned above, posing a number of important questions about the use of biodata, and we will provide methods and strategies for addressing concerns and enhancing the usefulness of biodata for organizations.

The books by Stokes, Mumford, and Owens (1994) and Gunter, Furnham, and Drakeley (1993) represent the most up-to-date research and thinking in the area of biodata. In addition, reviews by Owens (1976), Mumford and Owens (1987), Mumford and Stokes (1992) and Stokes and Reddy (1992) are excellent sources of information about biodata.

WHAT ARE BACKGROUND DATA?

Background data provide descriptions of a person's past experiences through a retrospective, self-report format. Some background data are collected in the form of application blanks, in which individuals fill in past job experiences, education, and other demographic information. More prevalently, biodata is collected using multiple-choice questions. The respondent may be asked such questions as "During your last job, how often did you volunteer to work on group projects?" or "In working with others on the job, how often have others come to you for advice on how to solve a technical or job-related problem?"

Biodata forms can be used to capture much of the same information one might obtain from an interview, but biodata forms capture the information more economically and with less bias, because the questions and responses are structured. The domain of items for a biodata form is very broad and may include attitudinal and personality type items, though many biodata users argue that items should be limited to objective, verifiable items. Though objective, verifiable items generally are best, attitudinal items often have been found to be highly predictive, and, thus, such items have an important place in a biodata inventory.

What uniquely defines biodata is its historical nature — its focus on past experiences. Biodata items should refer to events that have already occurred or continue to occur. They should not include broad statements about overall dispositions or hypothetical behaviors or situations. However, biodata forms differ in the extent to which they focus on remote past experiences (childhood and adolescence, first jobs) versus recent experiences (on the last job or in the past couple of years). More recent experiences probably are better than more remote events for predicting job performance.

Biodata items have been characterized in terms of a number of attributes in addition to their historical nature. Of particular interest to the user of biodata are some of the attributes discussed by Mael (1991). Some of the item attributes proposed by Mael deal with legal or ethical issues related to the use of biodata items for selection. One of these attributes is job relevance, the extent to which the biodata items reflect actual samples of work-related behavior. Many biodata form developers have relied on such items, but there is evidence that such job-related characteristics may be more able to be faked. Other concerns about biodata items are more controversial and more difficult to define. Mael's article summarizes current perspectives on these and other issues related to biodata item attributes.

FOR WHAT KINDS OF PERFORMANCE AND WHAT TYPES OF JOBS CAN BIODATA BE USEFUL?

Biodata forms have been used for a number of criteria in organizations, and their validity has been impressive for predicting training success, absenteeism, turnover, tenure, job proficiency, production, substance abuse, promotion, achievement or grades, wages, and teamwork. Criteria have been predicted across a wide range of job categories, including selection and promotion for supervisors, scientists, engineers, managers, salespersons, clerical workers, military personnel, and skilled and unskilled workers.

WHAT ISSUES MUST BE ADDRESSED IN DEVELOPING A BIODATA FORM?

Job Analysis

Considerable disagreement exists about the value of formal job analysis procedures, because most of these procedures do not provide the information needed to develop a biodata instrument. The goal of biodata is to identify the backgrounds of successful and less successful individuals based on the criteria. Most job analyses are not directly suited for this purpose. However, some type of job analysis is necessary to provide the rationale for inclusion of items in a biodata form. The job analysis should provide at least part of the material needed to develop hypotheses for item-level and construct-level relationships with the criterion measures. Use of job analysis may lead to a more face-valid questionnaire and may help if the procedure is attacked in court.

Criterion Development

An organization first must decide on the criterion of interest, whether it is reducing turnover, reducing accidents, job performance, or other outcomes. Criterion data available from the organization rarely are sufficient to serve as criterion measures in the development of a biodata form, because the circumstances under which typical criterion data are collected often lead to inadequate validity of the measures.

Biodata Items

Items typically are multiple-choice, with four or five response options. The choice of format may be determined to some extent by the type of form one wants to develop. Both continuous items (i.e., those items that are scored along a psychological continuum, such as "How often have you participated in group discussions? a — very often, b — often, c — sometimes, d — rarely, e — never") and discontinuous items (i.e., items that are not scored along a psychological continuum, such as "In what types of sports have you participated? a — karate, b — bicycling, c — white water canoeing, d — swimming") are common. Most important in the writing of items for a biodata form is to have a hypothesis about the item's relationship to the criterion of interest. These hypotheses are derived from a variety of sources, including hypotheses that emerge from job analysis information, from previous literature examining individuals in the particular occupations being investigated, from past biodata forms used to predict similar criteria in similar jobs, from life history essays written by successful and less successful job incumbents, and from detailed interviews with incumbents and supervisory personnel. The content of the biodata form is dictated by the information that one has about both individuals in the job and the criterion of interest. Russell (in Stokes, Mumford, & Owens, 1994) discusses item generation procedures for biodata forms and focuses on the role of theory in developing items.

Scoring Biodata Inventories

Scaling procedures have been categorized into three groups: external (empirical), internal, and intuitive. There is no clear evidence favoring any of these approaches. The empirical approach involves developing the scoring key on the basis of the ability of each item or item option to distinguish between high and low rated subjects. This technique is most likely to maximize prediction of a specific criterion and reduce faking. However, empirical keys generally lack face validity, possibly leading to negative reactions by applicants, and they tend to have low internal consistency reliability. In developing empirical keys, cross-validation is essential, requiring a large sample.

The internal approach requires that items on a questionnaire are scored in terms of their relationships to each other as determined by factor analysis or other item clustering procedures. The other subscales then may be used for prediction purposes in a multiple regression. This approach provides an understanding of what the biodata form is measuring, and the resulting biodata keys are more internally consistent. They may have greater face validity for applicants. One caveat, however, is that the application of factor analysis to large, heterogeneous item pools often results in factors that are difficult to interpret. In order to achieve a stable factor structure, large sample sizes are required when there are large numbers of items.

The intuitive approach uses expert judgments about which constructs the items are measuring and precisely how the item is to be scored related to the criterion. In practice, few researchers rely on a strict intuitive approach; instead, they use a mixture of the intuitive approach with some statistical analyses of internal consistency to finalize or "purify" their final scales prior to placing them into a prediction equation. This blending of the intuitive approach with some aspects of the internal approach has been called the "rational" approach.

It may be easier to satisfy concerns for legal issues in the application of biodata instruments using a rational approach. One is less likely to lose predictive power in dropping a problematic item from a rational scale than in dropping one from an empirical key should it be demanded by legal concerns. Biodata forms developed using this approach appear more job relevant, but their greater face validity makes them potentially more susceptible to faking. The approach relies heavily on the development of hypotheses based on theory, previous studies, or a detailed job analysis. Sample size requirements are somewhat smaller than for either the empirical or the internal approach, mostly because of the belief that cross-validation is less important with rationally derived scales. However, it is wise to develop and purify one's scales in one sample and validate them in a second sample, if possible, in order to increase the likelihood that the scales are stable across samples.

Faking

Faking has become an important issue for organizations that use any type of self-report inventory for selection, though its effect on the validity of biodata has not been established. Although there appears to be less faking than one would expect, it is necessary to reduce faking as much as possible in order to be fair to all applicants (and to meet legal challenges).

There are several strategies one might use to reduce faking. One must make sure that the applicant has not been coached by protecting the scoring key so that test administrators cannot coach favorite applicants and individuals cannot fake their responses to fit the key. Using warnings of verification of item responses has been shown to reduce faking, especially if there are a large number of verifiable items on the inventory.

Items or scales can be developed specifically to identify individuals who are faking. If the biodata form is composed of items that clearly are job-related types of tasks, it would be possible to develop a scale asking about performance of nonexistent tasks, use of nonexistent tools, or reading of nonexistent regulations or books, and so on. If items on the biodata form are less task oriented, it may be necessary to construct a measure of socially desirable responding, perhaps asking questions about a set of "unlikely virtues" that most people are not likely to truly possess. Another possibility is to repeat a number of items on the form to examine response consistency. This is likely to be effective only with computer-administered forms or with very long inventories.

Once a "faker" has been identified, there is little guidance available regarding the next appropriate step. Applicants could be told that there were problems in evaluating their inventory because of inconsistencies in their responses, and they could be asked to complete the biodata form a second time.

Other strategies for dealing with faking involve the use of empirical keying techniques, which weight for each item only those options that significantly differentiate the more successful from the less successful on the criterion measure. Each option is treated as an individual item, and individuals are scored based on whether the option was endorsed. (This is in contrast to those keying procedures in which each item is scored along a psychological continuum and a high score is obtained by selecting the extreme option on the continuum. Option keying may be applied to either continuous or discontinuous items.) Because option-keyed items do not necessarily make sense intuitively, the presumption is that it is unlikely that individuals can "guess" the right response in order to increase their score on the biodata form. Thus, option coding reduces score inflation because of faking.

In summary, it does not appear that faking has a great deal of impact on the selection decisions that an organization makes. However, it remains a concern that organizations will need to address. If organizations decide to use a faking scale to detect fakers and they wish to exclude otherwise acceptable candidates on the basis of their faking scores, then validation of the faking scale is important.

Reactions of Applicants

There has been increasing concern for the reactions of applicants to selection procedures. Procedures that are regarded as offensive or that do not appear to be job related may lead to lawsuits, reduced applicant motivation to do well (which can adversely affect the test's validity), or withdrawal of good applicants from the application process. Perceptions of the work relatedness of a selection procedure influence perceptions of privacy invasion. There are some types of items that individuals regard as unfair in a selection context, such as questions about friends, neighborhood, spouse, membership in political or community organizations, credit worthiness, psychological counseling, or arrest records. Organizations find that using panels to prescreen items in advance for "objectionability" is very helpful.

Legal Issues

Several legal issues emerge in the application of biodata forms for selection, including adverse impact on the basis of race, age, and gender, state and national laws related to privacy invasion, and the Americans with Disabilities Act (ADA). We will discuss current thinking in each of these areas related to biodata.

There is little, if any, adverse impact on the basis of race, particularly if items have been screened in advance by a knowledgeable panel of individuals. However, there is some evidence that there may be gender differences in biodata keys, which suggests the need for differential scoring for men and women.

Sackett and Wilk (1994) suggest that, if differential scoring is conducted for the purpose of enhancing the measurement properties of the instrument, rather than to reduce adverse impact, then it may be acceptable to do so under the Civil Rights Act of 1991. Because such practices have not been interpreted by the courts, it is best to screen items carefully on a biodata form that might be differentially answered by gender to develop a biodata form that is valid for both men and women.

Age differences may be important, particularly for those biodata forms that are likely to be used across a wide range of ages. It is critical to write items that apply to individuals of all ages. Here again, a panel of experts can prescreen items for potential age effects and can modify or delete those items that are problematic. For example, an item that asks about amount of insurance coverage is likely to be responded to differently by a 20-year-old compared with a 45-year-old. Also, items that refer to very early life experiences, such as amount of time spent watching television as a child, would be responded to differently by a 20-year-old compared with a 65-year-old, who may not have had a television set during childhood.

Regarding ADA, a literal interpretation would prohibit questions that indirectly identified a person's disability, such as not having participated in sports, debating societies, or cheerleading, because the ADA prohibits inquiries about an applicant's physical or mental condition. However, in practice, items that do not exclusively identify those with disabilities are likely to be acceptable. Developing biodata forms based on strong hypotheses about the job relatedness of each item would put organizations in a stronger position.

Privacy-prohibited items are found in categories related to classification and personal data, health, money, social class, and financial status, and many of these items are prohibited by state statutes. Because of concerns with state and federal regulations, as well as concerns for applicant reactions, it is increasingly important that organizations screen biodata items for offensiveness and invasiveness.

Generalizability over Time and Samples

The loss of validity across time can be prevented by conducting consortium studies involving multiple organizations to increase sample size. Stricter measures to protect the integrity of a key can be put in place, especially with increasingly sophisticated computer- and fax-based scoring procedures. However, changes in the performance requirements of a job may lead to an erosion of validity, which can be addressed only by revising the biodata form to fit the new job requirements. It is wise to reevaluate the validity of a biodata form, recognizing that range restriction will occur because of use of the key for selection, leading to an underestimate of the validity coefficient.

Biodata forms can be developed that will generalize to different organizations. Again, the use of consortium studies is very valuable, because it is then possible to construct a biodata form that includes items that are valid at all sites participating in the study, virtually guaranteeing that the resulting form is generalizable. Rationally developed composite keys may be more generalizable from one sample to another because they do not capitalize on sample-specific (or organizationally specific) variance in their construction.

Probably more problematic than generalization across time and across organizations is the issue of whether validities obtained in incumbent samples are generalizable to applicant populations when the form is both developed and validated using an incumbent sample. Motivational differences, as well as other experiential and demographic differences, may have unknown effects on the development of the biodata form. One solution, of course, is to develop biodata forms on applicant samples only, but this solution often is not feasible. Instead, it is very important that the incumbent sample is selected to be as closely matched to the applicant pool as possible. Also, it is important to compare applicant and incumbent data as soon as possible to check for differences in response distributions. Finally, validities in an applicant sample need to be reviewed as soon as sample sizes are adequate.

CONCLUSIONS

Biodata forms have been shown to be among the most valid selection procedures available, rivaling and sometimes surpassing the validity of cognitive ability measures. Properly developed, they can be generalizable across time and across organizations to predict a variety of important organizational criteria. Strategies exist for dealing with problems such as faking, invasion of privacy, and applicant reactions so that any negative effects are mitigated. Adverse impact on the basis of race or ethnic origin appears minimal, and with proper care and attention, biodata forms can be valid regardless of gender or age. Biodata forms continue to hold a great deal of promise as selection procedures.

REFERENCES

Civil Rights Act of 1991 (Pub.L. 102-166) (CRA).

Gunter, B., Furnham, A., & Drakeley, R. (1993). *Biodata: Biographical indicators of business performance.* London: Routledge.

Mael, F. A. (1991). A conceptual rationale for the domain and attributes of biodata items. *Personnel Psychology, 44,* 763–792.

Mumford, M. D., & Owens, W. A. (1987). Methodology review: principles, procedures, and findings in the application of background data measures. *Applied Psychological Measurement, 11,* 1–31.

Mumford, M. D., & Stokes, G. S. (1992). Developmental determinants of individual action. In M. D. Dunnette & L. M. Hough (Eds.), *Handbook of industrial/organizational psychology* (Vol. 3). Palo Alto, CA: Consulting Psychologists Press.

Owens, W. A. (1976). Background data. In M. D. Dunnette (Eds.), *Handbook of industrial and organizational psychology.* Chicago, IL: Rand McNally.

Sackett, P. R., & Wilk, S. L. (1994). Within-group norming and other forms of score adjustment in preemployment testing. *American Psychologist, 49,* 929–954.

Stokes, G. S., Mumford, M. D., & Owens, W. A. (Eds.). (1994). *Biodata handbook: Theory, research, and use of biographical information in selection and performance prediction.* Palo Alto, CA: Consulting Psychologists Press.

Stokes, G. S., & Reddy, S. (1992). Use of biographical data in organizational decisions. In C. L. Cooper & I. T. Robertson (Eds.), *International review of industrial and organizational psychology.* London: John Wiley.

V

TESTING WOMEN

21

Physical Ability Testing for Employment

Joyce Hogan and Ann M. Quigley

With the adoption of the Uniform Guidelines on Employee Selection Procedures (1978, hereafter Uniform Guidelines), it became clear that physical ability tests must meet the same standards of legal evaluation as other personnel selection devices. The framers of the Uniform Guidelines were concerned primarily with appropriate test use, particularly in light of race and ethnic group differences that resulted from cognitive ability tests. At the time, comparatively little attention was paid to gender differences resulting from physical standards and tests. Ironically, it is this area — selection for physically demanding jobs — that continues to be the source of substantial litigation from groups of women who fail to meet selection criteria set by employers.

LEGAL ISSUES

Civil Rights Act of 1964

Litigation under Title VII substantially affected the types of assessments and procedures used to evaluate applicants for physically demanding jobs. These legal challenges arise because physical performance tests — especially strength and endurance measures — tend to screen out proportionally more women and some ethnic group members than white males. The key for validating physical performance tests requires documenting the physical requirements of jobs and showing that the tests of these requirements are job related.

Since the passage of the Civil Rights Act of 1964, employers have attempted to defend three types of evaluations for personnel selection in physically demanding jobs (Hogan & Quigley, 1986). The first type involves weight-lifting restrictions, in which prohibitions were placed on women for working in jobs that required lifting "heavy" loads (e.g., 30 pounds in some states). In *Weeks v. Southern Bell Telephone & Telegraph Co.* (1969), Southern Bell refused to consider a female employee's bid for a job vacancy as switchman — a position with a 30-pound lifting requirement — claiming that sex was a bona fide occupational qualification. The U.S. Court of Appeals noted that Southern Bell was unable to show that the requirements of the switchman's job were so strenuous that most women could not perform them.

A second type of assessment employers have attempted to defend is height and weight standards. Most of the cases challenging employers' use of height and weight minimums for employment were heard during the 1970s, prior to the appearance of the Uniform Guidelines (1978). These requirements typically were struck down by the courts. Perhaps the most instructive and important height-weight case was the Supreme Court decision in *Dothard v. Rawlinson* (1977). At issue were Alabama's physical stature standards for state trooper (i.e., 5'9" and 160 lb. minimum) and correctional counselor (i.e., 5'2" and 120 lb. minimum) jobs. Regarding the job relatedness of the procedures, the Supreme Court stated that "if the job related quality that the appellants identify is indeed *bona fide*, their purpose could be achieved by adopting and validating a test for applicants that measures strength directly" (at 322).

The third type of evaluation — physical ability tests — is subject to the same standards as other employment tests and, therefore, is scrutinized for technical adequacy and documentation of validity. Litigation in which validation is used to justify the business necessity of tests is more recent than the challenges to height and weight requirements. Although the courts have recognized the major validation strategies, most litigation involves tests defended under content validity. Because content validity relies on judgment, use of work sample tests is subject to endless criticisms about test content and fidelity. In our view, it is more difficult to attack a validity coefficient, which may be why few challenges to empirically validated physical tests have been litigated. As "content valid" physical tests continue to reject women who question test fidelity and scoring, employers will begin to consider empirical validation strategies and more comprehensive, long-term research efforts.

Civil Rights Act of 1991

Section 106 of the Civil Rights Act of 1991 prohibits the adjustment of test scores based on classifications such as race or sex. This section arose specifically from controversial attempts to eliminate the adverse impact of cognitive ability tests through score manipulations, but once enacted, this provision applied to all types of employment selection tests. Perhaps the biggest question concerns norm-referenced physical ability tests. Norm referencing adjusts test scores according to gender — women are compared with groups of women and men are compared with groups of men. This appears to be a clear violation of Section 106. There is considerable interest in using this type of normative scoring, particularly among law enforcement agencies, and an exemption to the Section 106 prohibition of such scoring for physical ability tests may be sought by some agencies.

Americans with Disabilities Act

The Americans with Disabilities Act may make physical ability tests even more appealing to employers because they are not considered medical examinations and may be administered before a conditional job offer. Well-developed physical ability tests could replace less defensible medical standards that can be applied only after the employer extends a job offer. Such tests would permit employers to identify qualified persons who could meet the physical demands of the job. However, employers may have difficulty arranging appropriate reasonable accommodations for testing applicants with disabilities. Accommodations affecting test administration and scoring make the test vulnerable to psychometric flaws that may render it either invalid or uninterpretable. Unlike other employment tests, this may not be an issue, because well-developed physical ability tests measure skills and abilities required for job performance, so that a person not able to complete the test or requiring an accommodation to perform the test would face similar difficulty and require accommodations in performing the job. Such accommodation may not be feasible.

VALIDATING PHYSICAL ABILITY
TESTS FOR PERSONNEL SELECTION

We use the same strategies to validate physical ability tests as are used for validating paper-and-pencil tests. All include a job analysis or job review, an evaluation of the test's job relatedness, and final decisions about implementation.

Job Analysis

Research over the past 15 years now allows us to specify a taxonomy to describe the structure of physical performance in occupational tasks

(Hogan, 1991b). Minimally, we should evaluate the task requirements for strength, endurance, and movement quality. Any job analysis methodology that includes task evaluations of these requirements will provide adequate coverage of the physical domain, regardless of the job.

For physically demanding jobs, the objective of job analysis is to identify the critical job tasks and the abilities necessary to perform them so that performance tests and criteria can be specified. Typically, no one method of job analysis will accomplish all objectives. In addition, no one standardized job analysis procedure seems adequate for developing performance tests and criteria. The procedure we find most useful involves first developing a task and ability inventory based on observations, interviews, and panel discussions with incumbents. This procedure is explained in some detail by Goldstein (1993, pp. 54–69).

Next, the task and ability statements are listed in a job analysis questionnaire, rating dimensions and scales are developed, and the questionnaire is administered to a representative sample or the population of incumbents. Using the rating dimensions and scales, the job analyst specifies the critical and physically demanding tasks of the job and the critical abilities that the worker needs to do the job at the time of hiring.

Finally, and in service of content validity, the critical tasks are linked to the critical abilities needed to do them. This linkage process is accomplished by experts who evaluate the essential need for a worker's ability to perform each critical task.

These basic job analysis procedures result in comprehensive information sufficient to serve all validation strategies. Other job analysis methods are available to study physical requirements of work, but the choice of method depends on the goal of the analysis. In addition to the traditional job analytic approaches used by industrial-organizational psychologists, some test validation research relies on psychophysical, biomechanical, and physiological methods. For example, psychophysical evaluations of perceived effort provide reliable and valid data for quantifying work demands. Biomechanical methods are useful particularly for evaluating the stresses associated with manual material handling tasks. Physiolog-ical methods are appropriate for assessing the cardiovascular endurance or aerobic demands of performance.

Validation Strategies

Although we subscribe to the view that all validity is construct validity, the three validation strategies considered acceptable under the Uniform Guidelines (1978) clearly influence the way researchers label their investigations. In addition, the procedures used to satisfy the technical requirements for each validation type are different. These strategies are discussed briefly below with reference to physical tests.

Content-valid physical tests sample content of the job; they provide a description of performance. Validity of these tests comes not from empirical evidence but from the judgment that an applicant's performance on the test likely will resemble performance on the job tasks sampled. The key for validity is the judgment that the content of the test is a high fidelity representation of the critical job tasks. These test types (e.g., subduing and rescuing victims, dragging hoses, loading boxes) are used widely by police and fire departments, although the tests themselves differ across organizations.

Criterion-related physical tests involve showing that a predictor statistically is related to a measure of job performance. A general example is the correlation between scores on a physical test (e.g., isometric strength) and supervisory ratings of job performance. Although the strategy can use either predictive or concurrent procedures, most are concurrent studies in which the subjects are existing employees.

Construct-valid physical tests involve showing that a measure of a construct is significantly related to other test and nontest indicators of that same construct; conversely, a measure purported to assess one construct is not a measure of another, but a reliable network of convergent and divergent relations can be established. All physical ability tests are, to some degree, measures of constructs. For example, tests of lifting, pushing, pulling, and carrying are measures of the strength construct. Job performance criterion ratings of incumbents' effectiveness in lifting, pushing, pulling, and carrying also are measures associated with the strength construct, and these ratings should be related statistically to the test scores. The underlying construct provides the theoretical link between the predictor and the criterion measure. In our judgment, all physical ability test validation research is a form of construct validity. One of the best demonstrations of how such research is conducted is provided by Arvey, Landon, Nutting, and Maxwell's (1992) study of police officers.

Research Results

Physical ability tests are valid predictors of job performance when the critical tasks are physically demanding. We base this conclusion on four reviews of empirical validation studies. First, Lewis (1989) meta-analyzed 24 samples in which he classified predictors as strength tests, anthropometric measures, muscular power tests, and muscular endurance tests and criterion measures as work samples, supervisor ratings, and training performance. Validities for physical tests when nontest criteria are used range from 0.23 to 0.30. Second, Hogan (1994) classified predictors from 14 studies as constructs of strength, endurance, and movement quality and criteria as objective (e.g., production), subjective (e.g., ratings), and work sample measures. The highest average validities (mean r from 0.36 to 0.79) are for the strength tests across all criterion categories. Other construct measures also were significantly related to the criteria; however, the best pattern of relations was achieved with objective and work sample criteria. Correlations with subjective criteria were lower than the other criteria across all test types.

Third, Blakley, Quinones, Crawford, and Jago (1994) meta-analyzed correlations from seven different jobs that used isometric strength tests as predictors and supervisor ratings and work samples as criteria. Their results indicated significant mean validities for four different isometric strength tests and both types of criteria. Strength tests were better predictors of work sample performance (true validity 0.55) than of supervisory ratings (true validity 0.32). Finally, Arvey and others (1992) provide a compelling demonstration of the construct validity of strength and endurance for police officer performance. They developed their model from analysis of test and criterion data from 115 police officers and confirmed it using test scores from a second sample of police applicants. They demonstrate that the latent variables of strength and endurance explained much of the variance associated with test performance and supervisors' ratings. As further evidence of construct validity, they showed that the strength and endurance factors correlated in the expected direction with other physiological and anthropometric variables. In addition, their data suggest that the strength and endurance factors are virtually independent.

To summarize the results in these reviews, the valid predictors of performance are measures of strength, endurance, and movement quality constructs. For most jobs studied, the best pattern of prediction is accounted for by measures of the strength construct. The average validities of these tests is 0.34 and 0.68 when the criterion measures are supervisor ratings and work samples, respectively (Blakley et al., 1994). Physical ability tests always correlate higher with other performance measures (e.g., work samples) than with supervisory ratings. Finally, because measures of strength, endurance, and movement quality are relatively independent statistically, there is evidence of incremental validity when these measures are used in combination.

Although these results indicate that physical ability tests are valid predictors of job performance, the results also indicate that a user can expect adverse impact in application. The amount of adverse impact depends largely on test type and the cutoff scoring procedures. For isometric strength tests, women average 56 percent and 72 percent of the male maximum values on upper extremity and lower extremity tests, respectively. Women average about 70 percent of men's dynamic strength in weight-lifting tests. For endurance (aerobic) tests, women exhibit 10 percent to 20 percent less aerobic capacity than men in performing treadmill tests. For movement quality tests that measure balance, flexibility, and coordination, there are few gender differences. In many cases, the male and female score distributions overlap 85 percent to 100 percent. Implicit in these results is that choice of predictor will affect adverse impact. For example, a lower extremity isometric strength test will have equal validity but less adverse impact than a test of grip strength (Hogan, 1991a).

ISSUES OF TEST IMPLEMENTATION

Establishing Cutoff Scores

Consistent with the Uniform Guidelines (1978), to rank order job candidates based on test scores, the employer must show either through "job analysis or otherwise, that a higher score on a content valid selection procedure is likely to result in better job performance" (Section 14C(9)). The reality of rank-ordering physical ability test scores is that no women will score sufficiently high to qualify for the limited number of positions that typically are available. Consider Cleveland, where, in 1980 and in 1983, the highest ranked female firefighter applicants were listed at 634 and 334, and these women never came close to being hired.

When ranking is not possible, a cutoff score serves as a pass-fail decision. Applicants scoring above the cutoff score are considered equally well-qualified, while applicants scoring below the cutoff are considered below the standard of acceptable proficiency. A rational method to determine the cutoff score is to test a representative sample of incumbents who are all acceptable job performers, examine the distribution of their scores, and identify the lowest score in the distribution, minus the outliers. This becomes the cutoff score that can be announced to applicants and applied to their scores.

There are other decision models, including fixed and sliding bands; however, they must consider the "adequate job performance" guideline. For example, on a timed physical test, are persons whose scores range from five to six minutes better job performers than those whose scores range from six to seven minutes? For physically demanding jobs, the reality of bands as opposed to pass-fail is that women will be concentrated in the lower bands and will have little opportunity to be selected. Moreover, inappropriately established score bands are thinly disguised forms of rank ordering.

Test Preparation

There are a variety of test preparation activities that increase the success rate of qualified job applicants (Hogan & Quigley, 1994). At a minimum, they should receive information about the test in an oral, printed, or video format. This can include not only a description of the test but also recommendations for how best to prepare. A second option is to provide applicants the opportunity to try out or practice the test. A third possibility is to provide applicants a program of rigorous instruction and physical training. The key to successful training is to develop a level of performance that can be sustained on the job; marginally qualified applicants who overtrain to pass a test will be unable to sustain the appropriate level of fitness once hired.

These activities have several benefits. First, they will maximize the chances of success for all applicants. Applicants will have a better idea of the job requirements and will be better able to make a choice about the job. Problems of applicants being injured or doing poorly on the test because of unfamiliarity with test procedures will be reduced. Finally, employers who historically excluded women from physically demanding jobs can combat the chilling effect resulting from that exclusion and can demonstrate good faith in trying to select qualified women and minorities for these jobs.

REFERENCES

Arvey, R. D., Landon, T. E., Nutting, S. M., & Maxwell, S. E. (1992). Development of physical ability tests for police officers: A construct validation approach. *Journal of Applied Psychology, 77*, 996–1009.

Blakley, B. R., Quinones, M. A., Crawford, M. S., & Jago, I. A. (1994). The validity of isometric strength tests. *Personnel Psychology, 47*, 247–274.

Civil Rights Act of 1991 (Pub.L. 102-166) (CRA).

Dothard v. Rawlinson, 433 U.S. 321, 97 S. Ct. 2720, 53L. Ed. 2d 786 (1977).

Goldstein, I. L. (1993). *Training in organizations* (3rd ed.). Pacific Grove, CA: Brooks/Cole.

Hogan, J. (1994). Theoretical and applied developments in models of individual differences: Physical abilities. In M. G. Rumsey, C. B. Walker, & J. H. Harris (Eds.), *Personnel selection and classification* (pp. 233–245). Hillsdale, NJ: Lawrence Erlbaum Associates.

Hogan, J. (1991a). Physical abilities. In M. D. Dunnette & L. M. Hough (Eds.), *Handbook of industrial-organizational psychology* (pp. 751–831). Palo Alto, CA: Consulting Psychologists Press.

Hogan, J. (1991b). The structure of physical performance in occupational tasks. *Journal of Applied Psychology, 76*, 495–507.

Hogan, J., & Quigley, A. (1994). Effects of preparing for physical ability tests. *Public Personnel Management, 23*, 85–104.

Hogan, J., & Quigley, A. (1986). Physical standards for employment and the courts. *American Psychologist, 41*, 1193–1217.

Lewis, R. E. (1989). *Physical ability tests as predictors of job-related criteria: A meta-analysis*. Unpublished manuscript.

Uniform guidelines on employee selection procedures, 29 C.F.R. 1607 (1978).
Weeks v. Southern Bell Telephone & Telegraph Co., 408 F.2d 228, 1 Empl. Prac. Dec.
    (CCH) § 9970 (5th Cir. 1969).

22

Gender Issues in Employment Testing

Mary L. Tenopyr

The literature consistently shows that gender differences in scores on cognitive ability tests, except in the spatial visualization area, are relatively small and decreasing as society changes. Men are more variable in cognitive ability test performance than women. Some gender-based personality differences, particularly in aggressiveness, have been found. Women adopt a more participatory management style than men and tend to be undervalued as leaders. There is little evidence to support any notion that test results are biased against either men or women.

Gender issues are quite compelling in relation to physical testing, such as is done for many jobs requiring strength; in the area of mental testing, the issues are less glaring, but they are, nevertheless, important.

The two genders differ in many ways, but this discussion will be confined to differences on mental testing as it is used in employment settings. Cognitive ability, aptitude, knowledge, or achievement tests and personality measures will be considered mental tests. However, discussion of strength, psychomotor, and performance tests involving equipment of various sorts will be excluded.

DISPARATE IMPACT BY TYPE OF TEST

"Disparate impact," "disparate effect," and "adverse effect" (as the terms are used in legal settings) all refer to average differences in hiring rates for various groups. If one group scores, on the average, lower than the highest scoring group on a test or a group of tests, often referred to as a "test battery," the result, to the extent that test scores determine who is hired, is disparate impact. Various tests have different degrees of disparate impact relative to gender.

There are considerable differences of opinion among researchers as to what ability tests measure. Many researchers believe that most ability tests measure, to a large extent, general intelligence. Other researchers (e.g., Carroll, 1993, pp. 591–624) suggest that the human mind works in a more complicated way and that there are several distinct types of mental ability.

Despite the controversies, some conclusions about gender differences in scores on ability tests may be drawn. First, gender differences are much smaller than racial differences (Herrnstein & Murray, 1994, p. 295; Jensen, 1980, p. 622). The magnitude of gender differences in most tested abilities is relatively small; however, there is some dispute about how the magnitude of the differences should be interpreted (Eagly, 1995; Hyde & Plant, 1995). Women tend to excel in many of the language-based abilities, such as verbal fluency and spelling (Feingold, 1992; Maccoby & Jacklin, 1974, pp. 75–83). However, although men and women score about equal in tests of computational ability, adult males excel in tests of more complex mathematical problem solving (Hyde, Fennema, & Lamon, 1990). Burnett, Lane, and Dratt (1979) concluded that gender differences in mathematics scores on the Scholastic Aptitude Test disappeared when the effect of spatial ability was controlled statistically.

The difference between the genders in spatial ability is probably the largest mental ability difference between the two groups. This ability difference frequently shows up on tests of mechanical reasoning, and disparate impact relative to gender usually can be expected on such tests. This disparate impact has the practical effect of excluding women from high paying mechanical and engineering jobs. There is some evidence that most gender differences on ability tests are smaller now than they were some years ago (Feingold, 1988). Nevertheless, the difference in scores on spatial ability tests persists. Therefore, the validity and fairness of these tests should be scrutinized carefully before the tests are used as the basis for employment decisions.

There are indications that men are more variable in their ability test performance than women are, that is, that there are more men with extremely high or low scores than there are women. The size and the meaning of these differences is a matter of controversy (Feingold, 1993). The difference in variability is most pronounced in tests of spatial or mechanical ability. The difference has the most serious practical consequences in situations in which relatively few applicants are chosen from a rank-ordered list, as is often the case in civil service. In cases like this, the fact that there are more men with very high scores becomes apparent.

When personality inventories are used in employment, there is also opportunity for disparate impact. Feingold (1994) studied gender differences in personality that had been found between 1940 and 1992. Men were found to be more assertive than women and also had slightly greater self-esteem than women. Women scored higher than men in extroversion, anxiety, trust, and, especially, tender mindedness. There were no noteworthy gender differences in social anxiety, impulsiveness, general activity level, reflective thinking, orderliness, and beliefs about self-control.

Also, in this massive study, Feingold (1994) found that gender differences in personality traits generally were constant across ages, years of data collection, educational levels, and nations. It can be concluded that there is a potential for some personality inventories to result in at least some disparate impact for either men or women.

One of the major concerns of women is the prospect of obtaining managerial jobs that will position them for leadership roles high in employing organizations. Here again, there is the prospect of disparate impact. There is evidence that the genders differ in the manner in which they approach leadership (Eagly & Johnson, 1990). An important finding of this research, found across all areas of relevant research, is that women tended to adopt a more participatory or democratic style and a less auto-cratic or directive style than did men. Women who use such participatory styles may be assets in organizations that are adopting team approaches and emphasizing employee empowerment, as many organizations currently are.

However, as is clear from a report from the Federal Glass Ceiling Commission (1995), women face numerous barriers in achieving the highest levels in organizations. In fact, the report states that, in the Fortune 2000 industrial and service companies, only 5 percent of senior managers are women. The reasons that more women do not advance to top leadership roles are undoubtedly many and complex. In summarizing the literature on women in leadership roles, Eagly, Makhijani, and Klonsky (1995) found that women leaders tend to be devalued slightly by evaluators. This tendency was more pronounced when the women carried out their duties in a stereotypically masculine, directive style. Furthermore, devaluation of women leaders was encountered when the women occupied male-dominated roles and when the evaluators were male.

Thus, in selection of management and, particularly, in a situation where a mixed gender group of persons who are already leading is being considered for promotion to a higher level leadership position, possible differences in leadership style must be taken into account. In particular, references and performance appraisals for persons in leadership roles may result in disparate impact that adversely affects women.

GENDER DIFFERENCES IN VALIDITY

"Validity" refers to the extent to which inferences made on the basis of test scores are accurate. In employment situations, the validity question most often asked is, "How accurately can job behavior be predicted from test scores?" Do persons who score high on the test do the job better than those who score lower on the test?

The literature on gender differences in validity of employment tests is not definitive. However, there is no known accepted theory that would suggest that there should be gender-based differences in validity. At present, the proper strategy in employment is to assume that men and women are equally predictable as far as job performance is concerned.

VALIDITY DIFFERENCES IN PREDICTING
LEVEL OF JOB BEHAVIOR

There are two aspects to the prediction of job behavior. First, there is the question of how accurately the job behavior or performance is predicted from the test scores for different groups. This is the issue of differential validity. The second issue is that of differential prediction. The question here is whether a group's job performance is systematically predicted to be too much higher or too much lower than it should be, given a common validity coefficient. For example, if women's performance as a group is predicted to be better than would be expected, psychologists would say that a condition of predictive bias exists. In this case, not only would there be predictive bias, but the bias would be in favor of women.

In general, psychologists and the courts have held that, unless predictive bias is shown, a test's scores are not discriminatory (American Educational Research Association, American Psychological Association, & National Council on Measurement in Education, 1985, p. 93). Thus, when a test's scores show disparate impact, the employer may counter with proof that there is no predictive bias.

The research literature relative to possible predictive bias in employment testing of persons of different genders is sparse. Therefore, no firm conclusions about the extent of predictive bias of testing associated with the genders can be made on the basis of the research to date.

RESULTS OF LEGAL PROCEEDINGS

There is no substantial body of case law relative to gender and civil rights in employment as there is regarding minority employment testing. One reason may be that the gender differences in ability test performance are small and decreasing with the passage of time. However, some authors (Connor & Vargyas, 1992) do claim that gender bias in ability testing is prevalent. One cannot deny that there are gender differences in scores on some types of test; however, as was previously mentioned, gender differences in scores do not necessarily provide evidence of predictive bias. When an employer has an appropriate job performance measure, he or she will probably prevail legally if a showing of no predictive bias can be made. Again, it is inappropriate to claim that test scores are biased because of disparate impact on any group.

SUMMARY

Gender differences in the score on cognitive ability tests are much smaller than race differences. Furthermore, gender differences are getting smaller as society changes and educational patterns for the genders become more similar. Men's higher scores on tests of spatial ability, which affects performance in high level mathematics, still prevail. Also, there are more men with extremely high and low cognitive ability test scores. There are some differences between the genders in personality, particularly in aggressiveness.

Some differences in management style exist for the genders. In particular, women tend to adopt a more participatory or democratic leadership style than men. The performance of women as leaders tends to be undervalued. This effect is more pronounced when women adopt directive leadership styles.

There are no definitive findings concerning whether test results show predictive bias against either men or women. Furthermore, there is no accepted theory that would support any findings of such bias.

REFERENCES

Burnett, S. A., Lane, D. M., & Dratt, L. M. (1979). Shape visualization and sex differences in quantitative ability. *Intelligence, 3,* 345–354.

Carroll, J. B. (1993). *Human cognitive abilities: A survey of actor analytic studies.* New York: Cambridge University Press.

Connor, K., & Vargyas, E. J. (1992). The legal implications of gender bias in standardized testing. *Berkeley Women's Law Journal, 7,* 13–89.

Eagly, A. H. (1995). The science and politics of comparing women and men. *American Psychologist, 50,* 145–148.

Eagly, A. H., & Johnson, B. T. (1990). Gender and leadership style: A meta-analysis. *Psychological Bulletin, 108,* 233–256.

Eagly, A. H., Makhijani, M. G., & Klonsky, B. G. (1995). Gender and evaluation of leaders: A meta-analysis. *Psychological Bulletin, 111,* 3–22.

Federal Glass Ceiling Commission. (1995). *Good for business: Making full use of fact-finding report of the Federal Glass Ceiling Commission.* Washington, DC: U.S. Department of Labor.

Feingold, A. (1994). Gender differences in personality: A meta-analysis. *Psychological Bulletin, 116,* 429–456.

Feingold, A. (1993). Joint effects of gender differences in central tendency and gender differences in variability. *Review of Educational Research, 63,* 106–109.

Feingold, A. (1992). Sex differences in variability in intellectual abilities: A new look at an old controversy. *Review of Educational Research, 62,* 61–84.

Feingold, A. (1988). Cognitive gender differences are disappearing. *American Psychologist, 43,* 95–103.

Herrnstein, R. J., & Murray, C. (1994). *The bell curve: Intelligence and class structure in American life.* New York: Free Press.

Hyde, J. S., Fennema, E., & Lamon, S. J. (1990). Gender differences in mathematical performance: A meta-analysis. *Psychological Bulletin, 107,* 139–155.

Hyde, J. S., & Plant, A. (1995). Magnitude of psychological gender differences: Another side to the story. *American Psychologist, 3,* 159–161.

Jensen, A. R. (1980). *Bias in mental testing.* New York: Free Press.

Maccoby, E. E., & Jacklin, C. N. (1974). *The psychology of sex differences* (pp. 75–83). Stanford, CA: Stanford University Press.

Standards for educational and psychological testing. (1985). Washington, DC: American Psychological Association.

VI

IMPACT ON
PROTECTED CLASSES

23

Adverse Impact

Richard S. Barrett

Adverse impact occurs when there is a substantially different rate of selection in hiring, promotion, or other employment decision that works to the disadvantage of members of a race, sex, or ethnic group. (An analogous procedure is used with respect to age under the Age Discrimination in Employment Act, but not the Americans with Disabilities Act, which is not concerned with systemic discrimination.)

"Substantially different" is defined by the four-fifths or 80 percent rule of thumb. If the selection rate of members of a minority is less than 80 percent of that of the nonminority applicants, there is a presumption that there is adverse impact. The computation, which is discussed in more detail below, is easy. If the selection rate of the protected class is 20 percent and that of the nonminority group is 50 percent, dividing 20 percent by 50 percent gives a ratio of 2:5 (or 40 percent), well below the four-fifths standard (or 80 percent rule of thumb).

Determination of adverse impact is a relatively straightforward process, but one that can easily go awry:

1. Compute the selection rate (hired or promoted) for the time period in question for the highest scoring group, usually whites or men, by dividing the number hired or promoted by the number of applicants.
2. Compute the selection rate for the protected group in the same way.
3. Determine the impact ratio by dividing the selection rate of the protected group by the selection rate of the highest scoring group.

A selection rate for any race, sex, or ethnic group that is less than four-fifths of the group with the highest rate can be prima facie evidence of adverse impact. Some of the intricacies of this determination are discussed in more detail below.

RACE, ETHNIC GROUP MEMBERSHIP, SEX

The Uniform Guidelines on Employee Selection Procedures (1978, hereafter Uniform Guidelines), Section 4B, requires that data be kept and reported on applicants in five categories, "Blacks, American Indians, Asians, Hispanics, and Whites other than Hispanics." Because these racial and ethnic categories are not defined, there can be a question regarding the identification of an individual because of the procreating proclivities of his or her forebears. There is continuing debate about the classification of those with mixed ancestry. Classification by sex, despite certain surgical operations and controversy over genetic testing for athletes, is routine.

APPLICANT

Determining who is to be included in the list of applicants is addressed in Questions and Answers to Clarify and Provide a Common Interpretation of the Uniform Guidelines on Employee Selection Procedures (1979, #15, hereafter Questions and Answers). Questions and Answers says that there is no simple definition of an applicant. Graduating seniors, budding lawyers, and aspiring college professors sometimes send out hundreds of resumes; employers cannot be expected to explore the ethnicity or sex of each person. The Uniform Guidelines (1978) require only that the employer design and adhere to a definition of "applicant" that suits the employer's business needs.

NUMBER HIRED IN A TIME PERIOD

Judgment must be exercised to determine the time period to be covered. Some hiring data are kept on an annual or quarterly basis, but the hiring patterns do not necessarily follow the calendar. When business is poor, an employer may go for long periods without significant hiring. Then, when business picks up, there may be a rash of hiring and promotions. Only a careful examination of the history of the hiring practices can determine the appropriate time period.

Civil service lists may last as long as four years, which is a long time to wait. Adverse impact then can be computed on the basis of the employer's estimate of the number of positions to be filled if it can be assumed that everyone who is offered a job will take it.

DEMOGRAPHIC DATA

In the absence of hiring data, some light may be shed on the impact by comparing the present work force with the numbers of members of different races or ethnic groups or men and women in the labor pool. (*Wards Cove v. Antonio*, 1988, addressed this issue, the Supreme Court finding that the proper base for consideration of, for example, accountants, would be those with accounting degrees, not the total population.)

ADDITIONAL INFORMATION

Data from sources other than the employer's records may be brought to bear. Comparing the selection procedures with the results of similarly constructed procedures may clarify the situation. In *Griggs v. Duke Power Company* (1971), only three candidates for promotion had taken the test. Adverse impact was inferred from published studies of similar multiple-choice tests used with school children. Multiple-choice tests almost always have an adverse impact on Hispanics and blacks and sometimes against Asians.

SELECTION RATE AND IMPACT RATIO

The computation of the selection rate and impact ratio is straightforward. This example typifies data that might be presented relating to blacks and whites:

	White	Black	Total
Hired	24	6	30
Not hired	32	28	60
Total	56	34	90

The selection rate of whites is 24 ÷ 56 = 42.8 percent. The selection rate for blacks is 6 ÷ 34 = 17.6 percent. The impact ratio is, therefore, 17.6 percent ÷ 42.8 percent = 41.1 percent. Because 41.1 percent is less than 80 percent, adverse impact is indicated as specified in Uniform Guidelines (1978), Section 4D, Adverse Impact and the "Four-fifths Rule," which states that "a selection rate for any race, sex, or ethnic group which is less than four-fifths (4/5) (or eight per cent) of the group with the highest rate will generally be regarded by the Federal authorities as evidence of adverse impact."

STATISTICAL SIGNIFICANCE

There is a regrettable tendency for both statisticians and laymen to rely on tests of significance to decide whether there is adverse impact despite the explanation given in Questions and Answers #24 (1979), which points out that the Uniform Guidelines (1978) rely primarily upon the four-fifths rule of thumb rather than tests of statistical significance because, "Where the sample of persons selected is not large, even large real difference between groups is likely not to be confirmed by a test of significance" (Questions and Answers, #24).

CHI-SQUARE

Despite this disclaimer, part of the evidence on which basis findings of adverse impact are often made is the test of significance. With the caveat in mind that the level of significance is only one piece of evidence, the most frequently used statistical test of adverse impact is Chi-Square (more formally written χ^2). The application of Chi-Square is described in any elementary statistics text.

SMALL SAMPLES

Often, the number of applicants, particularly minorities, is so small that the existence of or freedom from adverse impact cannot readily be determined. Questions and Answers #21 (1979) addresses this issue through this example:

Applicants	Not Hired	Hired	Selection Rate Percent Hired
80 White	64	16	20
20 Blacks	17	3	15
White selection rate			20
Black selection rate			15

15 divided by 20 = 75 percent (which is less than 80 percent)

If the numbers of persons and the difference in selection rates are so small that it is likely that they could have occurred by chance, the Federal agencies will not assume the existence of adverse impact, in the absence of other evidence. In this example, if only one more black had been hired instead of one white, the selection rate of blacks (20 percent) would have been higher than that for whites (18.7 percent).

On the other hand, if a lower selection rate continued over a period of time, so as to constitute a pattern, then the lower selection rate would constitute adverse impact, warranting the need for validity evidence.

AVOIDABLE PITFALLS

There are many (often self-serving) errors in the application of the 80 percent rule. Consideration of these issues may save an employer substantial grief.

Records

Once upon a time, employers would claim that they did not keep records on the race and sex of their applicants, sometimes invoking state law that prohibited the practice. Those days are gone forever; state laws have been overridden by federal law, and records must be kept and the results reported.

Pass Rates

Employers sometimes compute adverse impact on the basis of the pass rates of the applicants. If those who fail are eliminated from further participation in the selection process or otherwise treated differently, this analysis is appropriate and should be considered with other data. However, if no action is taken as a result of failure, the analysis is worthless and may be misleading.

As is often the case in civil service testing, applicants are selected in rank order from the list. If the list is not exhausted, the passing score is meaningless; the effective passing score is the score made by the lowest scoring applicant who is accepted. Some jurisdictions set a low passing score, permitting many applicants to pass, then claim that they have eliminated adverse impact, even when there is a large difference in the hiring or promotion rates.

Sometimes employers like to consider the impact rates only of those who passed the test. When the test is at issue, this analysis begs the question by requiring that one assume that which has yet to be proven, namely, that the test is job related and, therefore, passing it determines that one is qualified.

Computing Adverse Impact by Combining Race and Ethnicity with Sex

Sometimes unsuccessful applicants believe that they are discriminated against on the basis of both race or ethnicity and sex simultaneously. Uniform Guidelines (1978) takes the position that these are two separate issues (Questions and Answers, 1979, #17). There is no obligation to make separate comparisons for subgroups (e.g., white male, white female, black male, black female). It always is possible to bring suit on the basis of the combined discriminations, but convincing the Court would be an uphill fight.

Bottom Line

Uniform Guidelines (1978) originally defined adverse impact using the bottom-line principle, which meant that there was no cause for action if the overall impact rate fell above the 80 percent line. However, the Supreme Court, in *Teal v. Connecticut* (1982), overturned that rule, making it possible to bring an action against any part of a process that had an adverse impact.

Accuracy and Completeness

Uniform Guidelines (1978) require that, "The report should describe the steps taken to assure the accuracy and completeness of the collection, analysis, and report of data and results." This provision was included because of the appalling number of errors found in reports of statistical analysis. The arithmetic should be checked for accuracy. The subjects on whom data is reported in different tables should all be present and accounted for.

SUMMARY

There is no simple touchstone that can be used to determine whether there is an adverse impact. Statistics is the mathematics of uncertainty. Statistical analysis, including tests of significance, helps to illuminate the issues, but it does not relieve one of the responsibility for making a decision, because significance is not an absolute standard. Significance is a statement of probabilities, not certainties.

To assess adverse impact, keep records of the race, ethnic group, and sex of applicants for hiring and promotion in the relevant time period. Categorize them by job or job family. Compute the relevant impact ratios. Evaluate the impact ratios in the light of the entire selection process and historical data from similar selection procedures, especially those used in other parts of the organization, and relevant statistical analyses.

Following these steps is good insurance against being embarrassed by inadequate records or incorrect conclusions.

REFERENCES

Griggs v. Duke Power Co., 401 U.S. 424 (1971).

Questions and answers to clarify and provide a common interpretation of the uniform guidelines on employee selection procedures, 41 F.R. 11996 (March 7 1979).

Teal v. Connecticut, 457 U.S. 440 (1982).

Uniform guidelines on employee selection procedures, 29 C.F.R. 1607 (1978).

Wards Cove v. Antonio, Sup. Ct. 87–1387 FEP Cases 163 (1988).

24

Alternative Selection Procedures

Richard R. Reilly

Prior to 1978, the chief concerns of professionals involved in employee selection were the validity and fairness of tests, especially cognitive ability tests. The Uniform Guidelines on Employee Selection Procedures (1978) introduced another concern by including a provision calling for employers to seek alternatives that have equal validity but less adverse impact than their existing selection procedures. This "alternatives provision" took another form with the passage of the Civil Rights Act of 1991. A seldom discussed provision of that act allows plaintiffs to shift the burden of proof back to an employer who has shown a selection procedure to be valid. If the plaintiff can show that a suitable alternative exists with at least equal validity and less adverse impact, the burden of proof is on the employer to show why the alternative was not used.

A paper in 1982 summarized the available evidence for the validity, adverse impact, and fairness of alternatives (Reilly & Chao, 1982). Since that time, several important developments have taken place within the field of personnel selection research. First, there has been an increasing use of meta-analytic methodology to arrive at conclusions regarding the validity of selection procedures. The application of meta-analysis has produced estimates of validity that are much higher than previously reported because of the recognition that range restriction and criterion unreliability serve to lower observed estimates of validity. A second related development has been an increase in the attention paid to several different alternative predictors, resulting in much more evidence regarding their validity. A third development has been a decrease in studies of selection fairness. ("Selection fairness," as it is used here, is based on the regression model that finds a selection procedure to be unfair if the regression lines for different groups are unequal.) The inattention to the issue of fairness may be a result of the consistent failure to find unfairness for any class of selection procedures.

The objective of this chapter is to provide a review of alternative procedures for employee selection. In the review of each alternative, the key considerations include the evidence for the validity of the alternative, the extent to which the alternative produces adverse impact, and the feasibility of the alternative from an organizational point of view.

ALTERNATIVES USED BY EMPLOYERS

What alternatives do employers use to select and promote employees? The most recent survey (Bureau of National Affairs, 1988) gives some answers. Although one-third of employers (31 percent) reported using cognitive ability tests, mainly to select clerical and other nonmanagement employees, other alternatives were used heavily. The most frequently used alternative (80 percent) was the interview, followed by work samples (63 percent). Other procedures, such as the assessment center approach (12 percent) and biodata (11 percent), were used less frequently. Physical abilities testing (11 percent) and integrity tests (7 percent) also were reported by a small but significant number of employers.

ALTERNATIVES AVAILABLE TO EMPLOYERS

We will review six different categories of alternatives to cognitive tests. Measures of maximal performance include work samples, trainability tests, and physical ability tests. Self-report measures include biodata, self-assessments, and personality tests. Judgments based on observed interpersonal behavior include interviews, assessment centers, and peer evaluations. Measures of past performance include behavioral consistency, academic achievement, reference checks, and experience measures. Expert judgments include those based on projective tests, handwriting, and individual assessments. Finally, a sixth category of special measures includes physical ability tests, integrity tests, and situational judgment tests.

Measures of Maximal Performance

Work Samples

Work samples have had a long and successful history in personnel selection. Perhaps the most frequently used work samples — typing tests — offer a good illustration of why work samples are valid. Work samples, or job simulations, allow the applicant to demonstrate job-related performance under standardized conditions. The correspondence between the tasks performed on the work sample test and the tasks performed on the job is clear and direct. More than two decades ago, Wernimont and Campbell (1968) proposed a "behavioral consistency model" that focused on the measurement of behavior samples relevant to dimensions of job performance. They argued that it would be better to "focus on meaningful samples of behavior rather than signs of predisposition as predictors of later performance" (p. 372). Work samples provide the kinds of standardized samples of relevant behavior that Wernimont and Campbell suggested.

The validity of work samples has been shown by several meta-analytic studies to be equivalent to or better than the validity of cognitive ability tests. In addition, where direct comparisons have been made, the adverse impact for work sample tests has been found to be lower than for cognitive ability tests. The inherent link between the work sample and job performance produces not only high validities but also tests that appear fairer and more relevant to applicants. Finally, work samples offer job candidates an opportunity to directly experience job-related tasks, thus, allowing a realistic preview of the job. There is some research evidence that this allows applicants to make better decisions about whether to take the job.

The work sample approach meets the definition of a suitable alternative; it has equal or greater validity and less adverse impact. Although the research is encouraging, it should be noted that the method has been criticized on the grounds that it fails to give the applicant an opportunity to demonstrate his or her ability to learn the job. Work samples assume that the examinee has been trained or has the experience necessary to effectively demonstrate the knowledge and skill measured by the test. The assumption of training also has implications for the reported adverse impact of work samples; prescreening or self-selection of untrained applicants may account for some of the reduction in adverse impact. Cost is a major limiting consideration with respect to work samples. The time and money involved in constructing and subsequently administering and maintaining valid work samples are significantly greater than for cognitive tests. In today's era of technological advancement, jobs change quickly, and work samples are, for many organizations, simply not feasible. Specifically, because of the close relationship that work samples have to the job, attenuation of content validity becomes likely without periodic revision.

Trainability Tests

Unlike work samples, which assess the existing knowledge and skill of an applicant, trainability tests allow applicants an opportunity to learn job-related material under standardized conditions. The learning period then is followed by assessment of learning with a paper-pencil or performance test. For example, an early trainability test developed for selecting telecommunications technicians presented training material relevant to the maintenance of digital electronic switching systems. Candidates were allowed a fixed period of time to study the material and then took a paper-pencil test to assess their knowledge of the material. Although their use is not widespread, trainability tests have been used for military personnel, a variety of employees in private industry, federal government employees, and employees in the United Kingdom.

Two major meta-analytic studies of the validity of trainability tests have concluded that their validity is equivalent to the validity of cognitive ability tests. In addition, the available evidence shows that trainability tests have less adverse impact than cognitive ability tests. In sum, trainability tests appear to meet the definition of a suitable alternative.

Trainability tests have other advantages shared with work sample tests. Like work samples, trainability tests offer realistic previews of the job and are linked to job content, making them both content and face valid. Trainability tests also overcome the disadvantage of work samples in that they do not assume that applicants have prior training or experience.

One reason that trainability tests are not more widely used is cost. Trainability tests are expensive to develop and, in cases where hands-on performance is involved, expensive to administer. In addition, trainability tests may be limited in occupations where technology is changing. Trainability tests must be reviewed on a regular basis to ensure content relevance.

Self-report Measures

Biodata

Biodata, in the context of personnel selection, refers to biographical information that may be collected as part of a standard application blank or with a special biodata form. Biodata can include information that is objective and verifiable (e.g., number of siblings) as well as information that is difficult or impossible to verify (one's favorite hobby; whether one is perceived as a leader by one's peers). Biodata items typically are presented in close-ended formats that allow objective coding. The approach to biodata that seems to work best is the antithesis of the work sample approach. In Wernimont and Campbell's (1968) terms, biodata are signs, rather than samples.

A standard approach to biodata validation involves five steps: the administration of a pool of items to a large sample of job applicants or employees, collection of criterion data for those employees, empirical analysis of the relationship between each biodata item and criterion performance, development of a scoring key based on the empirical analysis, and cross-validation of the scoring key on a holdout sample. The last step is necessary because capitalization on chance in the analysis sample almost always will result in an overestimate of the validity of biodata. The atheoretical, empirical nature of most biodata instruments presents special problems in assessing the generalizability of results across studies. Biodata instruments do not purport to measure specific constructs that might allow studies of discriminant and convergent validity, for example. Indeed, it is difficult to obtain information from study to study that includes the types of items that might consistently predict certain types of behaviors.

Despite these limitations, at least five separate meta-analytic studies have concluded that empirically keyed biodata instruments have validities approaching, and sometimes exceeding, those of cognitive ability tests for a wide variety of job-related behavior. In addition, several studies have shown the adverse impact of biodata to be less than that of cognitive tests. Other appealing features of biodata predictors are the ease with which biographical information can be collected and the low cost. Biodata instruments are untimed and, thus, involve minimal administration costs. The low cost of selection combined with reasonably high validities suggests high utility. However, several issues relate to the feasibility of developing and using biodata to select employees. These include the large samples needed to develop valid empirical keys, poor face validity of biodata items, and the possibility of faking or other purposeful distortion.

The evidence suggests that biodata instruments can be valid for a wide range of criteria and may have less adverse impact than cognitive tests. Whether biodata will have validity equal to cognitive tests may depend upon the criterion to be predicted. For overall job performance, the average corrected validities for biodata did not approach those reported for cognitive tests. For selected jobs and certain criteria (e.g., turnover), evidence suggests that biodata may have validity that is equal or superior to cognitive tests. In any case, employers considering alternatives to testing should consider biodata; at the same time, however, employers should be aware of the complex methodological issues surrounding the development and application of empirically keyed biodata instruments.

Self-assessments

Self-assessment, a direct and inexpensive way of obtaining information about employees, can be collected for abilities (such as intelligence), skills (such as typing), or competence in specific, job-related tasks. Research evidence suggests reasonably good validity for self-assessment, often approaching the validity of peer evaluations. Adverse impact for self-assessments would appear to be minimal, based on the research showing no difference in means for various subgroups. Self-assessment would appear to be an ideal alternative — reasonably good validity, no adverse impact, and low cost. Unfortunately, the most optimistic estimates of validity were obtained under research conditions. When subjects knew that self-assessments would be used for selection decisions and thought that no verification would be done, ratings were overly lenient and had limited variability, leading to no or very low validity.

The validity of self-assessment appears to hinge on the motivational set of the respondent. All self-report measures are vulnerable to the problem response distortion, but in the case of self-assessment, this concern is magnified, given the straightforward nature of the response. If the individual assumes that their self-assessment will be used in decision making and that no independent verification of the self-assessment will occur, then inflation is highly likely and validity will be suspect. Because most employment settings are characterized by precisely these conditions, it is unlikely that self-assessments can serve as a suitable alternative to other selection procedures.

Personality Tests

Personality testing has undergone a renaissance in recent years, primarily because of research suggesting that there are five core factors of personality, usually labeled Neuroticism, Extroversion, Openness to Experience, Agreeableness, and Conscientiousness. Armed with the "Big Five" as a taxonomic scheme, researchers have been able to produce meta-analytic evidence regarding the validity of personality measures for predicting job performance. This evidence suggests that conscientiousness, in particular, would appear to be worth considering as part of a selection system. Although the level of validity is lower than for measures of maximal performance, measures of conscientiousness have two characteristics that make them worth considering for selection purposes. The first is that personality measures, in general, do not appear to have adverse impact. The second is that personality measures have generally low correlations with measures of cognitive ability. This has led some researchers to suggest that an ideal approach to selection would combine a cognitive ability test with a measure of conscientiousness. The resulting combination would be a suitable alternative — one with higher validity and less adverse impact. One cautionary note to this optimistic picture has to do with the issue of faking. Almost all personality tests are measured using self-report inventories, which provide an opportunity for applicants to fake or otherwise distort their responses. The extent to which this problem is a serious one is not clear from the available evidence, but research evidence clearly shows that applicants can increase their scores by faking.

Judgments Based on Observed Interpersonal Behavior

The Interview

The term "interview" encompasses a wide variety of techniques, ranging from unstructured interviews to highly structured techniques resembling oral tests. For our purposes, the interview will be defined as an oral interaction between a job applicant and a representative of the employer for the purpose of predicting job-related behavior. Meta-analytic work done in the past few years has shown that the interview is a reasonably valid method of selecting employees for a wide variety of jobs. Structured, job-related interviews are best, but even unstructured interviews had useful validities. The limited data available also suggest that interviews have less adverse impact than cognitive tests and, so, should be considered as an alternative. Almost all employees are interviewed at some point in the selection process, therefore, most organizations could use the results of the interview to make better selection decisions, particularly if the interview is job related and structured.

Assessment Centers

An assessment center is defined as a comprehensive, standardized procedure in which multiple assessment techniques are used in combination to evaluate individuals for various organizational purposes. Although some assessment centers include paper-and-pencil tests and interviews, a special emphasis is placed on the use of situational exercises, such as in-basket and group exercises, which allow the observation of behaviors relevant to job performance.

Assessment center results usually are organized around dimensions of performance, such as leadership and decision making. Although research has suggested that construct validity of these dimension scores is lacking, the overall performance in assessment centers has been shown to be valid, especially for managerial jobs. In fact, the few studies comparing the assessment center approach with cognitive tests showed higher validities and less adverse impact, suggesting that, for managerial jobs, the assessment center approach is a suitable alternative. The greatest drawback to an assessment center approach for organizations is its high cost and labor intensive nature. Typically, an assessment for one individual might take anywhere from one to three assessor-days, depending upon the complexity of the process.

Peer Evaluations

Peers often have extensive opportunities to observe the behavior of a coworker under job-related conditions that are more revealing of typical, as opposed to maximal, performance. Judgments about a job candidate by coworkers or cotrainees have been shown to have good validities, similar to those for cognitive ability tests. Not as much is known about the potential adverse impact of peer ratings, though such issues as friendship bias (the tendency to rate one's friends higher) may affect the racial distribution of ratings. The major problem with implementing peer ratings has been the feasibility issue. Obviously, peer ratings are difficult to use for hiring external candidates. Even ratings made for the purpose of promotion or transfer can be manipulated or sabotaged, leading to perceived unfairness and lack of acceptance. More recent trends in organizational assessment may provide an opportunity to take advantage of the validity of peer ratings, at least for promotion and transfer decisions. So-called 360 degree assessment programs include ratings of performance by peers, usually for purposes of feedback. These ratings might overcome the obstacles that have been cited in the past — such as friendship bias — if the evaluations become a regular part of the organizational culture and are accepted as a legitimate organizational practice.

Measures of Past Performance

Behavioral Consistency Assessment

Relevant past performance should be a good predictor of future performance in an occupation. The behavioral consistency approach, developed at the U.S. Office of Personnel Management, requires applicants to describe their major achievements in job-related areas identified by experts as critical to job performance.

Although only a few studies of the behavioral consistency approach have been done, the results are promising. Validities have been as good as or better than cognitive ability tests when direct comparisons were possible, and behavioral consistency appeared to have less adverse impact.

The behavioral consistency approach involves a fairly elaborate developmental process and requires experts to be trained to evaluate the candidate protocols. Because there is a possibility that candidates may falsify information, policies need to be established to determine how much time and effort will be spent checking candidates' claimed experiences. Finally, the behavioral consistency approach requires a fair amount of time on the part of candidates. On the positive side, this may eliminate poorly motivated candidates; on the negative side, employers who are in competitive hiring situations may find it difficult to use the method. Also, behavioral consistency may be most useful for situations in which a pool of candidates with relevant experience is available and less useful for entry-level positions in which experience is not required or expected.

Academic Performance and Achievement

Many employers, as part of their initial selection process, consider grades (usually college) and level of education in making selection decisions. Grades, or rank in class, provide a convenient summary of performance in a quasi-standard setting. Although the available evidence suggests that grades appear to be correlated with job performance, the level of correlation is not nearly as high as for other available predictors. In addition, the difficulty of equating grades from different institutions poses a serious obstacle to using grades in a selection system. Eductional achievement measures show generally low validities with job performance and pose another problem — educational achievement measures usually produce adverse impact.

Reference Checks

Although it seems reasonable to assume that previous supervisors of a job applicant can provide relevant information regarding the performance of the applicant under job-relevant conditions, research shows generally poor results for reference checks. Several factors probably reduce the usefulness of reference checks for selection purposes. First, research shows a substantial problem of leniency with reference checks and a general lack of discrimination. One reason may be concern over litigation or the desire to place an unsatisfactory employee in another position. These problems may be exacerbated when candidates are given control over the selection of reference givers. It is unlikely that references will be sought from supervisors or others who would be likely to give poor evaluations.

Reference checks generally are a search for negative information and can serve a useful purpose by verifying prior employment. However, the general leniency and lack of discrimination combined with other difficulties of obtaining accurate information make reference checks unlikely to be useful predictors of occupational performance.

Experience Measures

Experience, either in a specific job or in a training program, frequently is used as a method of selecting employees. In some cases, the evaluation of the training and experience may be highly formalized, with points awarded for specific types of experiences. In other cases, as in many collective bargaining contracts, it is simply the amount of experience, or seniority, in a particular job that is important.

The research evidence shows poor validities for experience, whether it is evaluated by a formalized system or based on pure seniority. Although experience continues to be used by employers, the low validities, combined with potential for adverse impact, would appear to make this alternative one to be avoided unless it is part of a collective bargaining agreement.

Expert Judgments

Projective Techniques

Projective techniques include a variety of measurement processes that have as a common characteristic the presentation of ambiguous stimuli to which examinees provide responses that purportedly reveal standing on underlying personality constructs. Experts then interpret and score the responses, usually based on a predetermined scoring scheme.

The research evidence for projective techniques shows poor validity with the exception of the Miner Sentence Completion Scale (MSCS) (Miner, 1985). The MSCS, unlike most projective measures, was developed for organizational purposes, and the research suggests reasonably good validities with little adverse impact. Unfortunately, the research on the MSCS is limited with respect to the type of organization studied and the general lack of construct validity of the measure. The MSCS, like all projective devices, requires expert scoring, and it is not clear to what extent it is the expert or the device that is producing the validity. The limitations of the MSCS suggest that it cannot be generally recommended as an alternative. Because the MSCS appears to be the best of the lot, no other projectives can be recommended based on the available research.

Handwriting Analysis

One alternative frequently mentioned in magazines and management-oriented publications is handwriting analysis. Usually, these articles cite the popularity of handwriting analysis as a selection device in European countries and Israel and claim a large number of users in the United States. Although relatively few studies have been done on handwriting analysis, their conclusions are quite consistent. Handwriting analysts, regardless of the method used, appear to achieve reasonable interscore reliabilities, but there is no evidence that handwriting analysts can predict job performance or other job behaviors with any validity. Both review articles and individual empirical studies reach this consistent conclusion. It should be noted that, in at least one case, some apparent validity was the result of the biographical content of the writing sample provided by candidates. The research shows that, when standardized samples are used, there is no validity. Although handwriting analysis apparently continues to have appeal to some employers, this is not a method that can be recommended.

Individual Assessments by Experts

Judgments regarding future performance of job candidates represent a significant component of several selection devices, including assessment centers, peer ratings, and interviews. Consulting psychologists often are called upon to evaluate job candidates when empirical validation of selection procedures is not feasible (e.g., selection of a top executive for a corporation). The use of expert judgment typically is based on a combination of commonly used selection methods. A survey of industrial/organizational psychologists (Ryan & Sackett, 1987) found that the most commonly used assessment methods included personal history forms (82.7 percent), ability tests (78.4 percent), personality inventories (77.8 percent), and interviews (93.8 percent). Fewer respondents indicated that they used projective devices (34.0 percent) and simulation exercises (38.2 percent).

Because individual assessments typically are limited to only a few candidates, studies of the validity of expert assessment are rare. The available evidence indicates that expert judgments have useful validities, probably in the range of those reported for interviews. There is little evidence regarding the adverse impact of expert judgment, but it is reasonable to expect that adverse impact will be dependent upon the type of information relied upon by the expert (e.g., cognitive tests, personality tests). Organizations considering using expert judgments must consider the relatively high cost as a potential barrier, particularly when large numbers of candidates must be processed.

Special Measures

Tests of Physical Ability

Physical ability measures can play an important role in selecting personnel for physically demanding jobs. In most cases, however, the criteria of performance for physically demanding jobs are limited and specific. Physical tests have been used to predict the physical aspects of many different physically demanding jobs, such as firefighter, under-water demolition experts, telephone pole climbers, steelworkers, and miners. Despite the limited aspect of physical criteria, they frequently represent a highly critical component of job performance. Firefighter performance, for example, involves a combination of cognitive and physical performance, both of which may contribute to the safety of life and property.

As with cognitive predictors, a distinction can be made between tests of basic ability and work samples. Research for a number of physically demanding jobs has produced results that both types of physical tests can predict performance on job-related criteria at levels comparable with those for cognitive ability tests and work sample tests. Unfortunately, there is not enough evidence to compare the adverse impact and validity of the two types of tests, but the evidence is clear that physical ability tests will have substantial adverse impact for female applicants and little or no adverse impact for racial and ethnic minorities.

Physical tests can present some formidable problems for employers. Special equipment, careful medical screening, and risk of injury to candidates are some of the issues that must be considered by employers. One aspect of physical ability tests that differs from cognitive tests is that many physical variables are amenable to improvement through training. Because of this, employers implementing physical tests should consider providing information on training to candidates.

Integrity Tests

Integrity tests, or honesty tests, are paper-and-pencil instruments designed to identify dishonest job applicants. Originally developed as an alternative to polygraph screening, they are utilized mostly in settings where workers have direct access to cash or merchandise. Although their origins are distinctly different, integrity tests share a similar methodology and similar problems with personality tests. In fact, some integrity tests are "personality based" and use derived scores from items in an existing personality test. Other integrity tests are called "overt" tests because the questions overtly deal with dishonest behavior or attitudes toward dishonest behavior. It should be noted that, like personality tests, integrity tests have little or any adverse impact.

The history of integrity tests has been plagued by controversy and criticisms of validation research conducted by the test publishers. Because the tests purport to predict dishonest behavior, the measurement of the criterion in a traditional validation study is difficult. Recent meta-analytic work showed that integrity tests have validity for some criteria but that integrity tests appear to predict overall job performance better than the more limited criteria (e.g., theft) that they were designed to predict. The conclusion seems to be that integrity tests are an alternative measure of conscientiousness, and indeed, a perusal of the items embedded in integrity tests would seem to bear this out. In short, integrity tests may have some validity for predicting dishonest behavior, but the research evidence is limited. The validities in predictive studies with detected theft as a criterion were much lower than the validities for predicting overall job performance. More research is certainly needed, and a sensible recommendation for an employer would be to consider the use of a "big five" measure of conscientiousness, because integrity tests appear to measure the same construct and do so in a more invasive and potentially offensive way.

Situational Judgment Tests

Another emerging class of alternatives, called "situational judgment tests," were not reviewed because of the limited research evidence available. Situational judgment tests present job-related scenarios and ask applicants to choose one of several alternative responses. Scenarios can be presented in written formats or, more realistically, via CD ROM. Some limited research suggests that situational tests may have promise as an alternative, but data are too limited to make a judgment at the present.

CONCLUSIONS AND RECOMMENDATIONS

Table 24.1 shows the most promising alternatives to cognitive ability tests and summarizes the pertinent considerations for employers. Work samples, trainability tests, biodata, behavioral consistency measures, and assessment centers have demonstrated equal validity and less adverse impact than cognitive tests for certain criteria. To these five, a sixth alternative can be added by combining a measure of conscientiousness with cognitive ability, which should raise validity and lower adverse impact. Employers considering these alternatives should recognize that additional cost, elaborate development, or frequent revision may be necessary and that certain administrative issues will need to be considered.

TABLE 24.1
A Summary of Promising Alternatives

Alternative	Feasibility Issues
Cognitive plus personality-based conscientiousness measure	Faking and response distortion on personality test
Work samples	Cost of administration, need for experienced applicants, frequent revision
Trainability tests	Cost of development and frequent revision
Biodata	Cost of development, faking, and response distortion
Behavioral consistency	Cost of development, need for experienced applicants, possible negative applicant reaction
Assessment centers	High cost of administration

Source: Compiled by the author.

REFERENCES

Bureau of National Affairs, Inc. (1988). *Recruiting and selection procedures.* Personnel Policies Forum Survey No. 146. Washington, DC: Bureau of National Affairs, Inc.

Miner, J. B. (1985). Sentence completion measures. In H. Bernardin & D. Bownas (Eds.), *Personality assessment in organizations.* New York: Praeger.

Reilly, R. R., & Chao, G. T. (1982). Validity and fairness of some alternative employee selection procedures. *Personnel Psychology, 35,* 1–62.

Ryan, A. M., & Sackett, P. R. (1987). A survey of individual assessment practices. *Personnel Psychology, 40,* 455–488.

Uniform guidelines on employee selection procedures, 29 C.F.R. 1607 (1978).

Wernimont, P. F., & Campbell, J. P. (1968). Signs, samples, and criteria. *Journal of Applied Psychology, 52,* 372–376.

25

Sliding Bands: An Alternative to Top-down Selection

Sheldon Zedeck, Wayne F. Cascio,
Irwin L. Goldstein, and James Outtz

The purpose of this chapter is to describe sliding bands, a test score use or referral procedure, and how it has the potential to reduce or eliminate adverse impact against gender or racial minorities without severe or major impact on the utility of the selection process. This chapter will present the statistical procedure and its rationale used to calculate the bandwidths from which candidates can be chosen, an illustration of how the sliding band procedure is used, some pros and cons of the procedure, suggestions for adjusting the width of the band, and conclusions and commentary regarding the appropriateness of the procedure in light of the Civil Rights Act of 1991.

THE SLIDING BAND PROCEDURE

The essential process in test development and validation, briefly outlined, is as follows: conduct a job analysis; determine the performance domains you are interested in having the tests predict (i.e., specify the criteria for assessing success in the job of interest); hypothesize what kinds and types of "tests" might predict the criteria of job success (tests include paper-and-pencil aptitude and achievement tests, interviews, biographical information, assessment center results, and any other device used by organizations to make hiring or promotion decisions); purchase or develop tests that *reliably* measure the areas of interest; test your hypotheses by collecting data on the "tests" and demonstrate that the "test(s)" is valid according to one of the professionally acceptable strategies — content, criterion-related, and construct validation strategies; and, if there is validity evidence, adopt a procedure whereby the test results will be used to make decisions.

A traditional and common procedure by which to make hiring decisions or referral to jobs is known as top-down ranking. In this procedure, a rank-order list of test scores is established such that the highest scorer is at the top and is the first one considered for hire. If there are ten openings, the top ten scorers would be offered jobs (provided there are no other issues that might arise, e.g., as a result of background checks). If a candidate refuses, the next highest scoring candidate, in strict rank order, would be offered the job.

The question this chapter addresses is whether we should rely only on the scores on the test, given that most tests have less than perfect reliability and validity. If the top score in our distribution is 90, is 89 "truly" different from 90; is 88 "truly" different from 89 or 90; is 80 "truly" different from 80, 81, 89, or 90? The closer the scores are to each other (e.g., 89 to 90), the more likely it is that observers would guess they are not truly different from one another. The farther the scores are from each other (e.g., 80 to 90), the more likely it is that observers would think that the scores are truly different. What contributes to this lack of confidence? The answer is found in the concept of reliability.

The intent of psychological measurement is to provide quantitative descriptions of individuals in terms of the extent to which they manifest various psychological constructs, traits, and abilities. However, it is a fact of life that, if we administer the same measuring device several times to the same individual, we usually find that he or she does not obtain exactly the same score on all administrations. To develop an index of this degree of inconsistency, we compute reliability coefficients, which reveal the degree of consistency among the scores earned by an individual. Given that inconsistency within individuals exists, it is likely that, when we compare individuals based on different administrations of a test, there will be reversal of positions such that the individual who today receives a score of 90 may receive a score of 88 tomorrow and an individual who today receives a score of 87 may reverse tomorrow and score 90.

Given the likelihood of reversal in scores within and between individuals, we propose that a reasonable way in which to interpret scores and make decisions based on those scores is to create *bands* within which the lowest scorer is considered equivalent to the top scorer. Our use of the term "equivalent" should be interpreted to mean that there is a range of scores in which the scores are close enough to the top scorer in the band to warrant consideration for hire along with the top score. The questions, therefore, are, What range of scores can be considered to be equivalent? and If a set of scores is created in which the top and lowest score within the band are assumed to be equivalent, on what basis does the organization choose applicants for positions? The banding procedure provides a solution to the first question, while consideration of economic, political, and social issues influences answers to the second question.

The statistical question of what range of scores can be considered to be equivalent can be answered by calculating a statistic known as the standard error of the difference between scores (SED). The SED allows us to determine the differences between scores that can be considered equivalent or nonsignificantly different from each other. For our purposes, we calculate the SED to determine the scores within the band that are close enough to the top available score to warrant consideration for hire along with the top available score. As you will see, the underlying notion of SED is the reliability of the measurement device.

From an operational perspective, assume that we have the same distribution that we cited above in our discussion of top-down selection. Suppose, again, we have a rank-order list of test scores. Before we make a decision to hire the top scorer, we raise the question of what score in this distribution can be considered close enough to the top score in the distribution to also warrant consideration for hire. If we identify the score in the distribution that is not significantly different from the top score, then all those scores from that score to the top score compose the band of scores that is considered equivalent.

The formula for SED is as follows:

$$SED = C \times SEM \times \backslash R(2), \tag{1}$$

where C is a point on the normal curve that represents the likelihood that two scores are different from each other if the null hypothesis is true (e.g., 1.96 corresponds to the conventional 0.05 level of significance) and SEM is the standard error of measurement, as calculated by the following formula:

$$SEM = SD_x \backslash R(1 - r_{xx}) \tag{2}$$

where SD_x is the standard deviation of the test scores and r_{xx} is the reliability of the test. Examination of formula (2) shows the role of reliability. If tests are perfectly reliable ($r_{xx} = 1.00$), then, from a logical perspective, we have confidence that individuals' scores are measuring the construct of interest with consistency. Application of the SEM formula in this case produces a value of 0.00, which in turn produces an SED of 0.00. Thus, we have no reason to believe that scores of one individual could be reversed with another individual in subsequent testing. If, however, the r_{xx} is 0.00, then, from a logical perspective, we assume the scores to be a random distribution of numbers; thus, we have reason to suspect that the score is not measuring any construct, trait, or ability with consistency. In this case, SEM and SED will equal SD_x. From a practical perspective, in such situations, we have reason to believe that, on subsequent testing, a score today of 88 could be lower or higher on testing tomorrow; a score of 88 today could be 84 tomorrow, or a score of 84 today could be 88 tomorrow. Consequently, there can be reversal of position on rank-order lists from one occasion to another.

If application of formula (1) yields a value of 10 points, we can say that there is a band of scores that covers 10 points such that the lowest score in the band can be considered equivalent to the top score in the band. To use this information, we subtract ten from the top score in the distribution and conclude that all test scores from the top to bottom of the band are considered equivalent. Choices for selection can be made from anywhere within the band. Once the band is used up, a second ten-point band can be created and selections made from within this second band. This process, as described, is referred to as fixed bands.

An alternative to fixed bands is sliding bands. Sliding bands put the selection decision into a sequential mode, such that hiring decisions are made individual by individual, one at a time, until all positions are filled. If the top scoring individual is selected to fill a position, then one position is filled, and we then become concerned with filling a second position. A new band of individuals can be established by subtracting ten from the remaining highest top score and can be defined as containing all those scores that are considered equivalent to the top score. The width of the band remains ten points, but the referent score is now the top highest score that remains after the first decision for hiring was made (assuming the highest scorer in the distribution was chosen). In essence, the band slides as selections are made from the remaining top score and the band continues to slide every time such a score is selected. If the top score is not selected, then the band does not slide. In sliding bands, then, the bandwidth is constant but the number of candidates within the band fluctuates.

How does banding have the potential for influencing adverse impact? The literature shows substantial differences in the mean test scores achieved by majority members and minority members on certain types of tests (e.g., it often is found that there is a one standard deviation difference between racial minority and majority groups on cognitive ability tests), and this leads to adverse impact against minority members. If there is a band of scores that is considered equivalent, organizations can choose on the basis of secondary criteria that may include, as one of the criteria, racial or gender classification.

AN ILLUSTRATION

For our purposes, we will assume that there is a single test, such as a cognitive ability test, that measures quantitative reasoning and that it has been administered to 1,000 applicants (700 majority and 300 minority) who took the test to fill 50 openings. Also, assume that the test has a reliability of 0.75 and a criterion-related validity of 0.30; the range of obtained scores is between 80 and 20, with a standard deviation of 10. Table 25.1 contains part of the distribution of scores for this test (i.e., only the top 50 percent of scores). Table 25.1 also shows the racial distribution at each test score point (for the purposes of the illustration, we will use only "majority" and "minority" as the racial categories).

If we were to use a top-down, traditional referral procedure, we would recommend that all those with scores of 80 through 67 be hired; this would yield 50 hires, 43 of whom are majority and 7 of whom are minority. Using the 80 percent adverse impact rule specified in the Uniform Guidelines on Employee Selection Procedures (1978) produces an adverse impact conclusion against minorities (i.e., the hiring rate for majorities is 43 divided by 700, or 6 percent, while the hiring rate for minorities is 7 divided by 300, or 2 percent; 2 percent divided by 6 percent equals 33 percent, which is substantially below the 80 percent ratio).

In contrast, the following results are obtained with the sliding band procedure. Calculation of the SED (with a C value of 1.96) yields a bandwidth of 9.8 or 10 points. This means that the first bandwidth goes from 80 through 70 and that scores within that range are considered equivalent to the top score. In applying the bandwidth, as we make a decision about the highest scorer, the band slides, such that, if we hire the one person with the score of 80, the remaining 49 openings can be filled by looking at the remaining scores where 79 is now the top scorer. Subtracting 10 points from 79 indicates that 79–69 is the bandwidth, and this is the pool from which we can choose (there are 34 applicants within this band). We continue to slide the band as we select the remaining top scorers. Suppose the sliding band process has gone through the sequence such that we have chosen all those with scores down through 72. This yields a total of 19 hires, 16 of whom are majority and 3 of whom are minority; it leaves 31 openings to be filled. Given that we have hired all those with scores from 72 through 80, the highest remaining scorer is 71. Now, application of the ten-point bandwidth results in a band of 71 down through 61; within this band there are 122 applicants (102 of whom are majority and 20 of whom are minority) to fill the remaining 31 openings. Here is where we have most of our flexibility in that we are assuming that these 122 scores are not significantly different from the top score of the band, and, thus, the organization can choose any of the 122 to fill the 31 openings. If we want to maximize the number of racial minorities hired,

TABLE 25.1
Distribution of Test Scores

Test Score	N	Majority N	Minority N
80	1	1	0
79	1	1	0
78	1	1	0
77	1	1	0
76	2	1	1
75	2	2	0
74	3	2	1
73	4	3	1
72	4	4	0
71	5	4	1
70	5	4	1
69	6	5	1
68	7	7	0
67	8	7	1
66	11	9	2
65	13	11	2
64	14	13	1
63	14	11	3
62	18	14	4
61	21	17	4
60	24	18	6
59	25	16	9
58	26	17	9
57	27	16	11
56	28	14	14
55	29	14	15
54	30	13	17
53	31	16	15
52	33	16	17
51	34	17	14
50	36	17	19

Source: Compiled by the author.

we can choose all of the minorities in this band (20) and then take the remaining 11 from the majority subgroup. The total number of hires yielded by this procedure is 50, which includes 27 majority hires and 23 minority hires. These hiring numbers represent hiring rates of 4 percent and 8 percent, respectively, for majority and minority groups. This result yields no adverse impact against minorities.

From the perspective of the majority group, we find that the lowest scorer of this group has a score of 69 (note that there were five majority members with this score, but we only had to take one to fulfill our objectives). This illustration shows that minorities with scores of 68 down through 61 were selected while majorities with these scores were passed over and not selected. This difference may be *perceived* as unfair, but from the statistical perspective, it is not unfair; scores of 70 down through 61 are not considered significantly different from the score of 71.

PROS AND CONS

There are two major arguments against banding. First, critics argue that top-down selection is the procedure that maximizes utility or economic gain derived from using the test system, while sliding bands yield less than maximum utility. This is true in the traditional sense where utility is assessed by inputting the test's validity into the utility equation along with the other requisite statistical parameters. The utility calculation, however, typically does not include issues outside the scope of the test, such as the social and financial impact on the organization of a nondiverse work force, losses that may accrue to the organization because of a focus on a limited number of criteria, and other factors that are pertinent to the total selection concern. Putting aside such issues, is there a substantial loss in utility if there is some departure from top-down selection? Our research and that of others indicates that the answer is "no."

The second criticism is that it is illogical, on the one hand, to say that scores from 80 down through 70 are not different but that 69 is different but, on the other hand, as the band slides, to say that scores of 79 through 69 are not different but that 68 is different. Our response to the logic argument is that the system is logical if we focus on who is different from the *top* scorer available to be chosen for hire. An emphasis on the top scorer is consistent with the top-down procedure that chooses the top scores in succession. Thus, the issue is not whether 69 is different from 70 but whether 69 is different from 80, the score that the top-down procedure requires to be hired.

There are a number of advantages, as well as related precedents, for using a banding system. The primary advantage to using the sliding band procedure is that it provides flexibility for the hiring organization. It recognizes that test scores are not perfectly reliable and that tests do not have perfect validity. Given such a psychometric situation, the organization can consider secondary criteria to use in choosing among those who have equivalent test scores. The illustration focused on the interest in having a diverse work force, but there is no reason that other factors cannot be considered, either alone or in combination. These secondary criteria can include factors such as type or kind of education, training or continuing education acquired, attendance records, committee participation, and special skills. These factors are job relevant.

The factor we relied on to illustrate the procedure, racial composition of the work force, is one that has stimulated the most criticism. It is the factor that stems from political and social implications for testing, hiring, and affirmative action. We believe that having a diverse work force has important economic implications in both the short and the long term for an organization, particularly if survival of the organization is a goal. If the economic implication of having an all-majority work force were factored into the traditional utility analyses of test score use, we are not convinced that the resulting calculations would show as much utility as has been claimed for top-down selection, a situation for which the diversity factor has not been considered.

Aside from the reliability, validity, and social and political issues, there are other reasons for adopting a banding solution to hiring decisions. First, the criterion space that usually is tapped by tests is no more than 10 percent. Imposition of secondary criteria allows us to take into account factors that are not measured or predicted by our traditional tests and strategies. Sliding bands allow us to broaden the criterion space that job analyses indicate exist in most jobs.

Second, in practice, utility of a test system is not always the guiding factor in choice of a selection system. For example, in situations in which we look at test batteries, we may find that a test battery that yields a multiple correlation (R) of 0.45 is significant and the stepwise analyses indicate that each test component explains a significant amount of incremental variance. Calculation of the utility of this test battery, with its R of 0.45, will yield more economic gain than a test battery of three tests that may have an R of 0.43. Yet, from a practical point of view, we may decide to use only the three-test battery because it takes less time to administer and to score and it eliminates a less "face valid" component. The point is that we have a history of making decisions about what to include in test batteries that does not always rely *only* on economic, utility issues.

Third, there is precedent for using bands, but as we will show, this precedent is based on arbitrary rules as opposed to a statistical determination of what scores should be within the band. There are two examples of precedence. In educational situations, such as in high-school grading, we assign the letter grade of A to those who score 90 percent through 100 percent on tests, the letter grade of B to those who score 80 percent through 89 percent, and so on (we will assume no plusses and minuses are used). There is nothing magical about 10 percent intervals.

What is being conveyed is that, if a student averages 81 percent on tests and another student averages 89 percent on tests, they will both receive the grade of B and, therefore, are to be treated as equal with respect to the abilities being measured. In applications to college, both of these students look alike for this particular grade. In essence, the high school has determined that 81 percent is not different from 89 percent.

Another precedent situation is in civil service hirings. A number of jurisdictions have "rules of three," "rules of five," and so on. This means that the hiring supervisor is allowed to choose from the three (or five) highest scorers on the civil service examination. In practice, the supervisor interviews the three candidates and applies secondary criteria in making the decision of whom to hire. The scores could be 90, 89, and 79. The "tradition" of the "rule of three" is independent of the actual, absolute scores obtained and, in this example, would have the impact of stating to the supervisor that he or she can choose from a range of 11 points. If the third highest scorer was 69 instead of 79, the range now would be 21 points. In other words, the bandwidth is determined by the absolute values of the scores on the test and not by the psychometric properties of the test.

ADJUSTING THE WIDTH OF THE BAND

The above presentation has demonstrated that the sliding band procedure provides flexibility for the organization. Another opportunity for flexibility resides in the choice of the C value that is used in the formula to calculate the bandwidth. As stated above, C is the point on the normal curve that represents the likelihood that two scores are different from each other if the null hypothesis is true. We have illustrated the procedure by using the "conventional" significance level of 0.05. The interpretation given to banding with a C of 0.05 is that we are 95 percent confident that there is no reliable difference between scores within the band and that, in fact, the difference may be zero.

Those who have used the sliding band procedure have reported on occasion that the band has been perceived as too wide, making it difficult for many to see the equivalence in scores when a lower scoring individual is selected over a higher scoring individual when the actual test scores are quite discrepant. This is a real problem, to be sure, and one that can be addressed. From the perspective of perception, the procedure needs to be explained and illustrated clearly to those who are impacted by its adoption. It is particularly important to explain the procedure and rationale to those who believe that the width of the band is arbitrary and established with a wide range only to accommodate the hiring of minorities.

What needs to be realized, however, is that there is flexibility in what the width of the band can be and that this flexibility is found in the setting of the C value shown in formula (1). If the goal of the banding procedure is solely to reduce adverse impact, then one can use the value we used in the illustration, 1.96, plug it into the formula, and use the resulting bandwidth as the upper limit. If application of the formula results in a bandwidth of ten points, as it was in our illustration, we would state at the outset, prior to making any selection decisions, that ten points is the upper limit and that values less than ten points will be used to set the bandwidth if such values lead to no adverse impact. This strategy means that bandwidths can range from zero to ten points, with the bandwidths used being ones that yield no adverse impact.

To see how this works, we will return to our illustration (see Table 25.1), in which we were interested in hiring 50 candidates. In that illustration, use of the ten-point bandwidth and applying the sliding band logic took us from the highest score of 80 down through a score of 61. In that example, candidates in the majority group with scores of 69, 68, and so forth were passed over for candidates in the minority group with scores of 66, 65, and so forth. The results of this strategy yielded 27 majority and 23 minority hires. The strategy, instead, could have been to go down through the list in top-down fashion and skip higher scores only when necessary to achieve no adverse impact. Examination of Table 25.1 indicates that selecting all candidates with scores of 68 or better yields 36 majority and 6 minority, for a total of 42 candidates. The remaining highest scorer available for consideration is 67, but rather than employing a ten-point bandwidth, use of a four-point bandwidth would provide 60 candidates (51 of whom are majority and 9 of whom are minority members) from whom to fill the remaining eight positions. If seven minorities are chosen then the remaining one opening would be filled by a majority member and would come from the score of 67. The final composition of hires would be 37 majority and 13 minority hires. Adverse impact calculations for these numbers yield 37 divided by 700 equals 5 percent, 13 divided by 300 equals 4 percent, and 0.04 divided by 0.05 equals 80 percent, which satisfies the 80 percent rule. The bottom line for this strategy is that the lowest scorer chosen is at 63 and those majority members passed over are at scores 67 through 64. The range of scores passed over is less than in the previous illustration, but more importantly, passing over in this illustration is undertaken to yield no adverse impact, while the previous illustration maximized minority hiring. The former rationale of yielding no adverse impact might well be perceived as more fair than the situation that maximizes minority hiring at the expense of majority hires.

Another alternative, one based on a rational decision-making model, is to consider risks in decisions. In effect, the choice of the C value is a function of the risk the organization is willing to take in its decisions. In any situation in which hypotheses are being tested, there are two ways of being correct in the decision and two ways of making an error. For our purposes, we will focus on the types of errors — Type I and Type II errors. Type I error means that we have *incorrectly* concluded that there is a difference when there is no difference; this is represented by the alpha (α) level. In our illustration, there is a 0.05 chance that we have *incorrectly* concluded that 69 is different from 80. On the other hand, a Type II error occurs when we *incorrectly* conclude that there is no difference between scores when, in fact, there is a difference; this value is referred to as beta (ß). The value of ß is not based on convention but is a function, in part, of the sample sizes used to test the hypothesis. We cannot directly choose a specific value of ß but can affect its size by our choice of α. In our illustration, there is a probability value that can be placed on the *incorrectness* of concluding that 70 is equivalent to the top score of 80 when, in fact, 70 is different, and this probability is ß.

There are two important related points regarding α and ß that impact our choice of the C value. First, α and ß have an inverse relationship such that as α becomes smaller (goes from 0.05 to 0.01 with a concomitant increase in the value of C from 1.96 to 2.58), ß becomes larger — that is, attempting to reduce the error of incorrectly concluding that 69 is different from 80 when it is not increases the likelihood that we will incorrectly conclude that 70 is not different from 80 when it is. The second point is that the decision maker needs to determine whether a Type I error is more or less important than a Type II error for the organization. Is the negative consequence to the organization greater to incorrectly leave someone out of the band (Type I error) than it is to incorrectly include someone in the band (Type II error)? Our view is that the answer depends on the nature of the job and the risks involved.

Organizations need to think carefully about the relative risk they are willing to tolerate in judging a score to be significantly different or not different from the top score in the band of scores. The level of risk, in turn, is a function of the relative cost of a mistake in selection. Such factors as the criticality of a position and the economic and social consequences of an error in performance are relevant to such a determination. For some types of jobs, such as those of nuclear power plant operator or airline pilot, the positions are so critical and the consequences of error so great that organizations, justifiably, are unwilling to tolerate much risk of error in selecting someone who should not be selected. In other words, the organization's objective is to minimize erroneous acceptances. To accomplish this, we need to have ß as small as possible. To have ß as small as possible means that α is increased; α is increased when C is made smaller. Thus, organizations are likely to opt for narrow bandwidths in order to minimize any loss in validity relative to the economically optimal strategy of strict, top-down selection. The more crucial the job and the greater consequences that could result from poor performance, the more important it is to avoid a Type II error. In a high risk situation, we want to be very confident that the candidates hired are very good, and, therefore, if we use a band to select, we want to be very confident that the lowest scorer in the band is not different from the top scorer. We want to reduce ß as much as possible so that we will not incorrectly conclude that the two candidates are close enough when they are different. To accomplish this goal of reduced ß, we recommend that C values that are concomitant with increased α values be used. Increased values of α are associated with decreased values of C — for example, a C value of 1.0 is associated with an α of 0.16; previously, we showed that a C value of 1.96 is associated with an α of 0.05. In such situations, when we choose smaller C values than 1.96, all other things being equal, ß will be smaller than it was when α was selected at 0.05, and consequently, there will be reduced likelihood of a Type II error.

Alternatively, there are many jobs in our society in which the consequences of error are not as great, and, therefore, organizations justifiably can tolerate more risk of error (i.e., erroneous acceptances). For example, if new hires will be trained and the rate of success in training, based on past experience, is high, then organizations may want to set a wider bandwidth (e.g., 90 percent confidence), so that in concluding that any obtained score differs significantly from the top score in a band, the organization can say with a high degree of confidence (e.g., 90 percent) that the scores outside of the band really are different from the top score.

A point that needs to be stressed is that we are not advocating that organizations and decision makers can provide a simple declaration that the job of interest does or does not involve risk. Rather, the field needs to examine and develop formal methods that can be used to assess the risk involved, a topic that is beyond the scope of this chapter.

CONCLUSION AND COMMENTARY

The procedure of sliding bands is used to achieve a compromise between a sole emphasis on the economic value gained from valid tests and the social and political needs of communities. Sliding band has been demonstrated to reduce and eliminate adverse impact with minimal loss of utility. It also has been shown to result in diverse work forces. The procedure is based on an understanding and application of psychometric principles and the recognition that testing does not yield perfectly reliable or valid results.

A question that has been raised is whether banding is consistent with Section 106 of the Civil Rights Act of 1991, which states: "It shall be unlawful employment practice for a respondent, in connection with the selection or referral of applicants or candidates for employment or pro- motion, to adjust the scores of, use different cutoff scores for, or otherwise alter the results of, employment related tests on the basis of race, color, religion, sex, or national origin." It is our opinion that the application of the sliding band procedure does not involve the adjustment of scores, use of different cutoffs, or other alteration of the results of tests based on race, sex, and so on. Adoption of banding is merely a reliance on psychometric principles alone (e.g., reliability, variance, and confidence intervals) that acknowledge that there is a range of scores such that the lowest score in the band can be considered equivalent to the top score in the band. Selection from within that band can be based on random selection or secondary criteria. As stated in the U.S. Court of Appeals for the Ninth Circuit decision on banding (Officers for Justice, 1992), banding is: "A selection process which offers a facially neutral way to interpret actual scores and reduce adverse impacts on minority candidates while preserving merit as the primary criterion for selection. Today we hold that the banding process is valid as a matter of constitutional and federal law.

REFERENCES

Civil Rights Act of 1991 (Pub.L. 102–166) (CRA)
Officers for Justice v. Civil Service Commission of the City and County of San Francisco. 979 F. 2d 721 (9th Cir. 1992).
Uniform guidelines on employee selection procedures, 29 C.F.R. 1607 (1978).

SUGGESTED READINGS

Cascio, W. F., Goldstein, I. L., Outtz, J., & Zedeck, S. (1995). Twenty issues and answers about sliding bands. *Human Performance, 3*, pp. 227–242.
Cascio, W. F., Outtz, J., Zedeck, S., & Goldstein, I. L. (1991). Statistical implications of six methods of test score use in personnel selection. *Human Performance, 4,* 233–264.
Murphy, K. R. (1994). Potential effects of banding as a function of test reliability. *Personnel Psychology, 47,* 477–495.
Sackett, P. R., & Wilk, S. L. (1994). Within-group norming and other forms of score adjustment in preemployment testing. *American Psychologist, 49,* 929–954.
Schmidt, F. L. (1991). Why all banding procedures in personnel selection are logically flawed. *Human Performance, 4,* 265–277.
Schmidt, F. L., & Hunter, J. E. (1995). The fatal internal contradiction in banding: Its statistical rationale is logically inconsistent with its operational procedures. *Human Performance, 3,* 203–214.
Scientific Affairs Committee Report. (1994). An evaluation of banding methods in personnel selection. *The Industrial and Organizational Psychologist, 32,* 8–86.

VII

LEGAL AND REGULATORY CONCERNS

26

The Equal Employment Opportunity Commission and Other Government Agencies

Donald J. Schwartz

THE EQUAL EMPLOYMENT OPPORTUNITY COMMISSION

Its Role

The Equal Employment Opportunity Commission (EEOC) is often the place where employees and job applicants first go when they believe that they have been the victims of discrimination in the employment process and want to have their complaints resolved. The existence of such an agency can have considerable benefit to them and to their employers or prospective employers. Frequently, these applicants have been turned down, because they did not score high enough on a test or other selection procedure that does not appear to be relevant, for jobs they believe they can do. The EEOC can provide a mechanism by which the specific facts of their situations can be examined and explained, and satisfactory resolutions sometimes can be negotiated without these applicants incurring large personal legal fees or other expenses. In other cases, where legitimate complaints cannot be conciliated, the EEOC may file a lawsuit on their behalf, saving them additional legal fees and expenses. Their prospective employers also benefit, because the process by which charges are investigated can be a safety valve through which technical disputes

The views expressed in this chapter are those of the author and do not necessarily reflect those of the U.S. Equal Employment Opportunity Commission or any other government agency.

are resolved without private litigation that is expensive to both sides, regardless of the outcome, and often fosters ill will between employers and large segments of the communities that they serve and depend upon for their applicant pool.

The value of the process is critically dependent on accurate perceptions of what actually occurs when a charge is filed with the EEOC. If either side in a dispute believes that the agency has already prejudged the facts of the charge, has a hidden agenda, or misunderstands the law and relevant professional standards, the possibility of resolving charges is diminished greatly. Charging parties may hire private attorneys to pursue their claims or drop them simply because they do not believe in the system. Employers may simply not provide relevant data to support their positions and take their chances in court. There are, unfortunately, a number of widely held misperceptions about EEOC's responsibilities and procedures in charge investigation. One of the purposes of this chapter is to address these misperceptions. First, however, an overview of the Commission's procedures in the areas that are the subject of this book may be helpful.

The EEOC handles many types of charges that are brought under several laws. These charges include sexual harassment, mandatory retirement or dismissal because of age, unequal pay to men and women for the same work, refusal to accommodate individuals with disabilities, and intentional discriminatory treatment of individuals because of their race, sex, or ethnic group. This section addresses the handling of charges that arise from the personnel selection and promotion practices, including tests, that appear neutral on their face but may impact adversely the employment opportunities of members of one or more of these groups. These charges often involve complex issues that may be confusing for laypersons. For example, a woman applies for a physically demanding factory job that she has reason to believe she can handle and is given a physical abilities test that, although not replicating actual job tasks, is purported to measure the strength required on the job. She is told that she will not be hired because she failed the test. Another example might involve an applicant for a job who grew up speaking a different language and is rejected because of a low score on a mental abilities test that includes questions about the meaning of words or paragraphs, basic information about U.S. history and culture, and complex word problems measuring mathematical reasoning. These questions do not appear to be relevant to the specific job in question. Still another example might involve an applicant for an entry-level police job who is given a personality test that includes questions about life experiences, preferences, and habits designed to provide information about psychological disorders that are not obviously relevant to the work of a police officer.

The test or selection procedure in each of these situations appears to be more related to the applicant's gender, ethnic background, or psychological impairment than to the applicant's ability to perform the tasks required on the job; in fact, its use may be discriminatory, or it may be supported by evidence of validity that would be obtained and evaluated during the process of charge investigation.

The process typically begins when an aggrieved individual, or Charging Party, files a charge at one of the EEOC's district, area, or local offices. Occasionally, the charge is filed by an EEOC Commissioner as part of an investigation of a systemic pattern or practice of discrimination. In either case, the first step is to determine if the selection procedure has resulted in adverse impact against a race, sex, or ethnic group. This determination usually is made by an investigator at the district, area, or local office and requires the following information:

what the selection procedure is;

how it is used (e.g., to rank applicants or as a pass-fail screening mechanism with a specific cutoff);

the number of applicants from each race, sex, or ethnic group;

the number of applicants from each group who have been administered the selection procedure;

the number of applicants from each group who passed the selection procedure; and

the number of applicants from each group who are selected for the job in question.

The investigator obtains this information from the employer, or Respondent, and analyzes the data to determine for adverse impact in accordance with the type of charge. The impact standards contained in the Uniform Guidelines on Employee Selection Procedures (1978, hereafter Uniform Guidelines), which may include the "80 percent rule of thumb" and tests of statistical significance, are applicable to Title VII charges. Although these standards do not apply to the Americans with Disabilities Act (ADA) charges, tests of statistical significance may still be used appropriately.

If adverse impact is not found and there is no reason to suspect intentional discrimination or discriminatory treatment, the investigation stops at this point, and the District Director issues a letter of determination finding that there is no reasonable cause to believe that the Respondent's selection procedures have been discriminatory. If, however, adverse impact is found, the Respondent is asked for evidence that the selection procedure is job related. This evidence typically takes the form of a validation report, which contains data demonstrating the relationship between scores on the selection procedure and job behaviors. The validation report usually is referred to a psychologist in EEOC headquarters for review; in some cases, the report may be reviewed by a consultant working for a field office.

The technical standards that are used during this review for Title VII and ADA charges (when a test is claimed to be a reasonable factor other than age) are those of the Uniform Guidelines (1978). These Uniform Guidelines have been in use without modification since 1978 and represent the uniform position of the federal agencies as to what evidence will be required to support the use of a selection procedure. The Uniform Guidelines superseded earlier guidelines, issued in 1966 and 1970, which incorporated by reference the professional testing standards published by the American Psychological Association. The *Standards for Educational and Psychological Testing* (1985) were widely regarded as a set of ideal goals that were rarely, if ever, completely met in practice. Consequently, the EEOC guidelines that incorporated these standards also were perceived as so idealistic that employers using selection procedures that resulted in adverse impact were always in a state of noncompliance.

The technical standards of the Uniform Guidelines (1978), although intended to be consistent with generally accepted professional standards, were designed to reflect only those standards that were consensually regarded as minimally acceptable professional requirements for validity. This had the advantage of letting employers know in advance of a charge exactly what standards had to be met if validity became an issue. On the other hand, many highly desirable professional standards were not included in the Uniform Guidelines. For example, reliability is considered an important characteristic of tests, and the *Standards for Educational and Psychological Testing* devote a whole chapter to this topic. The Uniform Guidelines, although noting the desirability of reliability estimates, do not require evidence of test reliability for criterion-related validity studies, because low reliability works against the interests of the employer by limiting the size of criterion-related validity coefficients that can be obtained. If, however, validity coefficients are corrected for unreliability, it is particularly important that these adjustments are accurate and that low reliability coefficients are not used to inflate insignificant validities to the level of statistical significance.

If the validity evidence satisfies the requirements of the Uniform Guidelines (1978) and there is no evidence of another selection procedure that has substantially equal or greater validity and would result in less adverse impact, a no cause determination is issued, despite the adverse impact. If·the validity evidence does not satisfy these requirements, however, the District Director issues a letter of determination finding that there is cause to believe that the use of the selection procedures in question has resulted in discrimination. The Commission then attempts to resolve the charge through conciliation and negotiation of an agreement that provides appropriate remedies to affected applicants or employees and permits the employer to correct deficiencies in the selection or validation process. Appropriate remedies must be negotiated on a case-by-case basis. In some situations, a selection procedure clearly may not be a valid predictor of job performance and must be eliminated, revised, or lawfully used in a way so as to not result in adverse impact. In other situations, when a selection procedure probably is valid but the validity evidence does not completely satisfy the requirements of the Uniform Guidelines, use of the selection procedure on an interim basis while additional validity studies are in progress may be appropriate.

Settlement agreements that require the validation of new, revised, or existing selection procedures may provide for the review of validation strategies or validity evidence by the Commission prior to the operational use of these procedures. In these cases, an EEOC psychologist generally will provide comments on the design and results of the validity study, even if there are no new charges or evidence of adverse impact. These comments generally do not constitute prior approval of the procedures in question, unless the agreement requires EEOC approval before implementation. They do, however, provide a means to communicate concerns and resolve problems on a relatively informal basis, rather than in court.

If the issues cannot be resolved and an agreement is not negotiated and the Respondent is a private employer, the Commission may file a lawsuit on behalf of the charging parties or the affected class, and a Commission psychologist may be called on to testify. This action, however, requires the approval of the majority of the Commission and is taken only in a minority of testing charges. Only 10 of the 75 validation reports sent to an EEOC psychologist — after a finding of adverse impact — from August 1984 to March 1992 resulted in EEOC litigation. Even if the Commission does not file a lawsuit, however, the charging parties have the right to retain private attorneys and sue. It is highly important, therefore, that the positions taken by the Commission and its psychologists be defensible and consistent with applicable law and, to the extent possible, generally accepted professional standards.

Misperceptions

The role of EEOC and its psychologists in promoting the nondiscriminatory use of tests has been the subject of critical comment in published books, journals, and newspapers. Much of the critical comment is, as stated previously, based on misperceptions of the Commission's position. It is appropriate at this time to address some of these misperceptions.

The Uniform Guidelines and Affirmative Action

One prevalent misperception is that the Commission's policy on testing and its use of the Uniform Guidelines (1978) is nothing more than a mechanism to achieve affirmative action goals of proportional representation in the work force. The Commission is perceived as attempting to accomplish these goals by targeting employers who are underutilizing minority and female group members (i.e., do not have the right numbers) in their work force and requiring those employers to either correct the underutilization through quota hiring or produce validation studies that meet impossible technical standards. Because no validation study could satisfy these standards, employers are forced to adopt quotas that will eliminate the underutilization of women and minorities.

This perception is not accurate. In fact, the Uniform Guidelines (1978) have only a tangential relationship to affirmative action. The Uniform Guidelines' validation requirements are triggered by adverse impact in the selection process, not by underutilization of minorities or women. The adverse impact trigger applies to all race, sex, and ethnic groups. There have been situations (sometimes called "reverse discrimination" charges) in which adverse impact and discrimination against an overutilized group has been found. The Uniform Guidelines do include provisions that permit an agency to consider an employer's general posture with respect to affirmative action in carrying out its responsibilities, as well as statements encouraging lawful affirmative action programs where underutilization exists, but these provisions are used primarily by agencies that have the right to enforce affirmative action obligations, such as those that are derived from contractual agreements with federal contractors.

The validation requirements of the Uniform Guidelines (1978) are intended to be consistent with generally accepted professional standards with respect to validity evidence. These validation requirements have, in fact, been met in numerous charges, and the EEOC psychologists who reviewed the reports have so stated. The confidentiality provisions of Title VII prohibit disclosure of these charges or the tests involved by the Commission, but a survey of the Commission files several years ago indicated that about 75 percent of the validity studies meet the requirements of the Uniform Guidelines, either in whole or in part. It should be kept in mind, however, that charging parties have the right to file a lawsuit even if the Commission finds that a validation study meets the standards of the Uniform Guidelines. Such a situation occurred with respect to the Wonderlic Personnel Test. The Commission and the courts had found over the years that the validity evidence supporting the use of this test did not meet applicable guidelines and generally accepted professional standards. In one case (*Cormier v. PPG Industries, Inc.*), an employer conducted a criterion-related validity study that did meet guidelines requirements for a specific job group, and the Commission so found. A private lawsuit was filed, however, and, after a hearing in which evidence of the conclusions of the EEOC psychologist was introduced, the use of the test was found to be nondiscriminatory.

It should not be assumed that the Commission does not advocate and support lawful affirmative action programs, such as job redesign and outreach recruitment, that could provide more equitable representation of race, sex, and ethnic groups in the work force. Indeed, the Commission does support these programs as mechanisms to achieve the goal of equal employment opportunity. Nevertheless, the mere existence of under-utilization does not, by itself, mean that the use of a selection procedure has resulted in adverse impact or that the selection procedure is not valid. It would be foolhardy, in light of the well-established case law and the right of employers as well as charging parties to seek judicial review of Commission actions, for the Commission or its psychologists to base decisions on any other premise.

The Uniform Guidelines and Group Ability Differences

It long has been recognized that certain groups perform differently on certain tests. Specifically, the average scores of black and Hispanic examinees typically are lower than the average score of white examinees on tests that measure cognitive ability. It has been hypothesized more recently that cognitive ability tests are valid for all jobs and that the differences in average test scores reflect real differences in job perfor-mance. This would mean that adverse impact can be expected to result from the use of valid tests. These two observations have led to mutually inconsistent misperceptions about the Commission's testing policy and the Uniform Guidelines. One misperception is that the Uniform Guide-lines ignore the possibility that differences in test scores may reflect real differences in job performance and are, therefore, inconsistent with professional knowledge. The other misperception is that the Uniform Guidelines are based on the assumption that minority applicants are less competent than nonminority applicants and, therefore, need protection from the impact resulting from valid tests.

In fact, the Uniform Guidelines are based on the need for empirical evidence, not on any assumptions regarding validity and underlying ability distributions. If the use of a test results in adverse impact in the applicant pool (which may or may not reflect differences in the general population or relevant labor market), validity evidence is required. If the data are not there or not sufficient, mere assumptions of validity will not be sufficient to support the use of that selection procedure. If sufficient validity evidence is available, the test can be used notwithstanding its adverse impact, because members of any group who pass the test are more likely to perform well on the job than members of any group who do not pass the test.

OTHER FEDERAL AGENCIES

The major emphasis of this section is the role of the EEOC in the identification and elimination of discriminatory testing practices. Other agencies also have responsibilities in this area and also have adopted the Uniform Guidelines in this endeavor.

The Office of Federal Contract Compliance Programs in the Department of Labor has the responsibility for enforcing Executive Order 11246, as amended, with regard to federal contractors and subcontractors. This Order requires those contractors to agree, prior to accepting a government contract, to use nondiscriminatory selection procedures and to provide affirmative action to remedy underutilization. The standards used to determine whether selection procedures are discriminatory are the same Uniform Guidelines (1978) that are used by EEOC. The major difference is that discriminatory practices typically are identified in the course of contract compliance reviews, rather than through the investigation of charges of discrimination. In addition, the Office of Federal Contract Compliance Programs can require, based on contractual obligations, the establishment of affirmative action plans that are designed to provide employment opportunities to members of underutilized groups even if the selection procedures do not result in adverse impact or are validated in accordance with the Uniform Guidelines.

Title VII charges brought against state and local governments that are filed with EEOC are investigated in the same way as charges that are brought against private employers. If a reasonable cause determination is made and the issues are not conciliated, however, the charge may be referred to the Civil Rights Division of the Department of Justice for further investigation and possible litigation. The Department of Justice also has adopted the Uniform Guidelines (1978) as the basis for determining whether the use of selection procedures by a state or local government is discriminatory. Therefore, although the investigation by the Department of Justice generally is independent of the review by the EEOC, the same standards are used.

Federal employees or applicants for federal employment file charges or complaints alleging discriminatory use of selection procedures with the agencies involved. Agency decisions may be appealed to the EEOC or, in some cases, the Merit Systems Protection Board, which has assumed the regulatory functions formerly performed by the Civil Service Commission (now the Office of Personnel Management). The Civil Service Commission had adopted the Uniform Guidelines (1978) as a supplement to the Federal Personnel Manual governing its examination functions as well as those of the other federal agencies. The EEOC has continued to use these guidelines, where applicable, in charges brought against federal agencies as well as charges brought against private employers.

The Office of Revenue Sharing in the Treasury Department had responsibility for complaints against state and local governments that receive funds under the Revenue Sharing Act and also adopted the Uniform Guidelines (1978) as the standards for determining whether the use of selection procedures by employers covered under this act is discriminatory. The Revenue Sharing Act, however, was repealed in 1986, and the Office of Revenue Sharing now refers all complaints against employers who are still using funds previously provided under this act to the Department of Justice.

REFERENCES

Age Discrimination in Employment Act of 1967 (Pub.L. 90–202) (ADEA), as amended, 29 U.S.C. 621 *et. seq.*

Americans with Disabilities Act of 1990 (Pub.L. 101–336) (ADA), as amended, 42 U.S.C. 12101 *et. seq.*

Cormier v. PPG Industries, Inc., DC La, 519 F.Supp. 211, aff 702 F.2d. 567.

Executive Order 11246, as amended, 30 FR 12319; 32 FR 14303.

Standards for educational and psychological testing. (1985). Washington, DC: American Psychological Association.

Uniform guidelines on employee selection procedures, 29 C.F.R. 1607 (1978).

27

Interpreting the Ban on Minority Group Score Adjustment in Preemployment Testing

Paul R. Sackett

In the early 1980s, the United States Employment Service began making increased use of the General Aptitude Test Battery (GATB) in referring job seekers to potential employers. Because black and Hispanic GATB mean scores are lower than white mean scores, the United States Employment Service converted GATB scores to percentile scores within racial and ethnic groups and referred candidates to prospective employers on the basis of these within-group percentile scores. Thus, the same raw score would be converted to a markedly different percentile score if the examinee was white, black, or Hispanic. The result was that candidates from various groups were referred to employers at comparable rates: an employer requesting candidates scoring at or above the eightieth percentile would receive a list made up of the white, black, and Hispanic applicant pool members scoring above the eightieth percentile within their own group.

This practice of within-group norming was challenged by the U.S. Department of Justice in 1986 as unfair to white candidates. A National Academy of Sciences committee appointed to study the issue produced a book-length report (Hartigan & Wigdor, 1989) supporting referral based on normed scores. However, as public attention was drawn to the issue, there was a strong outcry against the practice, leading to a provision in the Civil Rights Act of 1991 prohibiting within-group norming. The act stated that it would be an unlawful practice for an employer "in connection with the selection or referral of applicants or candidates for employment or promotion to adjust the scores of, use different cutoffs for, or otherwise alter the results of employment related tests on the basis of race, color, religion, sex, or national origin" (42 U.S.C. 1981, Section 106).

The goal of this chapter is to review various findings from the psychological literature and discuss their implications for various possible interpretations of Section 106's ban on score adjustment. The chapter draws heavily on a detailed treatment of these issues by Sackett and Wilk (1994).

THE NATURE AND MEANING OF SUBGROUP DIFFERENCES

Substantial group differences are found on a variety of measures commonly used as bases for personnel decisions. Discussion of group differences on various tests can lead to confusion, because such statements as "there is a mean black-white difference of 15 points on test X, but only a 3 point difference on test Y" are meaningful only if the scale of measurement is comparable for the two tests (more specifically, if both tests have the same standard deviation). Thus, it is useful to convert raw score differences to standardized difference scores, which is done by taking the majority group mean, subtracting the minority group mean, and dividing by the pooled within-group standard deviation. This standardized difference commonly is referred to as "d." Two groups with a majority group mean 2 points above a minority group mean, and a standard deviation of 4 would, in this metric, differ by 0.5 standard deviation units; two groups with a majority group mean 10 points above the minority group mean, and a standard deviation of 10 would differ by 1.0 standard deviation units. If the minority group mean is higher than the majority group mean, d would have a negative value.

In order to give a sense of the practical implications of d values of a given magnitude, Table 27.1 presents the effects of group differences of varying magnitudes on the rates at which members of the groups would be hired. To aid in understanding the implications of the table, I note here some typical group differences. First, the male-female d on measures of the personality characteristic of "dominance" is typically about 0.5. Second, the white-black d on measures of general cognitive ability is typically about 1.0. Third, the male-female d on measures of muscular endurance is typically about 1.5.

For each of three prototypic selection strategies (high, moderate, and low selection ratios), the table presents the selection ratio for a minority group differing from the majority group by the specified d value. In other words, the table shows that, if the chosen test cutoff results in a majority group selection ratio of 10 percent, the minority group selection ratio will be 8.4 percent if d is 0.1 (i.e., if the two groups differ by 0.1 standard deviation units).

TABLE 27.1
Minority Group Selection Ratio when Cutoff for the
Majority Group is Set at 10, 50, and 90 Percent

Standardized Group	Majority Group Selection Ratio		
Difference (d)	10%	50%	90%
0.0	0.100	0.500	0.900
0.1	0.084	0.460	0.881
0.2	0.070	0.421	0.860
0.3	0.057	0.382	0.836
0.4	0.046	0.345	0.811
0.5	0.038	0.309	0.782
0.6	0.030	0.274	0.752
0.7	0.024	0.242	0.719
0.8	0.019	0.212	0.684
0.9	0.015	0.184	0.648
1.0	0.013	0.159	0.610
1.1	0.009	0.136	0.571
1.2	0.007	0.115	0.532
1.3	0.005	0.097	0.492
1.4	0.004	0.081	0.452
1.5	0.003	0.070	0.413

Source: Compiled by the author.

One clear pattern is that the effects of group differences are greater as the firm becomes more selective. For example, consider the effects of a test with a 1.0 standard deviation mean group difference. With a majority group selection ratio of 10 percent, the minority group selection ratio is 1.3 percent, 13 percent as large as the majority group selection ratio. With a majority group selection ratio of 50 percent, the minority group selection ratio is 15.9 percent, 32 percent as large as the majority group selection ratio. Finally, with a majority group selection ratio of 90 percent, the minority group selection ratio is 61.0 percent, 68 percent as large as the majority group selection ratio. Thus, it is clear that the degree of adverse impact produced by a test with a given d is lessened by the employer becoming less selective and lowering the cutoff score. However, doing so can dramatically reduce the value to the organization of using the test.

What Table 27.1 and the above discussion illustrate is that group differences on employment tests can have dramatic effects on the rates of selection from different groups. If the differences are because of biased measurement of the characteristic in question, there is clear need for some action to deal with the problem, perhaps involving some form of score adjustment and perhaps involving revision or replacement of the selection device. If the differences are not because of bias but, rather, reflect real group differences in the characteristic being measured and if the selection device is, in fact, related to job performance, then the employer faces the dilemma of wanting to achieve productivity gains through the use of the selection device but, at the same time, wanting to reduce or eliminate adverse impact against members of any group. It is this dilemma that drives many of the discussions of score adjustment as employers seek ways of balancing these competing goals.

ARE GROUP DIFFERENCES BECAUSE OF BIAS?

A well-accepted mechanism exists for determining whether group differences are real or are the result of bias, namely, the use of a model of predictive bias to compare test scores and measures of job performance across groups. The critical insight is that, if group differences are the result of bias, then a given test score would be linked to differing levels of performance for different groups. For example, if a ten-point mean difference on a test was, in fact, because of bias against a particular minority group, then minority group members should exhibit a higher level of job performance than majority group members with the same test score.

In domains where this model of predictive bias has been applied, such as cognitive and physical ability testing, the data do not support the position that group differences are the result of bias. This argues against continued insistence that group differences reflect nothing but test flaws. Note that this also is not a blanket acceptance of all group differences as real. For some types of selection devices, there is little or no research that applies the regression model, and there is no doubt that, within any area of testing, bad tests can be created through ignorance or through malice.

DIFFERENTIATING BETWEEN BIAS AND UNFAIRNESS

It is important to differentiate between the concepts of predictive bias as a technical characteristic of the use of a particular test in a particular setting and selection system fairness as a value judgment as to the appropriateness of a method of test use or a pattern of test outcomes. For example, one possible value judgment is that a selection system that produces a larger group difference (and, thus, a lower rate of minority hiring) than the group difference in job performance is unfair. For example, if an employer were to hire solely on the basis of cognitive ability, the employer would be choosing to focus on an applicant characteristic on which black-white differences are exceptionally large. The problem is not that the ability test is biased as a measure of cognitive ability but that the choice to rely solely on a characteristic on which blacks fare particularly badly, in comparison with other job-related characteristics, is unfair. That the ability test is job related and that ability tests can be part of the selection system is not under dispute. The issue is over-reliance on a selection device with a larger group difference than is found in job performance.

There is agreement within the psychological testing community regarding the assessment of predictive bias. There is no agreement as to the issue of fairness. The position on fairness articulated above requires a number of value judgments, such as whether increased minority employment per se is a goal to seek, and is but one of a number of value-based positions.

THE DIVERSITY-PRODUCTIVITY TRADE-OFF

The fact that many employers truly value both diversity and productivity needs to be faced head on. If a valid selection device has adverse impact, an employer using that selection device cannot simultaneously maximize both productivity and minority hiring. To assert that the two are not in conflict is to deny meaningful group differences, or at least to misunderstand and underestimate the impact of group differences. Approaches like within-group norming are attempts at compromise: *if* an employer values both diversity and productivity, then top-down selection within group achieves the diversity goal at the least possible harm to the productivity goal that would be maximized by strict top-down selection.

The act cannot prevent employers who value diversity from devising selection systems that will produce this result. The act may force employers to use less efficient selection systems to achieve diversity. Employers may eliminate valid predictors if they have adverse impact. They may "bury" predictors with adverse impact by using them in such a way that they have a negligible effect on selection decisions (such as setting a cutoff so low that virtually all applicants pass). They may use less reliable selection systems, as group differences are reduced by increasing the error variance in a test. They may have decision makers subjectively combine test scores and interview data, adding flexibility to the interpretation of test scores. In short, the act may force employers with a diversity goal to turn to selection systems that make a lower contribution to productivity.

SCORE ADJUSTMENT AND OTHER
GROUP-CONSCIOUS METHODS OF TEST USE

There are a variety of different ways of using tests that take group membership into account. Some of these directly involve score adjustment, such as the conversion of raw scores to within-group percentiles; others, such as banding, do not. The goal here is to facilitate an understanding of the similarities and differences between approaches.

Bonus Points

The most direct form of score adjustment involves adding a constant number of points to the scores of all individuals who are members of a particular group. Veteran's preference in application for civil service jobs typically is pointed to as an example of this practice. Thus, if there is a ten-point mean difference between men and women on a particular test, the mean difference could be eliminated by adding ten points to the score of all members of the lower scoring group.

Within-group Norming

Within-group norming involves converting individual scores to either standard scores or percentile scores within one's group. To use a physical ability test as a concrete example, being able to do 20 push-ups would put a woman at the seventieth percentile compared with female norms and would put a man at the thirtieth percentile compared with male norms. Despite identical performance on the physical ability test, the two candidates would receive different scores. Similarly, a man would need to do 44 push-ups to be at the seventieth percentile compared with male norms; thus, a man doing 44 push-ups and a woman doing 20 push-ups both would receive a within-group score of 70: both are at the seventieth percentile relative to their group.

At times, within-group norming may be undertaken as a pragmatic approach to eliminating adverse impact. In some domains, though, the rationale is that a given score has a markedly different psychological meaning in one group than in another and, thus, that the appropriate score for meaningful interpretation is one's standing within the group. The masculinity-femininity scale of the California Psychological Inventory illustrates this perspective: men and women respond in markedly different ways, and, therefore, the test developers' perspective was that the only meaningful way to interpret a score was in terms of one's standing within one's gender group.

Separate Cutoffs

The use of separate cutoffs for different groups is, in practice, identical to the bonus point approach: setting a cutoff five points lower for one group produces the same outcome as adding five points to the scores of members of that group. One at least symbolic difference is that the separate cutoff approach makes very clear what is being done: a lower standard is being used for one group than for another. If test scores are computed by the human resource department and made available to the hiring manager, it is not uncommon to find that, when score adjustment is used and adjusted scores are reported, the hiring manager is not aware that adjustment has taken place. With separate cutoffs, there is no ambiguity about the meaning of test scores.

Top-down Selection from Separate Lists

This approach involves ranking candidates separately within groups and then selecting from the top down from within each group in accordance with some preset rule as to the number of openings that will be allotted to each group. In many cases, this approach will be the equivalent of within-group norming and also equivalent to a bonus point approach. It also can be conceptualized as equivalent to the use of separate cutoffs, with the cutoff for each group being the score at which top-down selection fills the number of vacancies allotted to the group.

Banding

Banding refers to a set of approaches to test use in which individuals within a specific score range, or band, are regarded as having equivalent scores. A simple illustration of banding would be the situation in which all individuals with raw scores between 91 and 100 on a 100-item test would be assigned to Band 1, all between 81 and 90 to Band 2, all between 71 and 80 to Band 3, and so on. All individuals in Band 1 would be selected before turning to candidates in Band 2, but within Band 1, selection would not be in order of raw test scores: all within the band are seen as equivalent on the construct of interest. Order of selection of candidates within a band either would be random or would be on the basis of some additional selection criterion.

Banding discounts small differences between test scores and treats all scores within a specified range as essentially tied. Individuals within a band then can be selected randomly or on the basis of some additional characteristic, which could include minority group status. It is important to note that a variety of different approaches to banding exist. One crucial observation is that only when minority preference within a band is included as a feature of the banding approach does banding have the potential to markedly reduce group differences in selection rates. A second crucial observation is that an approach, recently articulated in the psychological literature, referred to as sliding bands with minority preference can be shown to be equivalent in outcome to adding a constant number of points to minority group members' scores. Thus, this banding approach can be seen as a way of achieving the results of score adjustment without the formal altering of scores.

Banding is another example of an approach to selection system fairness: it represents an espoused value-based position as to how test scores should be used to make personnel decisions. The position that a lower scoring minority group member should be preferred over a higher scoring majority group member unless the scores of the two candidates are significantly different at a 95 percent level of confidence is a value judgment.

The approaches to test scoring considered in the above paragraphs involve taking group membership into account *after* a test score is obtained. Other approaches take group membership into account in the test development process. These include the elimination of test items based on their performance in item tryout and the development of separate scoring keys for different groups. Taking group membership into account in item tryout is necessary in order to identify differentially performing items. Separate scoring keys for different groups are appropriate if it can be shown that differential keying produces higher levels of validity. The key is that the motivation for taking group membership into account is increased quality of the resulting selection devices.

Adding points to minority group members' scores, within-group norming, top-down selection from separate lists, setting differential cutoffs, and banding approaches that involve minority preference prove to be functionally equivalent in many circumstances. This relationship of banding and score adjustment does not seem to be recognized commonly. The permissibility of banding under the Civil Rights Act of 1991 is an issue yet to be fully resolved.

INTERPRETING SECTION 106 OF THE CIVIL RIGHTS ACT OF 1991

This chapter now turns to a consideration of the interpretation of Section 106 of the Civil Rights Act of 1991 in light of the above issues. It will pose and then address a series of questions about the interpretation of the act.

Should the Act Prohibit Any Approach to Test Use That Takes Group Membership into Account in Any Way?

This interpretation would require that any individuals responding in the same way on a test should receive the same test scores regardless of group membership and should have the same employment decision made about them regardless of group membership. Such a position can interfere with psychologists' goals of developing valid selection devices that lack predictive bias against protected groups. As noted above, taking group membership into account would be necessary should a given test be shown to exhibit some form of predictive bias, namely, a finding that performance is underpredicted for a particular group. Also as noted above, taking group membership into account would be necessary should research demonstrate that the development of separate scoring keys for different groups is needed to produce comparable levels of validity for the groups under consideration. This leads to a recommended interpretation of the act: "Section 106 of the Civil Rights Act of 1991 should be interpreted as prohibiting after-the-fact score adjustments undertaken solely to reduce or eliminate adverse impact. Taking group membership into account is permitted if doing so can be shown to increase accuracy of measurement or accuracy of prediction without increasing the adverse impact of the test." The act prohibits score adjustment "on the basis of race, color, religion, sex, or national origin." This could be interpreted as prohibiting adjustments done solely for purposes of reducing adverse impact against protected groups. Adjustments made to alleviate predictive bias and the development of different scoring keys by group are approaches that use group membership information in order to increase the accuracy of prediction of performance, not simply to alleviate adverse impact.

Should Banding Be a Permissible Approach under the Act?

Note that only banding approaches that take group membership into account come under scrutiny because of the act. A banding approach that uses random selection within a band, for example, does not take group membership into account. It also typically does not produce the gains in minority group selection that are obtained with approaches to banding that do incorporate minority preference. Banding approaches that give minority preference within a band often prove equivalent to approaches that are expressly prohibited by the act, such as the use of separate cutoffs. Given this equivalence, arguments for banding with minority preference must rest on arguments that banding procedures neither explicitly adjust scores nor explicitly use different cutoffs and, thus, do not violate the act.

Banding is premised on the observation that a test score difference between two people does not guarantee that the higher scoring individual truly possesses more of the characteristic being measured, given the less than perfect reliability of tests. There is considerable merit in the notion that small differences between candidates should not be overinterpreted; at that level, there is some appeal to banding. However, the notion that score differences should be ignored unless the scores differ significantly from one another is not a principle of test use that generally is held. At the level of the individual, there is the possibility that two individuals with cognitive ability test scores differing by, say, one standard deviation unit do not really differ in cognitive ability. However, in the aggregate, there is no doubt that the average level of cognitive ability among individuals scoring one standard deviation apart is markedly different. Thus, banding with minority preference cannot be viewed as mandated by psychometric theory. It represents a value judgment as to what constitutes fair test use, namely, ignoring score differences between majority and minority group members unless significantly different from one another, while, at the same time, treating nonsignificant differences within a group as meaningful. Decisions as to whether it should be permitted cannot, then, be driven by the requirements of psychometric theory but, rather, by issues outside the scope of psychological research. Descriptively, the approach does balance the competing goals of diversity and productivity. Arguments that banding with minority preference is not prohibited by the act may be very attractive to those who value such a balance.

Should Section 106 Apply Only to
Cognitive Ability Tests or to All Tests?

The issues are identical regardless of the type of test involved. There is no technical reason to apply the act to one type of test and not to another. However, to the extent that the act was passed without full information about its consequences, one can argue for as narrow an interpretation as possible.

Consider the following scenario: a firm valuing both diversity and productivity wishes to fill a job with a substantial physical strength component; a strength test has been developed and validated, showing a comparable linear relationship between strength and performance for both men and women; and the strength test has adverse impact by gender, and the adverse impact is "real" in that lower strength translates to lower performance. The firm cannot achieve its diversity goal without dropping the test and ignoring the physical demands of the job; setting a cutoff low enough that enough women pass to meet the diversity goal, thus, losing the productivity gains available through top-down selection of male applicants; or using some form of scoring adjustment, such as converting scores to within-group percentiles and then selecting top down, adding a caveat that no one scoring below some established minimum threshold be selected.

Note that all three of these approaches are similar, if not identical, in terms of the number of positions eventually filled by men and by women: all are comparable in achieving diversity. However, the approaches that do not involve score adjustment result in lower levels of productivity. This finding will obtain whenever the selection device under consideration both is a valid predictor of performance and has adverse impact against a protected group. Thus, the act will not thwart a firm seeking to meet a diversity goal; it will simply result in the firm accepting a larger productivity loss to attain this goal than would be the case if score adjustment were permitted.

Thus, a broad interpretation of the act may prohibit psychologists from using tests in a manner that balances these competing goals. If the goals are seen as legitimate and if one accepts that tests can both be valid and have adverse impact, then one concludes that Section 106 of the Civil Rights Act of 1991 is not an effective mechanism for regulating personnel selection and that the act should be interpreted as narrowly as possible.

REFERENCES

Civil Rights Act of 1991 (Pub.L. 102-166) (CRA).
Hartigan, J. A., & Wigdor, A. K. (Eds.). (1989). *Fairness in employment testing: Validity generalization, minority issues, and the General Aptitude Test Battery.* Washington, DC: National Academy Press.
Sackett, P. R., & Wilk, S. L. (1994). Within-group norming and other forms of score adjustment in preemployment testing. *American Psychologist, 49,* 929–954.

VIII

COMPLIANCE WITH TITLE VII AND RELATED LAWS

28

Related Federal Acts: Americans with Disabilities Act and Age Discrimination in Employment Act

Richard S. Barrett

Two laws that followed on the Civil Rights Act of 1964 bear sufficiently close relation to it to be included in this volume. They are the Americans with Disabilities Act (ADA) (1990) and the Age Discrimination in Employment Act of 1967 (ADEA).

ADEA protects workers aged 40 years or older from discrimination in employment. Section 4(f)(1) of the act provides that, "it shall not be unlawful for an employer . . . to take any action otherwise prohibited where the differentiation is based on reasonable factors other than age." The ADEA also states that business necessity of a testing procedure that has an adverse impact against older employees or applicants will be scrutinized in accordance with the Standards set forth in the Uniform Guidelines on Employee Selection Procedures (1978).

The ADA provides protection in employment for those with disabilities who can perform the duties of their positions satisfactorily, with or without reasonable accommodation. Employers are not required to accept substandard performance, but they are required to make modifications in the duty assignments, equipment, and architectural features to accommodate those who are impaired mentally or physically. If there are two qualified applicants, one with a disability and one without, the employer may select the more qualified, regardless of the disability. Employers are not required to lower safety standards to hire the disabled.

Because most of you are familiar with Title VII of the Civil Rights Act of 1964 and the Uniform Guidelines (1978), much of the treatment of the ADA is presented in contrast with Title VII.

DISABILITY

A disability is a relatively permanent physical or mental impairment that substantially limits one or more major life activities. A person with a temporary condition, such as a broken leg or pregnancy, is not protected, but an applicant with a record of past impairment, for example, alcoholism, is covered. Being considered impaired, even if one is not, also is covered; thus, a person known to be an epileptic whose condition is controlled medically is protected from discrimination. Dyslexia and learning disabilities are covered; mental retardation is not. Not covered are compulsive gambling, pederasty, current use of drugs, kleptomania, and similar antisocial behaviors.

A person associated with an individual with disabilities has some rights as well. For example, it is contrary to the law to refuse to hire an otherwise qualified applicant whose spouse may require his or her presence at treatment during working hours.

QUALIFIED INDIVIDUALS WITH A DISABILITY

The law protects only qualified individuals. Applicants who have the skill, experience, and education required by the job are qualified if they are able to perform adequately, with or without reasonable accommodation. Reasonable accommodation includes a modified work schedule, devices that accommodate the disability, and assigning marginal duties to another employee. An employer is relieved of the responsibility to make accommodations that demand undue hardship, for example, changes that are unduly costly or extensive.

POSITION DESCRIPTION

The report of the work duties differs from that required by the Uniform Guidelines (1978) in several respects. The description is confined to a single position, that is, the duties of a single individual, not of the members of a job category. If one manager likes to type his own letters but all others require their secretaries to type, an applicant whose disability prevents typing may be qualified.

The Uniform Guidelines (1978) are concerned with the duties performed by the incumbent; ADA requires that the position be described in terms of outcomes. If a conventional job description would say, "Carries tray of parts weighing 50 pounds to next work station," ADA would require that the description be rewritten to say, for example, "Transports parts weighing 2 pounds each to next work station," opening the door to changes in work methods, such as loading the trays with fewer parts, rolling the trays on a cart, or having the next operator in line pick up the parts.

The ADA uses classifications of "essential" and "marginal" that differ from the requirement in the Uniform Guidelines (1978) that the job description specify the importance and complexity of the duties. There is no clear rule for determining whether a duty is essential or marginal. A duty may be considered essential if the position exists to perform that function, if the consequences when the duty is not performed are severe, if only a few can perform the function, or if it requires a high degree of skill. An applicant who cannot perform an essential function may be rejected on that ground alone.

IDENTIFICATION OF INDIVIDUALS WITH DISABILITIES

The identification of an individual with a disability is touchy, because the privacy of the applicant must be protected. If the disability is visible, such as severe visual impairment or the loss of use of a limb, the employer is expected to act on the basis of the observation. Otherwise, the employer must ask very circumscribed questions. It is best to start with the application blank so that there is a record for all applicants' responses to inquiries if there are any reasons why they cannot perform the selection procedures for the positions they are seeking. Applicants who do not mention any impediments can be treated like other applicants.

INTERVIEW

Once it has been established that the applicant has a disability, an interview that follows sound professional procedures probably is acceptable. The interviewer may describe the selection procedure and job requirements and use the information to explore with the applicant the accommodations needed to perform the activities required by the selection procedures and the position.

The interview should be based on an exploration of relevant activities, either on previous positions or on related nonjob activities. Of course, there should be no questions asking directly about the applicant's disability or medical history.

SELECTION TESTING

Any selection procedure may be used if the results are not affected by the disability. If a test must be modified to be used, the results must be tempered by judgment. There is no way to interpret modified tests by making statistical adjustments to the existing norm tables. The safest procedure is to avoid any selection procedure whose results may be adversely affected by the disability. The Office of Personnel Management has prepared *Guide for Administering Written Employment Examinations to Persons with Disabilities* (Eyde, 1994).

REASONABLE ACCOMMODATION

The employment decision should take into account the changes that might make it possible for the applicant to perform adequately. Reasonable accommodations include redesigning the job, modifying testing procedures, or arranging flexible working hours.

MEDICAL EXAMINATION

If the applicant is judged to be qualified, that is, to be able to do the work with reasonable accommodations, a job offer may be made contingent on the results of a medical examination, which should be the same for all applicants.

PSYCHOLOGICAL TESTS

Some psychological tests are used like other predictive instruments and may be administered when other tests are administered. Some are used to identify pathology, are classified as medical tests, and can be administered only under the conditions described above. Some tests, such as the Minnesota Multiphasic Psychological Inventory, may be used for either purpose. The determination of the category into which a given test falls is decided by an Equal Employment Opportunity Commission investigator on a case-by-case analysis.

ADVERSE IMPACT AND AFFIRMATIVE ACTION

Unlike Title VII, there is no consideration of adverse impact under ADA, nor is there any requirement for affirmative action. There is no requirement that the employer seek out disabled workers. Because it is inappropriate to advertise for disabled workers, the best source of disabled applicants is local organizations that advance the interest of the disabled.

SUMMARY

The ADA treads a fine line between protection of the rights of the disabled and preserving their privacy. There are some tricky questions to which there is no specific response. For example, a current employee who is asked to take over some of the marginal duties of the disabled employee may be curious about the reason, but only the immediate supervisor and medical and safety officials have a need to know under the law. There are no fixed rules. The employer must use common sense.

The ADA is so new that there has not been time for many questions to be adjudicated in the federal or state courts. When in doubt, seek the advice of an attorney who specializes in this branch of the law. In the meantime, it is best to stick to work performance and related nonwork behavior, avoid initiating discussion of the disability itself, and make reasonable accommodations.

ADEA follows the same rules as Title VII.

REFERENCES

Age Discrimination in Employment Act of 1967 (Pub.L. 90-202)(ADEA), as amended, 29 U.S.C. 621 *et. seq.*

Americans with Disabilities Act of 1990 (Pub.L. 101-336) (ADA), as amended, 42 U.S.C. 12101 *et. seq.*

Civil Rights Act of 1991 (Pub.L. 102-166) (CRA).

Lorraine D. Eyde. (1994). *Guide for administering written employment examinations to persons with disabilities.* Washington, DC: Office of Personnel Management.

Title VII of the Civil Rights Act of 1964 (Pub.L. 880352), as amended, 42 U.S.C. 2000e *et. seq.*

Uniform guidelines on employee selection procedures, 29 C.F.R. 1607 (1978).

29

Zetetic for Testers

Richard S. Barrett

The Zetetic for Testers is a checklist that can help the builders and users of selection procedures to systematically evaluate their procedures and to determine whether they meet their needs and are fair to all of the applicants. ("Zetetic" is defined as "proceeding by inquiry" in *Webster's Third International Dictionary*.)

The Zetetic for Testers has two parts, recruitment and selection and validation. Recruitment and selection roughly follows the sequence of the selection process, starting with recruitment and ending with the selection decision. Validation covers points to be included in studies designed to show the business necessity of the selection procedure. It covers some related topics not covered in detail in this book, such as recruitment and test administration.

The questions are based on the Uniform Guidelines on Employee Selection Procedures (1978) as they were promulgated to clarify Title VII of the Civil Rights Act. They were later applied to the Age Discrimination in Employment Act. In the cases in which the requirements under the Americans with disabilities Act (ADA) differ, the difference is noted by "ADA" placed after questions that apply only to that law.

"Selection procedure" is broadly defined in the Uniform Guidelines (1978) as: Any measure, combination of measures, or procedure used as a basis for any employment decision. Selection procedures include the full

---

These questions are adapted from a longer Zetetic for Testers II available from the author at 5 Riverview Place, Hastings-on-Hudson, NY 10706.

range of assessment techniques from traditional paper and pencil tests, performance tests, training programs, or probationary periods and physical, educational, and work requirements through informal and casual interviews and unscored application forms."

No employer can be expected to have a complete and satisfactory answer to each question. For example, no employer has an up-to-date, detailed description of each position as required by ADA, but such a description should be prepared when a position is about to be filled. The courts have applied the Uniform Guidelines (1978) less strictly to the less structured procedures, such as the interview.

RECRUITMENT AND SELECTION

Recruitment

How are applicants, especially those in protected groups, recruited?

How are present employees informed of promotion opportunities?

Do recruitment programs aimed at the disabled respect their right of privacy? ADA

Application Blank

Does the application blank avoid questions regarding age, health, and other prohibited information?

Does the application blank ask if there is any reason why the applicant cannot perform on the job or on the selection procedures? ADA

Selection Procedures

Are copies of the selection procedure, manuals, and earlier studies available for inspection?

Do those who interview applicants, either staff members of the human resources department or prospective supervisors, avoid prohibited questions?

What steps are taken to assure that the applicants understand the instructions and can perform appropriately?

Do all applicants have equal access to test preparation programs?

What precautions are taken to maintain the security of the selection procedures?

What steps are taken to assure the accuracy of scoring, coding, and recording results?

Has reasonable accommodation been provided in the selection procedures or in the duties of the position to make it accessible to otherwise qualified applicants who are disabled? ADA

Selection Decision

How is each selection procedure used in making the selection decision?

Does the use of the selection procedures conform to the test manuals and the results of validation studies?

What is the rationale for the weight given to each element in the selection procedure?

How is the passing score, if any, established and justified?

Adverse Impact

(Adverse impact is not a consideration under ADA.)

What is the impact of each part of the selection procedure and of the whole selection process for each major job group?

If strict rank ordering is used, how is it determined that this procedure is more appropriate than the use of more flexible procedures, such as sliding bands?

How is the fairness of the selection procedure that has an adverse impact established?

What adjustments are made to fairly assess the qualifications of disabled applicants? ADA

VALIDATION

General

What is the purpose of the selection procedure?

What is the rationale behind the choice of the validation strategy that is used or for not validating the selection procedure?

How is it determined that specific jobs are included in or excluded from the study?

What efforts have been made to develop scores for unscored selection procedures?

Job Descriptions and Position Descriptions

(A position description is required by ADA. A position comprises the duties performed by one person. A job description is required by the Uniform Guidelines. A job is a collection of similar positions.)

When and by what method was the job last analyzed?

Does the job description describe the work behaviors, their relative importance and level of complexity, and the consequences of error?

Are duties for the position categorized as "essential" or "marginal"? ADA

Does the position description describe the work in terms of outcomes rather than work behaviors? ADA

Criterion-related Validity

How is the research population defined?

How well does the sample represent the expected applicant pool?

What are the pertinent demographic data of the members of the sample and of the expected applicant pool?

How does any departure from random sampling affect the interpretation of the results?

How is criterion performance defined, observed, quantified, and recorded?

How is performance on the criterion measures related to the employer's interest in safe and efficient work performance?

When a criterion other than work performance (such as tenure, attendance, or awards) is used, how is its relevance to the employer's interest determined?

When measures of success in training are used as criteria, how is it determined that the training is job related?

When paper-and-pencil tests are used as criteria, how is it shown that the scores are related to performance on the job?

What are the values of all basic statistics derived from the study for each selection procedure? Included, for each protected group and for the entire sample, are validity coefficients, item analyses, and means and standard deviations.

What corrections are made to the statistical results, and how are they justified?

What steps are taken to reduce or eliminate unfairness in the selection procedure and in the criterion measures?

Content Validity

Are applicants expected to bring with them the skills required by the job, based on prior training or experience?

Is the selection procedure a representative sample of important work behaviors?

Does the selection procedure generate a relevant work product?

How are the Knowledge, Skills, and Abilities defined and measured?

How are the Knowledge, Skills, and Abilities shown to be "necessary prerequisites" to performance on the job?

Do simulations adequately reflect the job circumstances?

How is the linkage between the performance on the test and performance on the job established?

Construct Validity (Validity Generalization)

(Note: The current popular term "validity generalization" is virtually identical to "construct validity" as it is used in Sections 14D and 15D of the Uniform Guidelines [1978].)

What is the definition of the construct?

What is the evidence from studies conducted by the user and by other researchers that shows that the selection procedure is validly related to the construct?

What evidence shows that the construct, as it is measured by the selection procedure, is validly related to work performance?

Are the research samples on which the construct validity is based sufficiently similar to those of interest to permit convincing generalizations?

When data from the literature are used to establish validity, how is it determined that there is no publication bias through underreporting of unfavorable results?

Do the studies on which construct validity is based meet the standards of the Uniform Guidelines?

REFERENCES

Uniform guidelines on employee selection procedures, 29 C.F.R. 1607 (1978).

IX

LITIGATION

30

Case Preparation for the Plaintiffs

Kent Spriggs

THEORIES OF PROOF

There are two major theories under which cases may be brought challenging selection procedures — disparate treatment and disparate impact. The first is a theory based on proving that the employer intended to discriminate against a protected class, such as gender, race, or national origin. It is grounded in commonsense concepts about ways in which one might infer discriminatory intent. Disparate impact theory is very different. This theory of proof has no commonsense analogue but is simply a creature of statute. Congress has legislated that, at some point, those practices that have adverse impact on a protected class and cannot be justified by their business necessity are illegal.

Disparate Impact

Many of the chapters in this book arise from the legal framework of disparate impact analysis. The plaintiff first must prove that a given selection device or procedure has an adverse impact on a protected class. This is sometimes very predictable. For example, most pencil-and-paper tests and formal educational requirements have a substantial adverse impact on blacks. Minimum height and weight requirements generally have an adverse impact on women. The first wing of the proof is to show the impact. This is generally a statistical presentation. With paper-and-pencil testing, it will be based on the impact that the results of the test have on hiring and promotion. With height and weight requirements, generalizations from census data will be possible. The Uniform Guidelines on Employee Selection Procedures (1978) are central. Among the requirements are that employers retain records that will disclose the impact that its tests and other selection procedures have on protected classes (29 CFR, § 1607.4). If an employer has not saved the required materials from which these answers can be inferred, for example, the testing results by race, a court is entitled to draw an adverse inference.

If disparate impact is proven, the employer must show that the procedure is required by business necessity. In the case of a test, it must be shown that the test is valid, as discussed in earlier chapters.

If the employer is successful, the plaintiff still may prevail by showing that there is an alternative selection procedure that fulfills the same function but has less adverse impact on the group in question.

Disparate Treatment

There are three basic patterns that plaintiffs can use to prove disparate treatment, that is, that the employer intended to discriminate.

The employee may try to show that there is a pattern and practice of discrimination against his or her protected group. This may be in the context of a class action. Pattern and practice proof may be used in an individual case to shift the burden of proof to the employer. These showings tend to be based on statistical proof. With this theory, the plaintiff may simultaneously attack all parts of a multipart selection process — the impact of nomination of one's supervisor and subsequent interview panels attacked in terms of the overall result when measured against the composition of those eligible for nomination.

In such pattern and practice proof, the choice of the benchmark or normative measure is often outcome determinative. The courts consistently have held that the best benchmark for hiring and promotion decisions is the actual applicant flow of those who meet those threshold qualifications not under attack by the plaintiff. Failing such data, benchmarks based on subsets of incumbent employees (for promotions) or census-based labor force data (for initial hiring) often are used. The court may look to the composition of those employed in similar jobs in the community.

If the plaintiff proves a pattern and practice from which discriminatory intent can be inferred, the employer cannot defend by showing business necessity. The employer essentially must prove that the statistics offered by the plaintiff do not show what the plaintiff alleges. The employer also may show that, even with the pattern and practice, the result of which the plaintiff complains is not a product of that pattern.

The plaintiff may also shift the burden of proof to the employer by providing proof of direct evidence of discriminatory animus. In most cases, there is no overt allusion to the protected characteristic being a part of the decisional process, but on occasion, allusions are made to the age, gender, or race of the plaintiff or stereotypical attributes of such qualities. The obvious kind of direct evidence is a manager who uses a racial epithet such as "nigger." More subtle but just as illegal are statements that reflect a stereotypical view of the employee's race or gender. Thus, in the Supreme Court's *Price Waterhouse v. Hopkins* (1989) decision, the direct evidence might not have been seen as a direct gender-biased insult per se but did reflect that the decision makers viewed Hopkins differently from male applicants for partner because of her gender. This is a powerful evidentiary tool for the plaintiff, because it supplies the element from which intent easily is inferred.

Failing either of the above, the plaintiff may use the method of proof discussed in a number of Supreme Court cases, perhaps most notably *Texas Department of Community Affairs v. Burdine* (1981). In such a model, the plaintiff bears a light initial burden, showing membership in a protected group and qualifications for the job. The employer then must merely "articulate" a "nondiscriminatory reason" or reasons. It then falls to the plaintiff to prove that such an articulation is pretextual, that is, that the articulated reason is not the true reason or is only part of the reason along with illegal motivation. The plaintiff may do this in many ways. A few indicia of pretext are the articulated reason is not the true reason, the selectee is less qualified, the employer departed from its normal selection processes to favor the selectee, the employer has precluded the employee from being able to compete for promotion, the employer changes the articulated reason during the litigation, and the employer treats the plaintiff different from other applicants.

DISCOVERY AND RECORD-KEEPING OBLIGATIONS

Often, pretrial discovery is the key to success for the plaintiff. It is the nature of the employment process that the employer has most of the relevant documents. Generally, most of the relevant witnesses still will be employed by the defendant employer.

Pretrial discovery procedures provided by the court rules allow the plaintiff's lawyer to use the litigation process to "discover" facts known to the employer. Interrogatories are questions that must be answered by the employer under oath. The plaintiff can request to inspect documents and premises. Often, documents are crucial to the plaintiff's case, because they may show that the company has not been fair in its selection process. They may show that a test has disparate impact on the plaintiff's group or that other competing applicants had inferior qualifications on their resumes. Electronic records are fully discoverable. The plaintiff may want to tour the workplace to familiarize counsel with attributes of a job in question. Counsel also will want to take depositions (examinations of witnesses under oath).

Title VII imposes record-keeping obligations on all employers. These are contained in the Code of Federal Regulations (C.F.R.). Records having to do with hiring, promotion, demotion, and termination must be kept for one year (29 C.F.R. § 1602.14). When a charge of discrimination is filed, all records relevant to a disposition of the charge must be kept until the case is completely disposed of, including appeals (29 C.F.R. § 1602.14). Records adequate to reveal the impact of selection procedures on all protected groups, for example, gender and race, must be kept regardless of whether any charges have been filed (29 C.F.R. § 1607.4). The failure to retain these records can lead the court to make adverse inferences concerning the employer's practices.

ATTACKING SYSTEMIC PRACTICES

Both the legislative history and court interpretations of Title VII have made clear that the intent of Congress was not only to provide a means of redress for individuals who were wronged but also to provide a statutory vehicle to root out illegal systemic practices. Authority was given to the U.S. government to bring suits. Being mindful that the government would not have adequate resources, Congress intended that private individuals would have authority to attack illegal systemic practices. Early on, the courts alluded to this concept by characterizing the individual plaintiff as a private attorney general.

The most common method by which one or more individual plaintiffs can attack practices is the class action. In such suits, the plaintiffs must show the court that they are appropriate representatives for all they seek to represent, for example, all blacks not hired, all women not promoted in the operations department. The plaintiff has a fiduciary duty to those he or she represents in the class, that is, he or she must act in their best interests and may not subvert those interests for his or her own gain. The burden is cast upon the plaintiffs to prove the illegal practice. If successful, others in the class as defined by the court are allowed to come forward in what are called "stage II proceedings" and file claims that they have been adversely affected by the adverse practices that are the subject of the litigation. Having done so, they are entitled to the normal remedies available to any Title VII plaintiff, such as back pay, front pay, reinstatement, and compensatory damages, even though, prior to the stage II proceeding, they had not been actual parties before the court.

Less commonly recognized but still useful in reforming practices are systemic injunctions. Even if the plaintiff does not seek class leadership status or is unsuccessful in obtaining class certification, if, in proving his or her own case, he or she shows that illegal systemic practices exist, the court may be asked to enjoin the practice at the end of the litigation. Illustrative of such relief would be an injunction against using a test or a formal educational requirement or a mandatory injunction that the employer post vacancies.

RETALIATION

Employment discrimination laws have antiretaliation provisos. These provisos are very broad. They protect employees or applicants who participate in enforcement proceedings or oppose practices made illegal under the antidiscrimination laws. "Participation" is construed very broadly. Illustrative is acting as a witness or assisting an employee in making a charge of discrimination. "Opposition" can be in a broad variety of ways limited only by opposition that is too disruptive of the employer's workplace.

Opposition to the employer's practices is protected even if it is determined subsequently that the law was not violated. It is sufficient that the employee have a good faith and reasonable belief that the practice is illegal.

Courts will tend to focus on the relationship of the protected activity to any adverse employment action, such as demotion or discharge. If the adverse action is proximate in time to the employer's knowledge of the protected activity, the case will be stronger.

It is most important for managers to instruct all those with supervisory responsibilities that there be no retaliation against those exercising protected activity. It is not unusual for an employee to have a mediocre discrimination claim but to suffer retaliation for filing a charge and have a very strong retaliation claim.

THE COMING OF JURY TRIALS AND DAMAGES

In 1991, Congress passed the most substantial group of amendments to Title VII of the Civil Rights Act of 1964 since extending coverage to federal employees in 1972. The act was passed largely in response to a number of Supreme Court opinions that had, in some cases, radically curtailed the guarantees of fair employment practices.

Probably the most significant change in the act was providing for the first time for compensatory and punitive damages for injured parties. (Blacks suing under Section 1981 had been able to seek damages prior to 1991. Section 1981 originally was passed in 1866 to enforce the Thirteenth Amendment prohibition of slavery.) with the coming of relief in the form of damages came jury trials. Interestingly, when the Civil Rights Act of

1964 was first passed, the impetus was largely afforded by the politics of the black Civil Rights movement, rather than women and ethnic groups other than blacks who were afforded its protections. The consensus of opinion was that, if Title VII cases were tried to juries in the South, blacks would lose. Thus, arose the tradition that back pay was an equitable relief, rather than legal, and no jury trials were afforded.

The political understandings of 1991 were substantially different. The general sense of advocates for Civil Rights was that plaintiffs could be successful before juries. There was also a concern that limiting monetary relief to back pay and front pay did not provide adequate inducement to employers to obey the law. The political climate was, in no mean degree, conditioned by the saga of Anita Hill in the hearings regarding Clarence Thomas and the greater realization of how widespread sexual harassment is in the workplace. The coming of jury trials also coincided with the rise of an ever more conservative federal judiciary.

Trials before juries very much change the calculus. Judges tend to focus on the complex rules governing shifting burdens of proof. Juries by and large are much more prone to focus on whether they feel that which has befallen the plaintiff is fair. Judges tend to be white, male, and well-to-do. They, like all of us, see the world through their own experience and often tend to identify with management. Juries are truly a cross section of the society. Thus, they bring to the process the perspectives of clerks and mechanics as well as managers. They are much more likely than judges to want to "send a message" to an employer who appears to have been unfair or meanspirited.

The coming of jury trials has had an impact on the cases that plaintiffs' lawyers choose. Now, more attention is given to questions such as how will the plaintiff seem to the jury, will the supervisors seem callous, has the employer acted in a way that seems underhanded, what is the degree of injury to the employee and his or her family.

One of the sad truths about the justice system is the prevalence of perjury. Sadly, perhaps through exhaustion, judges sometimes seem to take in stride conflicting testimony from which it is obvious that someone is lying. Juries are much more inclined to be very offended if they feel one side is lying. Plaintiffs' counsel experience that, after confronting an employer with an allegation of discrimination, a "nondiscriminatory" explanation is given. Often, after the appearance of counsel for the employer, the "nondiscriminatory reason" or reasons change, usually to one that is easier to prove in court. Juries presented with changes in what is supposedly the "true" reason for the action easily can take offense, as well they might.

Already, we have seen some very large damage awards. Again, as suggested above, juries are more inclined than judges to "send a message" to an employer that they feel has been meanspirited in violating the statute. This can be expressed in large compensatory damages for pain and suffering or in punitive damages. It is easy to understand how juries may take offense at the humiliation visited upon an employee who has suffered severe racial or sexual harassment and discrimination.

OTHER REMEDIES

One of the earmarks of employment discrimination has been the variety and inventiveness of remedies devised by courts. The Supreme Court has held that their duty is to "make whole" the plaintiff for the injury suffered.

For Individuals

Best known is back pay, which includes all fringe benefits. If the employee is not returning to the workplace and is making less than with the defendant employer or if the employee was deprived of a job that is not afforded him or her at the moment of judgment, the employee will be entitled to "front pay," lost earnings subsequent to the point of judgment.

The employee deprived of hiring or promotion or fired normally will be entitled to the job of which he or she was deprived. In some cases, the employer will be ordered to "bump" a wrongful jobholder from the job held in favor of the plaintiff.

If a seniority system is in place, an individual will be entitled to a modification of seniority in accordance with the judgment.

The court may modify the employment record (e.g., deleting negative references).

Systemic Remedies

If the proof shows that there were illegal components of the employment system or illegal results of the system, a number of remedies are available.

The court normally will enjoin any discriminatory practice, whether a test or job requirement, that has adverse impact without business necessity. The employer may be ordered to develop nondiscriminatory selection procedures.

The employer may be ordered to recruit differently or train a group of employees who have suffered discrimination. Courts have, on occasion, ordered that supervisors be trained to act in a nondiscriminatory manner.

The employer may be forced to report to the court.

Despite all the rhetoric in the media seeking to make quotas synonymous with affirmative action, quotas are legal when ordered by a court that has found severe discrimination.

ATTORNEYS' FEES

For those in risk management, there is sometimes inadequate consideration given to the implications of the presence of fee shifting, that is, the provision that the prevailing party is entitled to an award of attorneys' fees. Managers used to tort claims are very conscious that, as the litigation proceeds, they must continue to pay their own lawyers, but the "exposure" of the claim tends not to change. This is not the case in employment discrimination litigation, because, although the exposure of the employer to the claims of the employee may not increase materially, that is, the risk of back pay and damages, the fees for the lawyer are always increasing.

The method of calculating fees awardable under the statute is called the "loadstar" method. The fee is the product of a "reasonable hourly rate" determined by the court times all hours reasonably expended in prosecution of the claim. Thus, if an employer chooses extreme and time-consuming defense measures and if the employer is unsuccessful, he should understand that the fees owing to the prevailing plaintiff's attorney will be substantially greater. In what may at first seem counter-intuitive, the Supreme Court has held that, just because a monetary award is of modest size, this is not a basis for reducing the fees.

There are two constraints on plaintiffs in prosecuting suits. First, most employees cannot afford to pay a lawyer. Thus, most plaintiffs' lawyers work for no fee from the client or for a commercially unreasonably low fee; therefore, experienced plaintiffs' counsel will tend to screen cases very carefully and will tend to steer away from marginal claims. Further, if the plaintiff loses and the judge feels that the suit was frivolous, the Supreme Court has held that the employer may recover from the employee. Thus, in an era when there is much talk in Congress about the concept of "loser pays," such is, in part, a reality in employment discrimination practice. There does remain the substantial difference in standards — the plaintiff need only "prevail"; the employer must prevail and show that the suit was frivolous.

It is hoped that the foregoing has supplied a very brief introduction to unpleasant consequences of litigation that can befall the employer who fails to abide by the commands of Title VII. Further, the cost of litigation may suggest to the human resources professional faced with a Title VII lawsuit the wisdom of using alternative dispute resolution mechanisms, such as mediation, as intelligent risk management.

REFERENCES

42 U.S.C. Section. 1981.

Civil Rights Act of 1964 (Pub.L. 88-352) as amended, 42 U.S.C. 2000e.

Price Waterhouse v. Hopkins, 490 U.S. 228 (1989).

Texas Department of Community Affairs v. Burdine, 450 U.S. 248 (1981).

Uniform guidelines on employee selection procedures, 29 C.F.R. 1602, 1607 (1978).

31

The Industrial Psychologist as an Expert Witness in Testing Cases

R. Lawrence Ashe, Jr.

SELECTION OF THE EXPERT

Plaintiffs

A relatively small but gradually growing number of industrial psychologists has been used as plaintiffs' expert witnesses in employment testing litigation. Although these witnesses have had substantial experience under fire, it also has created the potential appearance of a proplaintiff prejudice, which may tend to erode the credibility of the witness as well as increase the likelihood of diligent defense counsel's unearthing prior contradictory testimony. Accordingly, plaintiffs may wish to consider someone such as an industrial psychologist from a nearby university who has significant practical industrial experience, whose professional views are neither polarized nor expressed in polemics, and who conveys to the court an attitude of professional detachment. Having appeared on more than a token basis for both plaintiffs and defendants is a potentially positive fact for any expert witness. Some plaintiffs' experts have fee arrangements that are expressly or essentially contingent in nature. This is neither professionally proper nor particularly useful for credibility.

Defendants

The major hazard for defendants lies in the selection of an expert more interested in (and perhaps qualified for) marketing for profit than professionalism in personnel selection or integrity in testimony. Such experts frequently are accompanied by soothing assurances of a complete answer to test validation and related equal employment opportunity problems.

Whether the actual work has been done in-house or by an outside consultant, prudent defense counsel will secure at least an informal appraisal from an independent expert and, if the opinion is favorable, consider using such an individual as an additional expert witness at trial. The same prototype as suggested for plaintiffs would apply.

Both

As in other fields of expertise, some professionally superb individuals regrettably make poor witnesses and sometimes are virtually incapable of communicating in lay language. Talking down to the judge or jury and a thin skin are other common faults. Checking attorney references where available and reading representative transcripts of prior testimony are recommended accordingly. Computer search capabilities should be utilized for both case law and other citations and discussion. Further, the attorney should find out whether the witness has expressed prior inconsistent views. If so, can new enlightenment be correctly and comfortably professed? Professional standing should be verified with peers as well as by client references. Litigation history should be checked by computer search.

Although there sometimes are battles of competing curricula vitae between the test validation experts, usually each will have a relevant doctoral degree and at least some appropriate experience. The plaintiff's expert frequently is more academic and accordingly has more publications, while the defendant's expert often has substantially greater "real world" experience. Assuming that the resume disparity is not too great, communications skills and witness demeanor become of overriding importance. The widespread advent of jury trials, even in some testing cases, has underscored this priority.

PRETRIAL USE OF THE EXPERT

The industrial psychologist can and generally should be involved in the initial analysis of the potential testing issues; statistical and qualitative evaluation of adverse impact data; preparation of interrogatories and interrogatory answers; research and counseling regarding relevant professional literature; preparation for and attendance and assistance at the opposing expert's deposition; assistance with documentary evidence; and analysis of strengths and weaknesses in each side's position on the test design and validation questions. Reports with specified rather complete contents now are required under federal discovery rules from each testifying expert.

If an expert consultant is going to explore numerous alternatives and a party wishes to present only the most advantageous of these alternatives at trial, it is advisable to have two experts, one who will experimentally explore a range of alternatives and one who will explore only the alternatives deemed most favorable and testify to them at trial. The purpose is, of course, to protect against discovery of one's work product in the form of the approaches not deemed advantageous. However, opponents will be entitled to explore who determined which studies were done by the testifying expert and that person's knowledge, if any, of studies done by others. Opposing experts may perform the "missing studies" and confront the "sheltered" expert witness with them. The sought-after aura of professional detachment may be eroded by persuasive evidence that counsel was the puppeteer for the testifying expert.

TRIAL ROLE OF THE EXPERT

The industrial psychologist should be thoroughly involved in the preparation of his or her own direct testimony, related evidentiary or illustrative exhibits, and possible cross-examination. Videotaped practice can assist in demeanor modification, though most witnesses ultimately revert to form over time and under the normal duress of the witness chair. The expert should devote sufficient time and effort to the case so as to avoid the form or substance of the "hip-shooting hired gun." If one is fortunate enough to have an expert who thinks quickly and in lay terms, the resulting cross-examination assistance can be invaluable.

DIRECT EXAMINATION OF AN EXPERT

The first task is to master the psychologist's jargon sufficiently and to get to know the expert well enough to insure effective communication during examination. The second is to discipline the expert and counsel to speak intelligibly in nontechnical language without talking down to the court, jury, or counsel. Ideally, both the lawyer and the expert will be fully familiar with the expert's professional writings and activities and prior testimony, because competent opposing counsel can be relied upon to have searched them for purposes of cross-examination. The attorney should deal directly with any prior arguably inconsistent positions taken by the expert by, for example, showing the evolution in professional thought accounting for the change in views. The attorney should try to introduce in exhibit form evidence that is detailed, dull, difficult to articulate, or self-praising, such as the expert's curriculum vitae. (The attorney should review that vitae first and edit out inappropriate or trivial contents.)

CROSS-EXAMINATION OF AN EXPERT

The attorney should do thorough and early discovery on test validation issues through interrogatories and requests for admission. If necessary, he or she should seek court assistance to force opposing counsel to delineate those testing issues that will, in fact, be tried. The attorney should accumulate, read, and master as much of the opposing expert's professional writings and prior testimony as possible. Where applicable, the attorney should insist upon the report required by the federal rules. A thorough deposition of the other side's expert is essential. Defendants will want to compare any job analysis and validation work done by plaintiff's expert with the standards now espoused as essential. Plaintiffs often will seek to apply every arguably relevant requirement of governmental and professional guidelines. If either expert has been uniformly and frequently identified with one point of view, impeachment potential exists.

POSTTRIAL ROLE OF THE EXPERT

The expert should be able to assist by critiquing each side's proposed findings of fact on testing issues. If settlement negotiations occur, the expert's advice on test validation language and terms is essential.

Use of Test Questions

There have been instances in which plaintiffs have effectively called to the court's attention facially unrelated questions contained on the test. In a criterion-related context, this fact should, of course, be irrelevant. Further, most courts and jurors are not well-equipped to evaluate individual test items in a professionally meaningful manner. Nonetheless, some courts have engaged in an analysis of specific test questions, requiring that the tests themselves become part of the record, despite claims of confidentiality. The Eleventh Circuit Court stated the view that it is "hopeless" for the trier of fact to determine content validity or job relatedness of a test without the questions themselves being placed into evidence (*Nash v. Consolidated City of Jacksonville* (1988). Test security is mandated, however, by both the Uniform Guidelines on Employee Selection Procedures (1989) and relevant professional standards (American

Psychological Association, 1985). Because of legitimate test security concerns, test items should be maintained under seal and not made a matter of open public record.

Job Analysis

The adequacy of defendant's job analysis efforts is often crucial in employment discrimination litigation. A professional job analysis requires substantially more than the job or position description used by many employers. It involves an accurate study of the various components of a job. It is concerned with not only analysis of the duties and conditions of work but also the skills and experience necessary to perform the work. A well-done job analysis is essential to prove content validity, may, in some circumstances, be required to justify the relevance of the criterion selection in a criterion-related study, and is almost always impressive to the court. With the advent of the Americans with Disabilities Act, job analyses (or, at least, more thorough position descriptions) increasingly are available.

REFERENCES

Americans with Disabilities Act of 1990 (Pub.L. 101–336) (ADA), as amended, 42 U.S.C. 12101 et. seq.

Nash v. Consolidated City of Jacksonville, 837 F.2d 1534, 1538, 53 FEP 672 (11th Cir. 1988).

Standards for educational and psychological testing. (1985). Washington, DC: American Psychological Association.

Uniform guidelines on employee selection procedures, 41 C.F.C. §§60-3.1 to 60-3.19 (1989).

32

The Expert Witness and the Attorney

Richard S. Barrett

This discussion of the role of the expert witness is based on my experience in fair employment cases, starting with *Griggs v. Duke Power* (1971) and continuing through about 100 others. Contrasting perspectives are provided in this book by Lawrence Ashe, who frequently works for the defense, and Kent Spriggs, who has written from the plaintiff's point of view.

When a testing psychologist meets attorneys in Title VII lawsuits, both bring with them the traditions, customs, and usages of their respective professions. They must each learn the other's ways and absorb enough of the other's lore to make an effective team. The purpose of this chapter is to help potential experts, attorneys, and clients analyze cases, prepare testimony, and participate in depositions and trials.

DIFFERENCES IN PERSPECTIVES

The objectives of the parties differ, but they are not mirror images of each other. Plaintiffs want relief for their clients, but in addition to winning the individual case, Civil Rights organizations, the Department of Justice, and the Equal Employment Opportunity Commission want to establish a precedent that will motivate other employers to eliminate unfair employment practices. The defendants are mostly interested in solving their own problems, either by winning on the merits or by minimizing the damage if they are found to be at fault.

Each side has its strengths and weaknesses, and they, too, are not mirror images of each other. Plaintiffs have the advantage of choosing who, when, where, and how to attack. Yes, Virginia, there is discrimination out there, and plaintiffs' attorneys have the luxury of picking the most promising cases. Plaintiffs know that defendants are motivated to settle because defense is expensive and an adverse judgment may lead to huge liability. Adding insult to injury, the court may order the defendants to pay the fees of the attorneys who sued them. Even if the defendants win, some of the revelations in court may be embarrassing.

Except for suits brought by the federal government, employers generally have more resources than the plaintiffs. Defense attorneys can, and sometimes do, introduce unconscionable delay to wear down and impoverish the plaintiffs, hoping to end the suit or to settle it on favorable terms. The defendants have control of the data, and although under the principle of discovery, they are required to produce it, there are countless ways to limit the disclosure and to delay the game.

CONTRAST BETWEEN LAWYERS AND PSYCHOLOGISTS

Lawyers work on the principle that everyone deserves a defense; some psychologists question the all-out attack on the unassailable and the dogged defense of the indefensible. Psychologists are more likely than lawyers to want to develop and use a procedure that improves the validity and fairness of the selection procedures. The serendipitous effect has been the proliferation of innovative procedures that otherwise would have not received the prominence that they now have. Some are discussed in the section on innovative selection procedures.

EXPERTISE VERSUS SCIENTIFIC EVIDENCE

A psychologist accepted by the court as an expert witness becomes the fountainhead. The court has limited interest in the research studies on which academics and professionals like to rely. They want to hear from someone who is subject to cross-examination, and that is you, the expert. Attorneys try to uncover flaws in the arguments of their adversaries through cross-examination, and they cannot cross-examine the absent author of the research study that you may cite. Courts suffer from the quaint delusion that they can tell on the basis of demeanor who is telling the truth, even though an accomplished psychopath can fool almost anybody and the nervous neophyte may be unconvincing. This position is foreign to the thinking of the psychologist, who has been brought up in a tradition of reliance on empirical evidence and knowledge of the difficulty of reading a person's state of mind. You must not only be correct, you must also be credible.

Because of their faith in the power of observation and cross-examination, attorneys direct much of their effort ad hominem rather than *ad verbum*. They try to show that opposing witnesses are not credible because of past identification with one point of view, inconsistencies in prior statements, or the promise of money. This principle is not without merit. I have watched one prominent psychologist blow his credibility by making contradictory statements in similar, almost simultaneous cases in which he represented opposite sides. If you plan to be an expert witness, review your prior testimony and published statements to make sure that they are consistent with your planned testimony or be prepared to explain how advances in the profession, differences in the situations, or some other circumstances account for what may seem to be a contradiction to the external observer.

CONCEALING BAD NEWS VERSUS STATING IT UP FRONT

Some lawyers work on the principle, "produce all that is true and good for your client, but no more," a strategy that leads some to want you to sweep bad news under the rug. No selection program is so bad that there is not some merit in it or so good that it is without flaw. You will be more comfortable and more credible if you willingly acknowledge your adversary's strong points and your own weaknesses before a seemingly reluctant concession is drawn out of you on cross-examination.

DISCOVERY

One of the great advances in U.S. jurisprudence in recent generations is the principle of discovery, which, when practiced, gives both parties the information they need to pursue their portion of the litigation. Each party can, under this principle, require the adversary to disclose data, such as number of applicants by race or the number hired; to describe the procedures for developing and validating the selection procedures; to identify the proposed testimony of their witnesses; and provide access to the witnesses for pretrial depositions.

Discovery removes the drama of the Perry Mason trial in which the witness, surprised by the sudden disclosure of some previously hidden information, breaks down and confesses all. It also means that much, but not quite everything, that you do is done in a fishbowl. Lawyers have, of course, built in ways to keep their private thoughts private. One is the principle of attorney's work product, under which some correspondence and other information is privileged and need not be disclosed. Be sure that you understand the rules before committing your thoughts to writing.

Discovery works like this. Each side prepares summaries of the testimony that they expect from their witnesses. Witnesses prepare reports. The adversaries may file interrogatories, formal written questions to which the other party must respond, or require that the opposing witness be deposed in an oral hearing similar to a trial. In principle, both parties have the information they need to make their cases before the court. However, no human institution is perfect, and discovery can be abused. Because the defendants have possession of most of the data, they are in the best position to stonewall, and stonewall some of them do, forcing the plaintiff to take the time, trouble, and resources to secure a motion to produce the information. Also, they can, and sometimes do, read the interrogatories very literally so as to avoid disclosing damaging information, leading the plaintiffs to write long, convoluted, and all-inclusive requests for every possible bit of information, some of which is not relevant.

The existence of discovery leads to a difficult question for defendant's expert, "Should one conduct analyses that may yield damaging results?" The quick answer, "No," is not altogether satisfactory. You can look foolish by not performing an analysis that any competent researcher would be expected to perform, especially one called for in the Uniform Guidelines on Employee Selection Procedures (1978). Besides, if the plaintiff's expert performs the same analysis, nothing is gained and your credibility is damaged.

Because it is generally in the interest of the plaintiffs to move ahead quickly to win relief for their clients and in the interest of the defendants to delay, most abuses stem from the defendants. If you are involved at this stage, work out your attitudes toward discovery, which may require some philosophic thought regarding the relative importance of furthering justice and winning the case.

GHOST EXPERT VERSUS EXPERT WITNESS

The issue is complicated by the ghost expert hired by the defendant, who may conduct a wide range of analyses and recommend that the expert who will testify redo only the ones that give the most favorable result. One must be aware of the possibility of being deliberately kept ignorant of essential information if the attorney asks only for certain limited analyses.

Lawyers defend this practice on the grounds that they need unbiased, frank information on which to base their defense. Many psychologists condemn this practice because they know that there is more than one way to conduct a study and to analyze the data. The effect of the efforts of the ghost expert may be that the attorneys mislead you by feeding you incomplete or misleading information or self-serving instructions.

If you are asked to fill this role, think carefully about the implications of your actions for the possible miscarriage of justice. If you suspect that there is a ghost in the background, take steps to make sure that you are not being deceived. I suggest that, if you are asked to analyze data and to give advice but not to testify, you insist that your participation be made known to the other side.

DATA ANALYSIS

Not performing analyses that are clearly indicated by accepted professional practice can be, for the conscientious professional, even more embarrassing than the results. Your opponents may insist on getting your data tapes, and they have access to the same computer programs that you do. Not only should the appropriate analyses be conducted, the results also should be reported in enough detail so that readers understand what happened and can draw their own conclusions. I have seen reports with long series of tables in which only positive, significant results were reported, leaving more gaps than there were data. One psychologist's explanation, that he was hired to find validity and that he reported it when he found it, did not wash.

Your adversaries will go over your report with great pains to find any flaws, and many reports have egregious flaws. I have seen such a simple statistic as chi-square computed incorrectly. Make sure that your computations are correct and that the data are reported completely.

ANECDOTAL VERSUS STATISTICAL PROOF

Lawyers are brought up on precedents and decisions based on the facts in front of them. Of course, there are exceptions, but many of them do not understand basic inferential statistics. It is not just a matter of their not knowing the specific formulas, many do not understand how generalizations about a population are drawn on the basis of information about a sample, the value of a validity coefficient, or the meaning of tests of significance. The expert witness must explain the basics to attorneys and the court, using diagrams and homely illustrations to make a point.

SETTLEMENTS BASED ON EXPEDIENCY
VERSUS SCIENTIFIC MERIT

Lawyers represent clients; psychologists, in addition, represent a scientific discipline. Lawyers sometimes ignore the merits to negotiate a settlement in pursuing their client's interest. The lawyers and their clients are satisfied because the suit is settled on acceptable terms; you may not be so pleased because settlements often run counter to psychometric principles, but there is nothing you can do about it. The only saving grace is that such settlements are not reported and do not become part of the precedents that establish case law.

PAPER TRAIL

Once a suit is under way, it is too late to plead ignorance of the need to preserve data and to conduct certain routine analyses. You are expected to leave behind a paper trail documenting what you did so that you can prepare a report as required by Documentation of Impact and Validity Evidence, Section 15C of the Uniform Guidelines (1978). This means, for example, that it is a good idea to keep notes on meetings, have subject matter experts sign attendance sheets, and generally keep compulsive records so that you can describe what happened, who did it, and when. Be careful not to destroy relevant information; to do so could lead to serious consequences, particularly if litigation is already under way.

INVOLVEMENT OF THE PSYCHOLOGIST

Line management, and especially attorneys, want to solve the problems on their own, calling in the psychologist only when they get stuck. If you have the forewarning and the leverage, get involved early. To do so will save you and your client a lot of grief. Ours is an arcane profession, involving as it does psychometric and statistical principles that may be foreign to your clients and that are difficult for them to deal with. They need training in these fields, and the psychologist needs training in the function of the adversarial process. To best foster this mutual education, you and your colleagues should work together to outline the conduct of the case. When you get through, everyone should understand the plan and be comfortable with it. If you do not, the resulting strain can interfere with your efforts and undermine your credibility.

Generally, opposing witnesses and attorneys treat each other with civility, sometimes sharing a drink or even a meal. It is wise, however, to be on your guard, because casual comments may come back, often out of context, to haunt you. It especially is important to be careful in making commitments to supply information. Insist on a written statement of what you have agreed to do.

YOUR DAY IN COURT

Your direct testimony should be a well-planned performance in which the attorney asks questions in a neutral way that allows you to put your testimony into the record. ("We prepare witnesses, not coach them," explained one attorney.) The court may interject questions but often is almost completely passive. Then comes cross-examination, in which the opposing attorney tries to point up the shortcomings of your direct testimony and of your character. No one is ever bored under cross-examination.

The rules of the game say that, on direct examination, your attorney must ask you nonleading questions with a foundation laid describing the preliminary activities. You and your attorney should know each question that will be asked and the answer that will be given. At the end of the testimony, you may be asked the "ultimate question," that is, the question on which the judge will rule, for example, "Is there an adverse impact?" or "Is the test valid?" Have an answer ready.

The rules for cross-examination are very different. The attorney is granted broad latitude in asking leading questions in an attempt to get you to say something that contradicts your direct testimony or undermines your client's case. A favorite trick is to quote your earlier work out of context. You can, and should, request to see the original document. If the context alters the meaning of the quotation, read both the quotation and the context into the record. Similarly, you have broad latitude in answering questions. You may have an opportunity to elaborate on points that you wish to emphasize.

ROLE OF ATTORNEYS AND EXPERT WITNESSES

Attorneys are in charge, but the best attorneys involve the experts early and make sure that everyone agrees on the conduct of the case. They plan the case in chief, prepare exhibits, discuss the data to be collected and analyzed, and prepare witnesses. As far as you, the witness, are concerned, an important function of your attorney is to protect you from the onslaughts of the opposing attorney. Your attorney should object to questions that are irrelevant, beyond the scope of your earlier testimony, ambiguous, or argumentative. Some alert attorneys object if they think that you are in trouble, even if they are sure that they will be overruled, to communicate that what you are saying is damaging and to give you time to think through your answer.

When the other experts are testifying, pay close attention to their testimony so that you can help your attorney to prepare questions for cross-examination. During cross-examination, you may pass notes to your attorney to help to guide the questioning, but often, things go by so fast that your questions are obsolete by the time they are written. Keep track of your comments so that you can discuss them before the cross-examination is finished. Typically, attorneys ask for a few minutes to discuss their response to the testimony with their experts before ending the cross-examination.

If there are some issues in your testimony or in the cross-examination that you believe may need clarification, you may suggest to your attorney that you take the stand again for redirect examination. Redirect is confined to the topics previously covered; the opposing attorney may object successfully if you try to introduce new material.

SUMMARY

Being an expert witness is a challenging and, to some people, a frightening experience. I have tried to help to remove some of the novelty and threat by describing how the system works and how you best can function in it. My fundamental advice to potential witnesses is to study the case thoroughly, examine the client's objective and methods, and work closely with the client's attorney so that there are no surprises. Follow the motto of the Boy Scouts, "Be prepared." Only then can you be satisfied that you have produced the best work for your clients and acted professionally.

REFERENCES

Griggs v. Duke Power Co., 401 U.S. 424 (1971).
Uniform guidelines on employee selection procedures, 29 C.F.R. 1607 (1978).

33

Cooperative Efforts among Potential Adversaries

Lawrence R. O'Leary

This chapter focuses on one strategy, the cooperative expert model, that the employer can use in some cases to save precious financial and time resources when the employer has already had or anticipates a legal challenge to an employment process for a given position. The strategy has been implemented successfully in a growing number of public jurisdictions and shows promise of providing some useful benefits to employers. My associates and I had been involved in the traditional adversarial model of litigation, in which some experts attacked and others defended the selection procedures in City A (a midwestern city with a population in excess of 250,000). The morale within the fire department deteriorated, and, more specifically, the racial tension among the candidates increased. The cooperative model, which dramatically changed the landscape of litigation in the promotion process, was brought forward by a federal district court judge in 1979 and subsequently has been applied in a number of agencies across the country. These include City B (an eastern city with a population in excess of 250,000) and City C (a similarly sized city on the West Coast).

The solution presented by the judge was fairly straightforward, and I have labeled this approach the "cooperative expert model." Under this approach, all litigants to the court action obtained the services of a test expert. Step two involved all of the experts agreeing to study the position to be filled (the "target position") and working as a team to develop a promotion system that they could all accept *before* it was implemented. In this first example, the city had its expert participating with the experts chosen by the African-American firefighters' group (Fire Fighters' Institute for Racial Equality), the International Firefighters Association, which is predominantly Anglo-American in City A, and an expert chosen by the Justice Department, which was one of the litigants.

The experts were called upon to contribute their specific areas of test expertise (e.g., job analysis, assessment centers, written tests) as well as serve as reviewers of the work of other members of the committee. The result of the committee's work was a selection system based on a thorough job analysis and a series of job-related promotion components upon which all members of the committee could agree before the promotion process was implemented.

Because the court did not appoint a chair for the committee and there was no voting procedure, all of the decisions were made by consensus. This procedure is cumbersome at the outset, but the pressure to produce a professional product motivated us to make the necessary adjustments. The members are acutely aware that their work will be reviewed by the court and, if it is not satisfactory, may be the subject of further litigation.

THE BENEFITS OF THE COOPERATIVE EXPERT MODEL

The basic benefits of this model are:

The suspicions of each litigant are dramatically reduced because they have their own expert.

The probability of litigation is reduced because each potential litigant had a hand in the creation of the promotion and selection process and approved it before the process was run.

There is a heightened probability that the promotion and selection system produced will be even more innovative, valid, and fair because it represents the synergistic results of several, as opposed to one, employment testing specialists.

There is the opportunity for the local agency to capture and structure a promotion process that the litigants created, that the local jurisdiction can administer, and that meets professional and legal requirements.

The success of this initial implementation of the cooperative model was sufficient for litigants in similar circumstances in City B to implement the model in that jurisdiction. It should be emphasized that this model is not presented as some kind of quick fix that is free of challenges. However, it is a strategy that can be used to save substantial and much needed financial and human resources (jurisdictional employees' time) as well as reduce the instances that create racial tensions within an organization.

WHO SHOULD USE THE
COOPERATIVE EXPERT MODEL?

Experience in using the cooperative expert model has provided some insight into when it should be used and who should use it. The rest of this chapter will address these issues as well as how the cooperative expert model might be implemented.

The conditions that would indicate that the cooperative expert model will provide substantial benefits include the following:

1. There is either overt distrust or potential distrust of the employer and their test administration agents on the part of significant portions of the candidate group.

2. The likelihood of a legal challenge of the results of the upcoming employment system (selection or promotion) is reasonably high. This would require the employer to take a number of expensive steps, which would not be necessary if the challenge were not presented. In using the cooperative expert model to address discrimination challenges in a proactive manner, it is absolutely essential that the expert possess:

    a. a basic competency in the field of testing and

    b. a commitment to work toward the reaction of a valid and fair selection and promotion system in an open and collegial manner. The overall success of the process can be compromised by hiring a consultant who will let his or her allegiance to a specific litigant interfere with the commitment to sound selection and promotion processes. Consequently, this expert also needs to enjoy the trust of all the litigants not to share "secure" information, such as testing materials or related information, with their litigant. Other issues to be addressed deal with how communication among the members of the test development committee (the group of test experts, subsequently referred to as "the committee") and the candidate group as well as the communication between the individual expert and his or her litigant should be handled. The rules governing these issues and others need to be laid out and published before the project begins. Any member of the committee could block adoption of a process.

3. All of the parties are predisposed to accept the results of the promotion or selection process that is jointly developed by the committee. Although none of the parties in the City A application of the cooperative expert model gave up their right to challenge the results of the committee's efforts, the judge initially pointed out that the burden of proof for any litigant trying to assert that the promotion process was not valid would be much more stringent as a result of their expert's participation in the creation of the promotion and selection process. The adoption of the cooperative expert model involves the litigants giving up something to

either break or prevent a stalemate among the parties. Each of them is giving up some control or perceived control in anticipation that a psychometrically sound selection system will produce acceptable results. However, the application of the cooperative expert model cannot and does not guarantee that pass rates for the Anglo male and protected class groups will pass the four-fifths rule.

HOW WOULD AN AGENCY IMPLEMENT THE COOPERATIVE EXPERT MODEL?

Schedules and Budgets

A budget must be prepared and schedules agreed upon. Consultants are typically from different firms and cities. The project scheduling is a potential problem but can be minimized if it is addressed early in the project.

Rules Governing the Functioning of the Members of the Test Development Committee

The rules under which the committee would function day to day were extremely important in the success of the past implementation of the model. These included the fact that all of the members of the committee were equal in status. There was no leader. This mixes general rules with our experience. However, the committee did agree that one member would have primary responsibility for one or more parts of the project. This frequently depended on the areas of expertise, experience, and training of the different committee members. Consequently, one member would take responsibility for conducting the job analysis; another would take responsibility for the assessment center if that were part of the selection and promotion system. The other members of the committee were still involved in a specific component in two ways, even though one member had primary responsibility: first, they would review and approve the plans that the primary team member proposed for this part of the project, and, second, the other members could and would assist the primary team member in completing that specific component.

Other Team Members Would Need to Approve the Results of a Specific Component before the Project Moved Forward

It is very important that a degree of professional collegiality exist among the team members. The committee members will have disagreements. This is not undesirable, and most of the time, these can be worked out. It is also important to publicize this rule to all litigants, not just the litigant representatives.

This brings up the question, "What if they cannot agree?" In those unusual circumstances when committee members are not able to agree on a commonly accepted version of a given component (e.g., a subset of questions of a written test or an assessment center exercise), that portion of the component will have to be replaced with a different set of questions or exercise. Another possibility is that different parties may have to go to court. A related issue, and one that was very important for the overall functioning of the committee, is that unanimous agreement among all committee members was essential at each step of the process before the committee would move on to the next step. Anything less than this would open the door to a dissenting member of the committee subsequently pointing out that he or she never agreed to a particular practice or part of the selection and promotion system when the results of the overall system did not produce the ideal pass rate for the litigant that he or she represented. This means that any committee member could stop the process at any time he or she disagreed with any part of the process. In point of fact, most team members are interested in producing quality results and do not mind using a component with which they may not be that familiar as long as they are clear about its validity and fairness.

Communication outside the Committee

The successful implementation of the model requires that the litigants are satisfied that the committee is doing its job in a professionally sound and impartial manner. Anyone who has worked in a public agency knows how rumors abound when a promotion or a selection system is established. Most of these rumors around the committee can be prevented or addressed by establishing the rules of communication between the committee and the litigants at the very beginning of the project. One possibility here is to limit any litigant-initiated communication with the committee to those situations in which all of the litigants are present. It is also productive to make all members of each litigant group aware of this rule early in the project.

On the subject of communication between the committee and the litigants, it is important to keep this line of communication open and, in some cases, even the direct dialogue between the committee members and the litigants instead of their representatives. This line of communication becomes more important when there are some delays in the progress of the committee. Even though the delays may be out of the control of the committee, there are forces within the organization that will use the all-powerful rumor mill to blame many of the organization's problems on the committee. For example, management of one of the author's clients blamed the lack of air-conditioned fire stations on the temporary delay on the committee's project and all the additional cost the delay was causing. Although this assertion was not accurate, it had the potential of impacting the morale of the candidates and resulted in a direct written communication to the candidates from the committee.

Saving Financial Resources by Placing One or More Local Personnel in the Working Meetings of the Committee

Just as using the cooperative expert model can produce savings of financial and other resources when compared with the cost of a protracted court battle, there is another step in using the cooperative expert model that can produce further savings. This step is the inclusion of one or more local people who have the technical background to benefit from the training that occurs by observing the committee work through the process of developing a highly valid, fair, and credible process. These local members would not have a vote on the deliberations of the committee, but they would have the opportunity to learn and to provide their input.

That learning can represent a massive financial savings to the local jurisdiction the next time the development of a promotion list for this specific position comes up. The jurisdiction then would have the option of developing and administering the promotion and selection procedure that the committee developed, thus, eliminating the cost of bringing in the committee altogether, or be able to conduct much of the actual implementation of the promotion and selection process under the direction of the committee.

The Role of the Local Jurisdiction in Working with the Committee

Typically, the members of the committee are from locations that are geographically distant from the client's jurisdiction and from the other members' home cities. Therefore, it is in the best interest of the litigant groups to provide the committee with assistance in completing such labor-intensive tasks as the job analysis, scheduling other meetings required by the committee, and office and clerical support. It has been the author's experience that early arrangements along these lines can pay big dividends for the litigants throughout the life of the project.

Summary of Committee Rules of Operation

There are many issues that arise in the day-to-day functioning of the committee. These can be dealt with effectively if there is trust among the members of the committee. This is why it is important to be cautious when initially selecting committee members. It is not easy to replace a committee member unless the request for the replacement is initiated by the litigant and that request relates to their own expert.

This brings up one final point, which is, "Who is the client of the consultant?" The author has been part of a committee under two arrangements. Each of them has advantages and drawbacks.

The first arrangement involves each consultant who is a member of the committee having one of the litigants as his client. Under this arrangement, the member would work with the committee within the rules described above and would periodically meet with the representative and the attorney of the litigant group. In these meetings, the progress of the committee would be discussed, and the committee member would explain how the litigant's interests are being served within the structure of sound testing practices.

A second alternative involves an arrangement in which each member of the committee works for the one common employer, such as an oversight committee made up of representatives of all of the litigant groups. The difference here is that none of the committee members would meet with the employer without all of the committee members and all of the employer's committee present.

Although there are positives and negatives to both of the models, either reporting arrangement is workable. The positive of the individual consultant–litigant model is that each litigant has an expert representing his or her interest in the test development process. The author has not experienced any negatives of this model while serving as a member of a committee. However, one potential negative is the possibility of substantial pressure on a consultant from the litigant who is being represented. The positive of the consortium model has been that the main focus of the committee on the development of a valid and fair selection system is unfettered by an allegiance to a specific group. The negative of this model is that the committee's picture of the views of the various litigant groups' opinions are more obscure, because no one on the committee has a clear and detailed picture of what a specific litigant's position is on a certain issue at a given point in time. The author has a slight preference for the individual litigant model simply because it provides an easier structure from which to monitor the viewpoints of the various litigants on an ongoing basis.

CONCLUSION

A promising and proven process of developing and implementing a valid, fair, and credible promotion and selection system in those situations in which there is a high probability of some legal action after the results of the process are published is described. It has been implemented by fire departments in highly litigious environments (e.g., cities with a population of over a quarter of a million people, one from the Midwest, a second from the East, and a third from the West Coast). However, it has the potential for being used in any job within the public sector in which the above conditions exist. Some of the major benefits are cost savings resulting from the prevention of a protracted court battle; cost savings resulting from the local jurisdiction being trained by the test development committee in how to create and administer a valid and fair selection system; reduced suspicion among the ranks of the potential litigants, because each litigant has a specific expert involved in all of the work to develop, administer, and score the promotion and selection system; and a reduced time frame in which promotions or selections are not delayed in court, leading to the avoidance of the creation of substantial resentment between the litigants, who usually are from different ethnic backgrounds. The application of this model can be useful under certain conditions. The cooperative expert model does work, but new users are encouraged to take the time to address many, if not all, of the issues mentioned in this chapter. Of particular importance is the competency, credibility, and capacity of your expert to work with the various litigants and the other experts.

Suggestions for Further Reading

Arvey, R. D., & Faley, R. H. (1988). *Fairness in selecting employees* (2d ed.). Reading, MA: Addison-Wesley.

Bureau of National Affairs. (1992–present). *Americans with Disabilities Act cases.* Washington, DC: Author.

Bureau of National Affairs. (1992–present). *Americans with Disabilities Act manual.* Washington, DC: Author.

Cascio, W. F. (1989). *Managing human resources: Productivity, quality of work life, profits.* New York: McGraw-Hill.

Cascio, W. F. (Ed.). (1989). *Human resources planning, employment and placement.* Washington, DC: BNA Books.

Cropanzano, R. (Ed.). (1993). *Justice in the workplace: Approaching fairness in human resource management.* Hillsdale, NJ: Lawrence Erlbaum.

Dillon, R. F., & Pellegrino, J. W. (Eds.). (1989). *Testing: Theoretical and applied perspectives.* Westport, CT: Praeger Publishers.

Equal Employment Opportunity Commission. (1995). *EEOC compliance manual,* EEOC Order 915.002. Washington, DC: Author.

Equal Employment Opportunity Commission. (1991). *The Americans with Disabilities Act, your responsibilities as an employer.* Washington, DC: Author.

Equal Employment Opportunity Commission. (n.d.). *Americans with Disabilities Act, employment regulations.* Washington, DC: Author.

Equal Employment Opportunity Commission, & U.S. Department of Justice. (1992). *Americans with disabilities handbook.* Washington, DC: Author.

Eyde, L. D., Nester, M. A., Heaton, S. M., & Nelson, A. V. (1994). *Guide for administering written employment examinations to persons with disabilities,* PRDC-94-11. Washington, DC: U.S. Office of Personnel Research.

Fiedler, J. F. (1994). *Mental disabilities and the Americans with Disabilities Act: A concise compliance manual for executives.* Westport, CT: Quorum Books.

Frierson, J. G. (1992). *Employer's guide to the Americans with Disabilities Act.* Washington, DC: Bureau of National Affairs.

Geisinger, K. (Ed.). (1992). *Psychological testing of Hispanics.* Washington, DC: American Psychological Association.

Gold, M. (1993). *An introduction to the law of employee discrimination.* Ithaca, NY: ILR Press.

Gottfredson, L. S., & Sharf, J. C. (Eds.). (1988). *Fairness in employment testing.* San Diego, CA: Academic Press.

Grossman, V. (1979). *Employing handicapped persons: Meeting EEO obligations.* Washington, DC: Bureau of National Affairs.

Gutman, A. (1993). *EEO law and personnel practices.* Newbury Park, CA: Sage Publications.

Hansen, C. P., & Conrad, K. A. (Eds.). (1991). *A handbook of psychological assessment in business.* Westport, CT: Quorum Books.

Hartigan, J. A., & Wigdor, A. K. (Eds.). (1989). *Fairness in employment testing: Validity generalization, minority issues, and the General Aptitude Test Battery.* Washington, DC: National Academy Press.

Johnson, C. D., & Zeidner, J. (1991). *The economic benefits of predicting job performance.* Vol. 2: *Classification efficiency.* Westport, CT: Praeger Publishers.

Jones, J. W. (Ed.). (1991). *Preemployment honesty testing: Current research and future directions.* Westport, CT: Quorum Books.

Kramer, J. J., & Conoley, J. C. (Eds.). (1992). *The eleventh mental measurements yearbook.* Lincoln: University of Nebraska-Lincoln, The Buros Institute of Mental Measurements.

Ledvinka, J., & Scarpello, V. G. (1991). *Federal regulation of personnel and human resource management* (2d ed.). Boston, MA: PWS-Kent.

Lowman, R. L. (1989). *Pre-employment screening for psychopathology: A guide to professional practice.* Sarasota, FL: Professional Resource Exchange.

Nester, A., & Colberg, M. (1991). *Legal and psychometric concerns in testing persons with disabilities.* Washington, DC: U.S. Office of Personnel Management.

Normand, J., Lempert, R. O., & O'Brien, C. (Eds.). (1994). *Under the influence? Drugs and the American workforce.* Washington, DC: National Academy Press.

Schmidt, F. L., Pearlman, K., Hunter, J. E., & Hirsh, H. R. (1985). Forty questions about validity generalization and meta-analysis with commentaries. *Personnel Psychology, 38*, 697–801.

Schmitt, N., Borman, W. C., & Associates (Eds.). (1993). *Personnel selection in organizations.* San Francisco, CA: Jossey-Bass.

Schneider, B., & Schmitt, N. (1986). *Staffing organizations* (2d ed.). Glenview, IL: Scott, Foresman.

Spriggs, K. (1994). *Representing plaintiffs in Title VII actions.* New York: Wiley Law.

Stokes, G. S., Mumford, M. D., & Owens, W. A. (Eds.). (1994). *Biodata handbook: Theory and use of biographical information in selection and performance evaluation.* Palo Alto, CA: Consulting Psychologists Press.

Thornton, G. C., III. (1992). *Assessment centers in human resource management.* Reading, MA: Addison-Wesley.

Turner, R. (1990). *The past and future of affirmative action: A guide for human resource professionals and corporate counsel.* Westport, CT: Quorum Books.

Weatherspoon, F. D. (1986). *Equal employment opportunity and affirmative action: A sourcebook.* New York: Garland.

Weiss, D. H. (1991). *Fair, square, and legal: Hiring and firing practices to keep you and our company out of court.* New York: AMACOM.

Zeidner, J., & Johnson, C. D. (1991). *The economic benefits of predicting job performance.* Vol. 3. *Estimating the gains of alternative policies.* Westport, CT: Praeger Publishers.

Zeidner, J., & Johnson, C. D. (1991). *The economic benefits of predicting job performance.* Vol. 1. *Selection utility.* Westport, CT: Praeger Publishers.

Name Index

Anastasi, A., 39
Arvey, R. D., 187, 188
Asher, E., 90
Ashworth, S., 145

Barrick, M. R., 100, 145
Bentson, C., 100
Blackmun, H., 6
Blakley, B. R., 188
Borman, W. C., 148, 150
Bray, D. W., 12
Brogden, H., 73, 85
Buller, P. F., 159
Bullock, R. J., 99
Burnett, S. A., 193

Camara, W. J., 6, 8
Campbell, J. P., 210
Campion, M. A., 140
Caplan, J. R., 101
Carroll, J. B., 193
Carter, G. W., 122
Chao, G. T., 208
Conley, J. J., 148
Connor, K., 196
Costa, P. T., Jr., 147

Crawford, M. S., 188
Cronshaw, S. F., 135
Crouch, D. J., 159

Dobbins, G. H., 140
Dodge, G. E., 88
Draft, L. M., 193
Dunnette, M. D., 122

Eagly, A. H., 193, 194
Erwin, F. W., 100
Eyde, L. D., 12, 262

Farh, J., 140
Fay, C., 139
Feingold, A., 193, 194
Fennema, E., 193
Finn, S. E., 148
Finnegan, B., 140
Flanagan, J. C., 135
Frei, R. L., 145
Freid, C., 89
Friedman, T., 91
Furnham, A., 171

Gast-Rosenberg, I., 101

Gaugler, B. B., 100
Gebbia, M., 91
Ghiselli, E. E., 94
Goldstein, I. L., 30, 32, 41, 186
Goldstein, L., 5
Gooding, R. Z., 96
Gottier, R. F., 144
Gough, H. C., 146
Guion, R. M., 144
Gunter, B., 171
Gwartney, J., 90

Haan, N., 148
Hanson, M. A., 120, 121, 145
Hartigan, J. A., 246
Hartke, E., 148
Harvey, R., 32
Haworth, J., 90
Hayes, T. L., 150
Heilbrun, A. B., 146
Helson, R., 148
Herrenstein, R. J., 193
Hirsh, H. R., 100
Hogan, R., 148, 150
Hogan, J., 148, 150, 184, 186, 187, 189
Hough, L. M., 145
Howell, W. C., 150
Hunter, J. E., 91, 93, 95, 96, 99, 100, 103, 135, 149
Hunter, R. F., 95, 96, 135, 149
Hyde, J. S., 193

Jacklin, C. N., 193
Jackson, D. N., 101, 145
Jago, I. A., 188
Janz, T., 139
Jensen, A. R., 193
Johnson, B. T., 194

Katoka, H. C., 139
Kelly, E. L., 148
Kirk, J. R., 89
Kirsh, M., 96
Klonsky, M. G., 194
Kowal, D. M., 12

Lamon, S. J., 193
Landon, T. E., 187

Landy, F. J., 27, 42
Lane, D. M., 193
Latham, G. P., 135, 138, 139, 140
Law, K. S., 99
Lee, C., 138
Lefkowitz, J., 91
Lempert, R. O., 153
Lerner, B., 90
Lewis, R. E., 187
Lin, T., 140
Locke, E. A., 135
London, M., 12
Lorber, L. Z., 89
Lowman, R. L., 13

Maccoby, E. E., 193
Mael, F. A., 172
Mahoney, J. J., 160, 162
Makhijani, M. G., 194
Maurer, S. D., 135, 139, 140
Maxwell, S. E., 187
McDaniel, M. A., 100, 135, 139, 145, 148
McDowell, D. S., 88
McHenry, J. J., 145
McRae, R. R., 147
Milsap, R., 148
Miner, J. B., 2197
Moane, G., 148
Motowildo, S. J., 122, 148, 150
Mount, M. K., 102, 145
Mowry, H. W., 122
Mumford, M. D., 171
Murray, C., 193

Newcomb, M. D., 162
Newman, R. F., 150
Noe, R. A., 96
Normand, J., 153, 158, 160, 162
Northrop, L. C., 100
Nutting, S. M., 187

O'Brien, C. P., 153
Ones, D. S., 145
Orlav, E. J., 162
Outerbridge, A. N., 90
Owens, W. A., 102, 171

Pearlman, K., 100
Pearson, K., 73
Perry, B., 139
Petrson, L. V., 159
Plant, A.J.S., 193
Prussell, E. D., 140

Quaintance, M. K., 12
Quigley, A., 186, 189
Quinones, M. A., 188

Reddy, S., 171
Reilly, R. R., 208
Rollings, D. E., 159
Rosen, N. A., 124
Rosenthal, D. B., 100
Rothstein, H. R., 100, 101, 145
Ryan, A. M., 218
Ryan, J., 162

Saari, L. M., 140
Sackett, P. R., 177, 218, 247
Salyards, S. D., 158, 160, 162
Schmidt, F. L., 94, 96, 99, 100, 101, 135,
    145, 149
Schmitt, N., 27, 42
Schneider, B., 7, 30, 41
Sheridan, J., 159

Skarlicki, D. P., 140
Sparks, C. P., 101
Stark, D., 148
Stokes, G. S., 171
Syvantek, D. J., 99

Tett, R. P., 101, 145
Thorndike, R. L., 134
Thornton, G. C., 100
Toquam, J. L., 145

Vargyas, E. J., 196
Viswesvaran, C., 145

Webb, D. O., 159
Weisner, W. H., 135
Wernimont, P. F., 210
Whetzel, D. L., 135
Whyte, G., 139
Wigdor, A. K., 246
Wiggins, J. S., 145
Wilk, S. L., 177, 247
Williams, E. B., 91
Williams, R. E., 88
Winkler, H., 159

Zedeck, S., 30, 41
Zwerling, C., 162

Subject Index

Abilities, differences in, 193–95
Academic achievement, 216
Accommodation, reasonable, 262
Accuracy of data, 17, 206
Adjective checklist, 148
Adverse Impact. *See* Impact
Affirmative action, 242–43, 262
Age differences, 177, 249
Age Discrimination in Employment
    Act, 201, 264
Agreement Score, 114
Alcohol, 156
Alternative selection procedures,
    14–15, 148–50, 209
American Psychological Association
    (APA), 3–4
Americans with Disabilities Act
    (ADA), 9–10, 149–50, 177, 185, 201,
    239, 264
Amicus curiae brief, 5–6
Anecdotal evidence, 289
Applicant, 202
Application blank, 168, 265
Artifacts, statistical, 95–100
Assessment, individual, 218
Assessment centers, 214–15
Attorneys' fees, 278

Background data, 172
Banding, 252, 254–55
Bar examination, 54
Behavioral consistency, 215–17
Benefit to employer, 85–87
Bennett Mechanical Comprehension
    Test, 127
Berger Programming Test, 42
Bias, 18, 55, 139, 249–50. *See also* Impact
Big Five, 145–48, 213
Biodata, 149–50, 171, 173–74, 211–12
Bonus points, 251
Bottom line, 206
Burden of proof, 273
Business necessity, 7. *See also* Validity

California Psychological Inventory,
    148
Charging parties, 238–39
Chi-Square, 204
Civil Rights Act of 1991, 7–8; Sec. 106,
    253–56
Civil Service Commission, 244
Cognitive ability, 255
Confidentiality of test materials, 16–17
Construct validity, 187, 268
Constructed response, 55
Contamination, 29

Content-construct scale, 49–50
Content validity, 36, 40, 210, 283;
    apparent content validity, 41–42;
    sample items, 56–59, 61, 62
Context, performance, 148
Cooperative model, 294–97
Corimer v. PPG Industries, 242
Correct answer, 59–60
Corrections, statistical, 70
Cost, 123
Cost of validation, 89–92
Criterion, 71, 173
Criterion-related validity, 187, 267
Cutoff scores, 248, 252

Damages, 275–77
Data, accuracy of, 17, 206
Data analysis, 289
Defendants expert, 280–81
Deficiency, 29
Demographics, 203
Department of Justice, Civil Rights
    Division, 244
Dictionary of Occupational Titles, 89
Difficulty, 62
Dimension, 127
Disability, 150, 260–62
Discovery, 19, 273–74, 287–88
Discrimination, systemic, 274–75
Disparate impact. *See* Impact
Disparate treatment, 271–73
Distractors, 51
Diversity, 250
Documentation, 35
Dothard v. Rawlinson, 184
Drug testing, 154–59; errors in, 158–50;
    program effectiveness, 159–62

Educational requirements, 167-68
Equal Employment Advisory Council,
    88
Ethical standards, 13, 17; cases, 15–18;
    bias, 18; discovery, 19
Examination of expert, 282–83
Executive Order: 11246, 244; 12564, 154
Experience measures, 217
Expert witness, 15–16, 285–87, 290–93;
    ghost, 18–19, 288–91

Face validity, 39–40, 116
Fairness, 5–7, 161–62, 249–50
Faking, 117, 175–76
Federal Glass Ceiling Commission, 194
File drawer, 99
Fire Scene Simulation, 107–11
Fit, 115–18
Five Factor, 145–48, 213
Fourth Amendment, 155

Gender. *See* Sex
General Aptitude Test Battery (GATB),
    9, 91, 95, 96, 127, 246
Ghost expert, 18–19, 288–89
Griggs v. Duke Power Company, 6, 134.
    See also under substantive topic
Group differences. *See* Bias; Impact
"Guidelines and Ethical
    Considerations for Assessment
    Center Operations," 125

Handwriting analysis, 217–18
Hires, 202

Impact, 14–15, 63–64, 116, 123, 150,
    161–62, 166, 177, 188, 192–95, 201–2,
    203, 205–6, 243, 247–49, 262, 266,
    271–72. *See also* Bias
Implementation, 131, 189
Integrity tests, 219–20
Interpersonal skills, 59
Interview, 214–61; development,
    135–38
Item-by-item analysis, 51–54

Job analysis, 30–33, 126–27, 129, 173,
    185–86, 284
Job description, 23–25, 50–51, 71, 266
Jury trials, 275–77
Justice, Department of, 244

Knowledge, 50; needed to perform, 52;
    tests, 44–45
Knowledge, Skill, and Ability (KSA),
    23, 28–34, 43–44, 50

Language, 61
Larry P. v. Riles, 10

Legal issues, 38–39, 154–55, 176–77, 183–85, 195–96
Legal proceedings, 195
Licenses, 168
Linkage of test to job, 41, 52–54
Local jurisdiction, 298

Medical examination, 262
Meta-analysis, 99, 135, 188
Minnesota Multiphasic Personality Inventory (MMPI), 149
Multiple assessment techniques, 127

Nash v. Consolidated City of Nashville, 283
National Institute on Drug Abuse, 153

Office of Federal Compliance: Executive Order 11246, 244; Executive Order 12564, 154
Office of Personnel Management, 244
Office of Revenue Sharing (Treasury Department), 245
Officers for Justice v. Civil Service Commission of the City and County of San Francisco, 234
Organizational climate, 114

Pass rates, 205
Passing score, 51, 63, 166
Pattern and practice, 272
Peer evaluations, 215
Performance, past, 215–16
Performance Priority Survey, 112–18
Personality tests, 194, 213–14
Physical ability, 182, 219, 249
Plaintiffs expert, 280–81
Position, 8; description, 260–61, 266–67
Posttrial use of expert, 283–84
Practicality, 140
Prediction, 122
Preparation, 189–90
Pre-trial preparation of expert, 281–82
Price Waterhouse v. Hopkins, 6, 273
Privacy, 116, 177
Productivity, 250
Projective techniques, 217
Protected classes, 202

Psychological tests, 262

Qualifications to conduct validation, 88–89
Qualified individual, 260
Quality, indications of, 54–55
Question and Answer, 25; applicant, 77, 202; task analysis, 25

Race norming, 8, 251
Ratings, 68
Reasonable accommodation, 262
Recognition of correct response, 58
Record keeping, 205, 273–74, 280, 290
Recording procedures, 127–28
Recruitment, 72, 265
Reference checks, 216
Reliability, 138–39, 229
Remedies, 277–78
Reputation, 147
Results, 100–101, 128
Retaliation, 275
Retranslation, 34–35
Rule of three (five), 230

Sample, 71, 204
Sample item, 56–59, 61, 62
Scatter plots, 74–84
Scholastic Aptitude Test, 193
Scientific evidence, 286–87
Score adjustment, 8–9, 177, 182, 251
Scoring tests, 109, 121, 130, 167, 174–81
Selection procedure, 71, 261–62, 264–66
Selection rate, 203, 248
Selective efficiency, 69
Self-assessments, 213
Semantic validity, 39
Settlement agreements, 241
Sex, 6, 168, 195
Simulation, 49, 53–54, 57, 107–11
Situational judgment tests, 220
Sliding bands, 224–28; illustration, 226–28, 252
Society of Industrial and Organizational Psychology Principles, 28, 30. See also under substantive topic

Standards for Educational and Psychological Testing, 240
Statistical artifacts, 95–100
Statistical proof, 289
Statistical significance, 201, 204
Statistics, 68–69, 72, 95
Subgroup differences, 247
Subject matter expert (SME), 32, 40
Systemic discrimination, 274–75, 277

Task analysis, 25
Task performance, 148
Teal v. Connecticut, 206
Test development, 41
Test development committee, 296–97
Test plan, 34
Test wiseness, 55, 63
Testing disabled, 261
Texas Department of Community Affairs v. Burdine, 273
Textbook answer, 62
Time pressure, 60–61
Top-down selection, 223, 252
Trainability, 210
Training: to take tests, 63; as criterion, 68
Training Assessors, 128, 132–33
Treasury Department, Office of Revenue Sharing, 245
Trial, 282
Trivia, 60

Uniform Guidelines: development of, 4; Sec. 3B Alternatives, 117; Sec. 7B, C, D Use of Other Studies, 102; Sec. 8B Cooperative studies, 102; Sec. 14B(2) Job Analysis, 24, 67; Sec. 14B(3) Criterion, 68; Sec. 14C(1) Appropriateness, 31, 35, 43; Sec. 14C(4) Standard for Content Validity, 43; Sec. 14C(9) Performance, 189; Sec. 15C(1) Utility, 228–29; Sec. 15C(3) Job Analysis, 25; Sec. 15C(5) Relationship to Job, 51; Sec. 15E Use of Other Studies, 102; Sec. 16 Definitions, 24, 43, 67. *See also under substantive topic*

Validity, 27, 128–29, 133, 138–39, 159–61, 162, 166, 186–89, 195, 229, 266
Validity generalization, 94–95; study, steps in, 96–100; results, 100–101, 176
Variance, 69–70

Wanted answer, 51, 59–60, 62
Wards Cove Packing Co., Inc. v. Antonio, 7, 88, 203
Watson v. Fort Worth Bank and Trust, 5, 88
Weeks v. Southern Bell Telephone & Telegraph Co., 184
Width (of band), 230–33
Within-group norming, 8–9, 179, 251
Work samples, 209–10

About the Contributors

R. LAWRENCE ASHE, JR., is a partner of Paul, Hastings, Janofsky & Walker, where he chairs its East Coast Employment Law Department from its Atlanta office. He served as Management Co-Chair of the American Bar Association Labor and Employment Law Section's Equal Employment Opportunity Committee and is a Fellow of the American College of Trial Lawyers. He authored or coauthored the Scored Tests in several editions of Schlei & Grossman's *Employment Discrimination Law*. He specializes in serving as counsel regarding personnel testing cases for test users, designers, and publishers and is a frequent presenter at the Society of Industrial and Organizational Psychology conventions.

RICHARD S. BARRETT is the principal of Barrett Associates, a consulting firm specializing in fair employment issues. He served as Professor at New York University and Stevens Institute of Technology. He testified for the plaintiffs in *Griggs v. Duke Power Company, Moody v. Albemarle Paper Company,* and *Davis v. Washington,* all of which were decided by the Supreme Court. He has testified in more than 100 cases brought under Title VII of the Civil Rights Act and the Age Discrimination in Employment Act for both plaintiffs and defendants. As an employee of the Equal Employment Opportunities Commission, Barrett participated in writing the Uniform Guidelines on Employee Selection Procedures and Questions and Answers to Clarify and Provide a Common Interpretation of the Uniform Guidelines on Employee Selection Procedures. He was a member of the Ad Hoc Committee on

Testing of the Society of Industrial and Organization Psychology that made the society's formal comments to the committee that wrote both *Standards for Educational and Psychological Testing* and the second edition of *Principles for the Validation and Use of Personnel Selection Procedures* (1975). He was a consultant to the Commission on Testing and Public Policy and chair of the New York State Advisory Committee for Bias in Standardized Testing. He has written more than 50 books and professional publications.

WILLIAM C. BURNS is the principal in William C. Burns and Associates. He served as Chair of California's Technical Advisory Committee on Testing to the California Fair Employment Practice Commission. He was a member of the committee of the Society of Industrial and Organizational Psychology that developed *Principles for the Validation and Use of Personnel Selection Procedures* (1975). He has testified on testing issues before committees of both houses of Congress.

WAYNE J. CAMARA is Research Scientist for the College Board and a member of the Executive Committee of Division 1 (General Psychology), Division 5 (Evaluation, Measurement and Statistics), and Division 14 of the Society of Industrial and Organizational Psychology. He served as Assistant Executive Director of Science at the American Psychological Association and Project Director for the preparation of *Standards for Educational and Psychological Testing* and is a Fellow of the American Psychological Association. He has served on congressional advisory and review panels concerning testing. He is Associate Editor of the *Journal of Occupational Health Psychology* and a reviewer for several journals.

WAYNE F. CASCIO is Professor of Management and Director of International Programs at the University of Colorado. He has taught in several universities from Hawaii to Switzerland and consulted internationally. He was President of the Human Resources Division of the Academy of Management and of the Society of Industrial and Organizational Psychology. He has authored or edited five texts on human resource management. Editorial board memberships include *Journal of Applied Psychology, Academy of Management Review, International Journal of Selection and Assessment, Human Performance, Asia-Pacific Human Resource Management,* and *Organizational Dynamics.*

IRWIN L. GOLDSTEIN is Professor of Psychology and Dean of the College of Behavioral and Social Sciences at the University of Maryland. He has served as President of the Society of Industrial and Organizational Psychology, from which he received the Distinguished Service Contribution Award. He also received the Richard Swanson Award for

Research Excellence from the American Society for Training and Development. He is Series Editor of *Frontiers of Industrial and Organizational Psychology* and Associate Editor for the *Journal of Applied Psychology* and *Human Factors Journal*.

MARY ANN HANSON is a Research Scientist at the Personnel Decisions Research Institutes in Tampa, Florida. She has developed situational judgment tests as part of her dissertation and for the Army and the city of New York. She is coauthor of a chapter on Personnel Selection in the *Annual Review of Psychology*.

SARAH E. HENRY is a Consultant with Gunn Partners Inc., which specializes in reengineering, restructuring, and large-scale changes for Fortune 500 companies, and Vice President of the Metropolitan Association for Applied Psychology and a member of the Society for Industrial and Organizational Psychology's Program Committee. She was a Managing Consultant with the Renaissance Strategy Group and a Senior Consultant with Towers Perrin. Her corporate experience includes direction of Organization Development for Warner Lambert and Irving Trust, where she also directed Executive Development and International Human Resources.

JOYCE HOGAN is Professor of Psychology, University of Tulsa. She is a Fellow of Divisions 5, 14, and 21 of the American Psychological Association, Editor of *Human Performance*, and on the Editorial Board of *Human Factors*.

ROBERT HOGAN is the McFarlin Professor and Chair, Department of Psychology, University of Tulsa. He is a Fellow of Divisions 5, 8, and 14 of the American Psychological Association. He was formerly Professor of Psychology and Social Relations, Johns Hopkins University and Editor of the Personality Section, *Journal of Personality and Social Psychology*. He is the author of more than 100 articles, chapters, and books.

GARY P. LATHAM is the Secretary of State Professor of Organizational Effectiveness in the Faculty of Management, University of Toronto. He has served as an expert witness in numerous Title VII cases involving selection and performance appraisal decisions. In the human resources field, his creative achievements include the development of the situational interview, behavioral observation scales for performance appraisal, and self-management training techniques based on goal setting.

RODNEY L. LOWMAN is the Chief Executive Officer of the Development Laboratories (Houston) and Consulting Faculty, Duke University Medical Center and Editor-in-Chief, Ethics Casebook Revision Project of the Society of Industrial and Organizational Psychology. He has been on the faculties of the University of Michigan, Duke University, and Rice University, was Chair of the Professional Affairs Committee, and a member of the Ethics Committee, American Psychological Association. He has held editorial positions with *Personnel Psychology* and *Professional Psychology*. He is the author of more than 50 publications including five books and monographs.

JACQUES NORMAND is a study director at the National Research Council of the National Academy of Sciences in Washington, D.C., where he directed a National Research Council/Institute of Medicine committee study on drug use in the workplace and coedited its 1994 report, *Under the Influence? Drugs and the American Work Force*. Prior to joining the National Research Council he held research psychologist positions in both the private and public sectors with responsibility for the development, validation, and implementation of various organizational intervention programs. He has published in various professional research journals and has spoken at numerous professional meetings on evaluation issues.

JAMES OUTTZ is a private consultant in Washington, D.C. He specializes in the development and validation of tests involving audio and video media for both public and private sectors. He developed the concept of sliding bands for a police department. He is a frequent participant on panels and commissions concerned with selection and fairness.

LAWRENCE R. O'LEARY is the owner and manager of O'Leary, Brokaw and Associates, a corporation of consulting psychologists and graduate students, and teaches Industrial and Organizational Psychology at Webster University and the University of Missouri–St. Louis. He is President of Gateway Industrial/Organizational Psychology and a founding member of the Society of Industrial and Organizational Psychology, in which he was a member of the Membership Committee. He is the author of *Interviewing for the Decision Maker* (1976), *The Selection and Promotion of the Successful Police Officer* (1979), *The Police Assessment Center*, and *The Firefighter's Assessment Center*, as well as journal articles.

ANN M. QUIGLEY is a Research Psychologist with the United States Postal Service. She is a member of the American Psychological Association.

ROBERT A. RAMOS is an Independent Consultant at Ramos and Associates, Davis, Florida. For most of his career he was an Industrial Organizational Psychologist at American Telephone and Telegraph, Bell Communications Research, and NYNEX. He was a psychometrician for the city of New York. He has served on several committees of the Society of Industrial and Organizational Psychology, including the Board of Ethnic and Minority Affairs and the Committee on Psychological Tests and Assessment, of which he was Chairman.

RICHARD R. REILLY is President, Assessment Alternatives, Inc., and a Research Psychologist, American Telephone & Telegraph Company. He served as Professor of Management Sciences at Stevens Institute of Technology. He is a Fellow of the American Psychological Association and a member of the Editorial Board of *Personnel Psychology*.

PAUL R. SACKETT holds the Carlson Professorship in Industrial Relations at the University of Minnesota. He has served on the faculties of the University of Kansas and the University of Illinois at Chicago. He was President of the Society for Industrial and Organizational Psychology. He coauthored (with George Dreher) *Perspectives on Employee Staffing and Selection* (1983).

STEPHEN D. SALYARDS is a Research Psychologist in the Office of Employment and Placement, U.S. Postal Service, performing job analysis, test development, validation, and survey research.

NEAL SCHMITT is University Distinguished Professor of Psychology and Management at Michigan State University. He is Chair of the Committee on Psychological Tests and Assessments of the American Psychological Association and member of the Board of Testing and Assessment of the National Academy of Sciences. He has served as President of the Society of Industrial and Organizational Psychology and of the Michigan Association of I/O Psychology. He is coauthor (with Benjamin Schneider) of *Staffing Organizations* (1986) and (with Richard Klimoski) of *Research Methods in Human Resource Management* (1991); he is coeditor (with Walter Borman) of *Personnel Selection in Organizations* (1993), and part of the series *Frontiers of Industrial and Organizational Psychology*.

DONALD J. SCHWARTZ is the Chief Psychologist at the U.S. Equal Employment Opportunity Commission. He has been chief psychologist at the office of Federal Contract Compliance Programs and the U.S. Department of Labor, a personnel research psychologist at the U.S. Office of Personnel Management, and represented all three agencies in the development of the Uniform Guidelines on Employee Selection Procedures and interpretive questions and answers on these Uniform Guidelines. He is a member of the American Psychological Association and the Society for Industrial and Organizational Psychology. He has been a contributor to *Personnel Psychology, Public Personnel Management,* and *Law and Human Behavior* and has written chapters in two books on job analysis and test policy.

LANCE W. SEBERHAGEN is Director, Seberhagen & Associates. He is a member of the American Psychological Association, American Statistical Association, and the Society of Industrial and Organizational Psychology and was President of the Personnel Testing Council of Metropolitan Washington. He has been an expert witness in more than 60 cases.

KENT SPRIGGS is the principal of Spriggs and Johnson. He has practiced law for 30 years, specializing in Civil Rights and has served on the Executive Board of the National Employment Lawyers Association. He is author of the two-volume work, *Representing Plaintiffs in Title VII Actions* (1994).

GARNETT S. STOKES is Associate Professor and Chair, Applied Psychology Program, University of Georgia and a consultant on selection procedures. She is a member of the American Psychological Association and the Society of Industrial and Organizational Psychologists. She is a member of the Editorial Board of the *Journal of Applied Psychology* and editor of *Biodata Handbook: Theory, Research, and Use of Biographical Information in Selection and Performance Prediction.*

CHRISTINA SUE-CHAN is a doctoral student on the Faculty of Management, University of Toronto. Her research interests include selection, performance appraisal, and training.

MARY L. TENOPYR is Measurement & Selection Systems Director at American Telephone & Telegraph. She is President of the Division of Evaluation, Measurement and Statistics of the American Psychological Association. She is on the editorial boards of *Journal of Applied Psychology, Journal of Vocational Behavior,* and the *International Journal of Selection and Assessment.*

CHERYL S. TOTH is Instructor, Applied Psychology Program, University of Georgia and has been a Statistical Consultant for Career Pathways.

SHELDON ZEDECK is Professor of Psychology and Chair of the Department of Psychology at the University of California at Berkeley. He has consulted and conducted research and is author of *Measurement Theory on the Behavioral Sciences, Work, Families, and Organizations* and other texts.